Ongar Music Club

Records to Recitals

A Personal History

1975 – 2021

RODERICK ELMS

The Choir Press

First published in the United Kingdom in 2021 by
The Choir Press

Body text typeset in 11pt Palatino

Cover Design by Colin Foo MCSD
Cover photo of the High Street, Chipping Ongar
by Brian Gibbs / Alamy Stock Photo

ISBN 978-1-78963-220-0

The Choir Press

Foreword by John Lill CBE

It has always been a remarkable achievement for a music club to continue over the years and never more so than now, when real music is systemically attempted to be starved out of all existence. It is now falsely labelled 'élitest' and continually replaced by yet more 'pop'. Of course, this gigantic dumbing down of the spiritual art of classical music creates temporary fortunes for those who permeate it but at the huge loss of the proper development of mind, soul or civilised behaviour.

In the light of all this destruction (and I do speak from experience, having given well over 5,000 concerts worldwide), I find it astonishing that a modest sized market town as Ongar has created such a dynamic and successful music club, which has lasted over so many decades. The organisers and public alike have remained resilient, purposeful and unaffected by trendy, cheap fashion. The results are admirable, including the creation of the Ongar Music Club's Essex Young Musician of the Year competition, rapidly evolving since 1984.

I am so proud to have been President for many years. I remember dear Barry and Jean Hall very vividly. What an extraordinary duo they were, conquering all odds with their enthusiasm, strength of purpose and sheer hard work in order to keep the Club firmly on the map! It rapidly developed as a result and has continued to do so.

I warmly congratulate all connected with this outstanding enterprise and wish you every future strength and success!

John Lill
President – Ongar Music Club

*This book is dedicated to the founding fathers of
Ongar Music Club with great affection and admiration*

Presidents of Ongar Music Club

Lord Yehudi Menuhin OM KBE, President 1975 – 1999

John Lill CBE, President 1999 –

Contents

Preface

My long association with Ongar Music Club dates from its first public concert on 15th October 1975 when I was asked to page-turn. My good friend and colleague Geoffrey Timms, a founder member of the club and instrumental in establishing it, also invited me to give a piano recital in December of that year. So began a close relationship with the club that lasts to this day. Along the way, I saw the birth of the 'Essex Young Musician of the Year' competition in 1984 and many other exciting developments. I served on the committee from 1985 until 2020 and as a trustee from 2019 to 2021, witnessing the planning of recitals by such icons of the classical music world as Lord Yehudi Menuhin OM KBE, John Lill CBE, Sir Peter Pears, Dame Janet Baker and Dame Eva Turner.

I've long felt that the history of Ongar Music Club deserved proper acknowledgement, although doing so was always going to be problematic due to the passing of so many years. Researching the detail brought many challenges, although I was fortunate to have access to the club's records, immaculately ordered and dating back to the first meeting.

The subtitle of this book, *Records to Recitals*, acknowledges the simple beginnings of the club and how it transformed into a fully-fledged organisation presenting musical performances of the very highest standards. Four chapters trace the club's development from 1975 to 2021, and in writing these, I have drawn extensively on the records covering the period from 1975 to 2016 – these records are now kept at the Essex Record Office and available for public viewing. There are also separate chapters on specific aspects of the club's activities.

I am indebted to many club members and friends for their considerable support and encouragement in embarking on this project. I would particularly like to thank Jeremy Hall, Nicola Harries, Tonia Hart, Peter Jackson, Catherine Jennings, Dr Michael Leach, Peter Lewis, Patti and Howard Nicholson, Dr Janet Pope, Roger Roles, John Root and Sylvia Terry, without whose invaluable help and generosity of spirit, the writing of this book would not have been possible.

Roderick Elms, September 2021

1. Small Beginnings

The small town and parish of Ongar is situated in Essex, some eleven miles west of Chelmsford and twenty-one miles north of London – Ongar meaning 'grass land'. The town's full name is Chipping Ongar – the word Chipping deriving from the Old English for Market. Its oldest building, St Martin's Church, dates back to the eleventh century. Many other buildings in the town are rather classical and date from 1841. The original police station was the first large building in Ongar to depart from this style.

A railway line between London and Ongar was established in 1865 and ran as a shuttle service north of Epping using steam locomotives. Its ownership was transferred to London Underground in 1949 when it became part of the Central Line. The line was eventually closed in 1994, and it now runs as the Epping and Ongar Railway – a 'heritage transport experience' where you can 're-live the romance of travel in bygone times'. Bus services have operated to Ongar since the 1920s.

The Budworth Hall is named after Captain Philip John Budworth, who lived in nearby Greensted Hall. He died in 1886 and bequeathed the area of land on which the hall stands. This Grade II listed building was built in memory of Captain Budworth and has been home to the club for most of its life. It was erected in 1886 as a combined assembly, reading, and coffee-rooms, and still serves the community today. It is built of red brick and is of a complex but vaguely 'Tudor' plan.

Tony Moore • St Martin's Church, Ongar, May 2014

For a very long time, music has played an important part in the lives of many living in Ongar and the surrounding area. By the early seventies, a small group of local friends were meeting regularly in each other's houses to listen to gramophone records. This tradition expanded somewhat, and with encouragement from Tony Moore [1], who was

[1] Tony Moore also founded the Three Valleys Male Voice Choir in 1994. He is seen in the photo singing with the group in Ongar. Since its inception, the choir has raised thousands of pounds for charity. Sadly, Tony passed away in May 2020 following twenty-six years of devoted service.

chairman of the relatively new Ongar Community Association and also very much involved in the local Rotary Club, these activities expanded and moved into the Budworth and other local halls. With growing audiences, a logical progression was the creation of a more formal music club, and this suggestion was made by Tony Moore to David Kirkwood, one of the great enthusiasts of the informal music group, with a view to setting up an 'Ongar Music Club'. This was done informally in late 1974 as part of the Ongar and District Community Association. By the end of that year, four meetings had been held with an average attendance of fewer than five people. The first meeting of 1975 was on 8th January, being attended by six members. Unfortunately, the nature of that meeting is not recorded.

It's difficult to imagine the challenges involved in getting such a venture off the ground – not least the financial considerations involved in any form of public presentation, ranging from hall booking, ticket and programme production, publicity materials and artiste's fees. It's fairly clear that in the early days, such fees were set at a bare minimum, if paid at all. It's remarkable to note that the membership went from a basic five to around forty-one in a little over a year (November 1976) and that there was a financial surplus of £35.

This journey, acknowledging the founders' love of music and their wish to share that love, would progress in broadly the same form for some forty years, albeit it with a few inevitable twists and turns along the way. At the time of writing (late 2021), the club has a strong membership, although the style of concert-giving is currently significantly different from that in 1975 – having necessarily accommodated the changing needs of a fairly consistent local demographic. Advances in technology have also brought new possibilities for the arts and their audiences with options for 'online' presentations – something which has been of particular significance during the pandemic of 2020–2021, when live concert-giving has not been possible. However, until March 2020, live music was still being presented regularly in Ongar's Budworth Hall, giving pleasure to large and very enthusiastic audiences.

2. 1975–1984 The First Ten Years

The first formal business meeting [1] of Ongar Music Club was held on 22nd January 1975 when ten 'members' attended. The details of that meeting are recorded as follows [2]:

Club Meeting – 22nd January 1975

Following some discussion, those present agreed to form a committee, and the following elections were made:

Chairman / Secretary	Mr D. Kirkwood
Treasurer	Miss M. Greatrex
Press Secretary	Mr A. Bennett

It was proposed and agreed that all members would make a flat payment of 50p, from which the treasurer could make all payments. This rule would apply to new members. Future payments would be levied by the treasurer as circumstances required.

The chairman would check the requirements of membership of the Community Association (CA).

The chairman would endeavour to obtain the use of a notice board at the Budworth Hall, and would obtain suitable stationery.

It was decided that the first concert visit would be to the [Royal] Festival Hall on either 21st or 28th February, the programme on each occasion being Mozart piano concerti.

The next meeting would be held on Wednesday 12th February 1975 at the Budworth Hall. The meeting would include a short talk by the chairman on the works to be heard in the first concert visit.

There being no further business, the meeting closed at 10:00 pm, those present appreciative of the hospitality of Mr & Mrs Terry in making their home available for the meeting.

[1] Initially, the word meeting referred to concerts but was later used to mean committee or general meetings.

[2] This is an extract from the committee's minutes. Similar quotations are shown throughout in a similar manner.

A second meeting is recorded for 12th February 1975:

Club Meeting – 12th February 1975

The meeting was held in the Budworth Hall and was attended by twelve members. The chairman gave a short talk illustrated by musical extracts on the Mozart piano concerti K. 246, K. 459 and K. 466, which formed the programme for the club's first concert visit to the Royal Festival Hall on 21st February.

The chairman gave details of the information received, and following consideration by members, it was decided to subscribe to the following organisations – the annual cost being shown:

Wigmore Hall	No charge
Royal Albert Hall	£1.00
Triad Bishops Stortford	£0.50
Royal Festival Hall	£1.00
English National Opera	£1.00
Royal Opera	£1.00
Royal Ballet	£1.00
BBC Concerts	No charge
English Chamber Orchestra	£1.15
London Mozart Players	£1.65

Membership of the English Chamber Orchestra and London Mozart Players includes certain privileges, which it was hoped would apply to all club members.

Following discussion, it was agreed that at the next meeting we should endeavour to arrange a programme for future club activities and Mrs Beale[1] agreed, in this respect, to approach the music staff at the Ongar Comprehensive School.

After discussion, it was agreed that the next meeting would be a Gilbert and Sullivan evening, and Mrs. Terry agreed to give a short talk on this subject. It was agreed that the next meeting would be held in the Old Library Building [2].

After discussing the subject, members travelled to the Old Library Building to see the facilities, and it was agreed that a notice board and club facilities could be made available by arrangement with the warden.

---

[1] Unfortunately, it has not been established who Mrs Beale was.

[2] The building referred to as the old library building had previously been the offices of the Ongar Rural District Council, erected in the mid-1980s. Now known as Essex House, the building sits at the junction of the High Street and Castle Street. When the new library was built, the old building was sold to Edwyn Gilmour who redecorated and refurnished it. The old Council Chamber (upstairs) was hired to local societies. This was the Arts Centre in which early concerts took place. Historical information courtesy of Dr Michael Leach.

The first concert visit

The first concert visit was held on Friday 21st February when thirteen members of the club attended a concert at the Royal Festival Hall.

The programme was as follows:

> Mozart Piano Concerto in C K. 246
> Mozart Piano Concerto in F K. 459
> Mozart Piano Concerto in D minor K. 466

The conductor and soloist was Daniel Barenboim, the orchestra being the English Chamber Orchestra.

It's recorded that the evening was enjoyed by all attending, and general satisfaction was expressed with the seats in the choir. The highlight for Tony Moore had been rubbing shoulders with the journalist and broadcaster Bernard Levin in the cloakroom!

An undated meeting is recorded as follows:

Club Meeting – Wednesday

Seven members attended, and the evening started with a musical quiz which proved successful – most could recognise the music – the difficulty arose in trying to guess the name of the piece and the composer.

The rest of the evening was given over to discussion of the club programme [presumed to be for 1976]. The framework was agreed as follows:

April 9th	Gilbert & Sullivan – Mrs Terry
May 8th	Visit to Brentwood Music Society
June	Proms talk – guest speaker
July	Music in Education – guest speaker

The chairman would finalise details of the programme and produce a news sheet for members, and it was agreed that the ladies would organise a supper for the June meeting and possibly for July.

Details of possible concert visits would be published by the chairman.
Thanks were expressed to Mrs Terry for organising coffee facilities.

The first AGM of the new club was held on Wednesday 17th September 1975 at the Arts Centre in Castle Street, Ongar. It was necessary to formally elect the committee and the following nominations were made and approved:

Chairman / Secretary	D. Kirkwood
Treasurer	Mrs M. Greatrex
Committee members	Mrs S. Terry
	Miss P. Musgrave
	Mr A. Bennett
	Mr G. Timms

It was agreed that the committee should finalise as soon as possible, details of the future programme and club membership, and general discussion took place on these.

The first formal concert to be given for the club was scheduled for 15th October, and this would be given by the flautist David Jewell, the cellist Hilary Jones, with club member Geoffrey Timms playing the piano. This would be held in the hall of Great Stony School. The next committee meeting contained details of the preparations for this event, as well as a good deal more substance relating to future plans:

Committee Meeting held on Friday, September 26th 1975

Present
D.A. Kirkwood – Chairman
Mrs Terry
Miss Greatrex – Treasurer
Miss Musgrave
Mr Timms
Apologies for absence – Mr A. Bennett

i) Sponsorship

We have received several offers of assistance as follows:

Great Stony School – use of the school hall
Rank Hovis McDougall Ltd. – all printing requirements
May and Baker Ltd. – financial assistance
Ongar Community Association – use of piano
Offers of assistance from Midland and Barclay's Banks and
Ongar Rotary Club would be progressed by the chairman.

It was agreed that we would advertise the assistance we receive in all appropriate literature, e.g. concert programmes and that we would give two complimentary tickets to each sponsor.

ii) Concert – October 15th 1975

Admission charges were fixed at 50p for adults and 25p for OAPs / students. Mr Roberts would be asked to act as doorman, and refreshments would be dealt with by the lady members of the committee – charging 10p for coffee and biscuits. The charge for programmes would be 10p. Mr Timms would provide programme notes, and programme details would include:

> Programme details
> Programme notes
> Performers' details
> Future programme details
> Details of committee
> Details of refreshments
> Detachable slip for potential members

The chairman would approach Mr Playford regarding moving the piano, and would also arrange insurance. Mr Timms would also arrange tuning on the day. Mr Bennett would be asked to arrange publicity for the concert.

iii) Future Programmes

Provisional details are as follows:

Date	Event	Venue	Adults	OAP/Student
November 19th	Ongar School Band	Great Stony	25p	Free
December 27th	Roderick Elms, piano	Great Stony	50p	25p
January 14th	Music Boxes	Arts Centre	25p	10p
February 18th	Keith Gurry, violin	Great Stony	50p	25p
March 17th	Members Concert	Great Stony	25p	10p
April 14th	Talk Barrie Hall	Great Stony	25p	10p
May 19th	Choral Evening	St Martin's Ch.	60p	30p
June 23rd	Quiz	Arts Centre	-	-

iv) Club Membership

Mrs Terry was unanimously elected Membership Secretary, and the committee expressed their thanks to Mrs Terry for taking on this task. Membership fees were fixed at 25 pence for adults and OAPs and 10 pence for students (n.b. – where reference is made to students, the maximum age for this category is 18 years on 1st September of each year of membership, the club year starting on 1st September each year.)

v) Club Rules

Mr Bennett had suggested a basis for the rules and principles of the club. These were agreed as a sound basis for discussion, but due to the lateness of the hour, this topic was held over to the next meeting. The meeting closed at 10:40 pm, the date of the next meeting having been arranged for Wednesday 22nd October 1975 at 27 Bowes Drive.

The first public concert went ahead as planned, and I officiated as page-turner for the occasion. The programme was:

> Concertino for flute, cello and piano, *Werner*
> Fantaisie for flute and piano Op. 79, *Fauré*
> Sonata for cello and piano, *Valentini arr. Piatti*
> Papillons for piano Op. 2, *Schumann*
> Sonata for flute and piano, *Hindemith*
> Piano Trio in G minor Op. 63, *Weber*
>
> David Jewel *flute*, Hilary Jones *cello* and Geoffrey Timms *piano*

At the following committee meeting held on 22nd October, it was agreed that October 15th concert had been a great success with an attendance of around eighty people. Epping Forest Arts Council had been approached for a donation of 'approximately £5' towards the cost of putting on the concert.

Plans were made for the forthcoming cheese and wine quiz evening – this was to be ladies vs gentlemen. It was also noted that we should be members of the Community Association. With regard to the club rules, the following were decided:

i)   The Chairman could stand for a maximum of three years

ii   The Committee to be elected annually at the AGM

iii) The Constitution of the Committee to be decided by the AGM

iv) The AGM of the club would be held in September each year

v)   Committee members could claim all reasonable expenses through the treasurer after approval by the committee

vi) It was decided to open a bank account at the Midland Bank

ONGAR

MUSIC

CLUB

Wednesday 15th October 1975

at 8 pm

Great Stony School, Ongar.

The front cover of the very first programme from 15th October 1975.

Financial assistance has always been crucial for classical arts organisations and this was sought from the very start – over the years, this has become increasingly difficult to achieve. The organisations listed to the right, are acknowledged in the first programme as supporting the opening season.

ACKNOWLEDGEMENTS

We are extremely grateful for the help we have received from the following organisations, without which the promotion of our concerts would not have been possible:

May & Baker Ltd. - Ongar Research Station

Midland Bank Ltd. - Ongar

Epping Forest and District Arts Council

Ranks Hovis McDougall Ltd. - Harlow

Great Stony School - Ongar

Ongar Community Association

R.V. Playford (Builder) - Ongar

Details of the first season were printed in the first programme from October 1975.

Date	
November 19th	Quiz - Ladies v Gentlemen followed by a Wine and Cheese Party
December 17th	Piano Recital - Roderick Elms
January 14th	Music Boxes - Bruce Moss
February 18th	Violin Recital - Keith Gurry
March 17th	Members Concert
April 14th	BBC Speaker (Barrie Hall)
May 19th	Chorale Concert
June 23rd	Arts Week - Quiz

Discussion subsequently took place regarding the issue of the piano that was currently in the Budworth Hall:

> It was decided to approach the Community Association with the suggestion that the grand piano be transferred to the Arts Centre [based in the Old Library Building] for the use of the Music Club. The Music Club would maintain the piano in reasonable condition and would provide a suitable upright for use in the Budworth Hall.

> The chairman would write to the appropriate authority in the CA. It was noted that a good upright had been purchased at a total cost of £16. It was also agreed to donate a proportion of any surplus we make each year to the CA.

The minutes of the meeting held on 26th November 1975 indicated a profit of £15 on the cheese and wine evening and the ladies were congratulated on the standard of refreshment provided. It was noted that the funds available would enable the club to pay for the replacement piano. It was agreed that this matter would be discussed at the next meeting of the CA executive committee. The grand piano would remain the property of the CA. The record shows that by then, there were forty-one members. The treasurer reported that the available funds stood at £35 after paying for the upright piano.

Venue	Admission	
	Adults	OAP/Students
Arts Centre	50p	25p
Great Stony School	50p	25p
Arts Centre	25p	10p
Great Stony School	50p	25p
Great Stony School	Free	Free
Great Stony School	25p	10p
St. Martin's Church	60p	30p
Arts Centre	Free	Free

By 6th February, the piano move was being planned, and the cash in hand was now around £80. On 19th March it was noted that the piano had been moved to the Arts Centre for the use of the Music Club and that the committee was still looking for suitable crockery. By then, discussions were underway for Antony Hopkins to give a BBC broadcast from Ongar, and the chairman was to write to the Ongar Comprehensive School to ask about the possibility of using the hall for this occasion. Plans were also well underway for a club visit to the ballet at Sadler's Wells.

The meeting minutes for 21st May 1976 show a record attendance for the choral concert held in St Martin's Church, with an audience of over two hundred – a donation of £15 was made to Christian Aid. There was, in fact, a small loss of £2.50 on the concert, mostly due to the hiring of a professional orchestra. Details were finalised for the club to have a stall at the Great Stony School fête. This meeting also decided that concerts for the following season would be arranged for Friday evenings and the same meeting also discussed, for the first time, the idea of running children's concerts. This was pursued at the next meeting (10th June 1976) when it was agreed that this was a good idea and that planning should be completed by the time of the forthcoming Cheese and Wine evening. It was suggested that this should run in mid-September – see Chapter 8. The minutes also contain an interesting note saying that "The chairman would write to the CA expressing our displeasure over the hiring of the piano to a band in Harlow".

June was something of a month for committee meetings – a further one on 25th June agreed to a new committee structure as follows:

> Executive Committee
>
> Chairman
> Secretary
> Treasurer
> Membership secretary
> Publicity Secretary
> Artistic Adviser
> Concerts Committee Member
>
> Concert Committee
>
> Chairman
> Five members

1976–1977

The second season brought with it the introduction of season tickets priced at £4 for adults and £2 for students and OAPs. That meeting (3rd September 1976) also saw the first mention of a raffle. This became a regular feature of concerts and other events for a good many years. This particular raffle is indicated as being drawn at the remarkably late hour of 11:00 pm on 21st January 1977. The subsequent AGM (17th September) notes the election of Barrie Hall to the committee as Publicity Officer.

An Extraordinary General Meeting (EGM) was held on 10th January 1977 to discuss the venue for concerts, the piano, the use of club funds and membership of the CA. The committee felt that the Arts Centre was no longer a suitable venue for concerts – primarily due to the lack of a public entertainment licence which restricted the sale of tickets to club members. Other adverse factors included excessive extraneous noise and inadequate seating.

Various options were discussed and it was decided to hold the forthcoming concert in the Budworth Hall to assess its suitability. The storage of the grand piano (by then in the Arts Centre) was a major consideration in considering alternative premises. It was explained that the club's piano needed much expensive renovation and that the money might be more wisely spent in purchasing another instrument. This could be either a secondhand instrument or a new one from Danemann's, which had been offered at the cost price £2,500 – as opposed to its usual price of £5,000. Most agreed that if financially feasible, they should try to take the second option. As moving forward with the piano situation would involve large sums of money, it was felt that the membership should be consulted in the matter. Those present expressed their confidence in the judgement of the committee.

Membership of the Community Association – the facilities available to the club as a 'Membership Section' of the CA were explained, and the alternatives of becoming either an 'Affiliated Group' or completely independent were also discussed. It was generally agreed that for the time being, the club would benefit most by remaining a 'Member Section'. Although this meant the club would pay slightly more to the CA in hiring fees, the CA would probably be more willing to store the piano for a Section than for an Affiliated Group. Mr Kirkwood explained that in this case, individual members must also pay CA membership subscriptions.

At the February meeting (4th February 1977), the chairman presented figures for the financial commitment in purchasing a new Danneman piano. It was felt that the full-size concert grand was not only beyond the club's means but not necessary for the club's purposes. This particular instrument would also incur greater problems of storage and insurance. The National Federation of Music Societies (NFMS) had offered an interest-free loan for half the cost of a piano. The chairman proposed that expenditure be limited to a figure of £1,500. It was agreed that Geoffrey Timms and I should visit the Danemann showroom together with an NFMS representative, and meanwhile, Barrie Hall would look into alternative instruments. This meeting also saw the first reference to investigating charity status, and 'Mrs Wilson' was deputed to investigate the club's application. It was also suggested by the chairman that the club loan the CA £200 for one year in order that they commence building work on the upstairs Concert Room – the Budworth Hall actually housing two large rooms – the upstairs Concert Room and the rather larger, ground floor Ballroom.

Reports on the piano situation were made to the next meeting (4th March 1977). By good fortune, as the result of ongoing searches by Geoffrey Timms and Barrie Hall, a full size (nine feet) concert grand piano by the firm of Weber had been located for sale by a Mrs Grace Green – this had been recommended by the pianist Rhondda Gillespie who had played it. After a visit to look at the instrument, the committee decided unanimously to accept the offer at the cost of £1,500, towards which an NFMS interest-free loan of £750 would be put. Additional interest-free loans were made by members of the committee and others to facilitate the payment. It's noted that:

> Miss Musgrave offered to call a meeting of the Concerts Committee to discuss fundraising as an alternative to forming a third committee for this purpose.

There was also a discussion about the following season, and it was agreed that the May (orchestral) concert would be called the 'Jubilee Concert'. Suggestions for the programme from Geoffrey Timms included Richard Strauss' oboe concerto, Haydn's 'Clock Symphony', a Mozart Overture and Beethoven's fourth piano concerto. It was also proposed by the chairman that concerts be arranged for the second Friday of the month whenever possible.

The piano was moved to the Budworth Hall during the week of the 14th March in good time for its inaugural recital by Rhondda Gillespie, to be given on Sunday afternoon, 3rd April. The subsequent meeting on 15th April noted that the piano had been installed and paid for. Barrie Hall also reported that he had approached Denis and Brenda Matthews, John Lill, Katerina Wolpe, the Lawrence Leonard Wind Ensemble and Yehudi Menuhin to appear for the club – all of these had offered to give concerts to help the piano fund. Yehudi Menuhin had also agreed to become President of Ongar Music Club as well as offering to let the club have some of his records for raffling. As might be expected, the committee received this news with considerable enthusiasm.

David Kirkwood, Chairman of Ongar Music Club acknowledging the arrival of the 'new' Weber concert grand piano.[1]

The idea for the club's series of children's concerts had come from Geoffrey Timms, who had been Head of Music at Beal Grammar School for Boys in Ilford (this later became Beal High School) and who was expert in dealing with young people and arranging suitable musical ventures. The children's concert on 22nd May resulted in five winners who were awarded three record tokens and two book tokens for their involvement. There was an attendance of eighty-five for the concert, with forty children submitting paintings for the attendant art competition; this being judged by Mr & Mrs Stevens of the Ongar Art Society.

At the June meeting, the ever-recurring topic of ticket prices was discussed, and the chairman proposed that these increase to £6 for the following season, including the necessary membership of the CA. He also made the suggestion that when planning concerts, the club might try to develop a theme during the season to maintain interest from year to year – possibly the complete cycle of Beethoven's piano sonatas over a period of several years.

[1] Unfortunately, I've not been able to establish the identity of the lady sitting on the piano

At the committee meeting on 20th July 1977, Phoebe Musgrave's proposal of an increase in number on the 'Executive Committee' by two was approved, and one of the names mentioned as a possible candidate was that of John Harrop, who was to become a stalwart member of the club for the rest of his life. We also read that at that same meeting came the first suggestion from Barrie Hall that he would keep a permanent record of all events and reviews by way of a scrapbook – this would be displayed regularly at club events.

The minutes also note that Peter Katin (due to give a recital) had written to the club to say that he would like to 'check the piano' as it was not a Steinway. The committee agreed to this, providing he paid his own expenses. If he was not agreeable, then the engagement was to be considered cancelled. Following his visit, Peter Katin withdrew from the engagement.

1977–1978

During late 1977, several of the loans made towards the purchase of the piano were repaid, to the point that it is noted in the minutes for the meeting held on 3rd January 1978, that all loans were repaid in full. That meeting noted that since the CA was again in financial difficulties, various ideas were discussed to allow the Music Club to offer some support. The meeting also recorded the sad loss of club member Hugh Terry, with a donation of £10 being made to the Essex Burns Unit in his memory. It was also recorded that the eminent Essex-born pianist John Lill, who had a home in the Ongar area, had been awarded an OBE, and it was agreed that the chairman would write to congratulate him. The meeting concluded with a suggestion from Barrie Hall that artistes should be requested to wear formal evening dress – to which the committee agreed.

1978 – A Turbulent Year

It was reported at the committee meeting on 31st January 1978 that there had been a meeting of the CA on 30th January at which it was stated that funds were urgently required in order to avoid closure.

A loan of £2,000 was available, but only if sections were willing to pool their funds. A vote was taken on the motion that those present recognise the legal right of the CA to call in the funds of the member sections. Those present were told that this was a formality as the Charity Commissioners had confirmed the legal position.

The motion was carried. Music Club representatives voted against the motion. Not all member sections were represented, nor were all those included in the vote, members of a section. Equal representation of those sections in attendance was not observed.

Mr Harrop reported that a letter had been sent to Mr Kirkwood requesting that a statement of the club's accounts be presented to the CA by 2nd of February and funds to be made available by the following week.

Committee requested that Mrs Wilson reply informing CA executives that as both the Chairman and Treasurer were away, it would not be possible to comply with this request at present.

Mr Hall was requested to contact the NFMS regarding the legal ownership of the piano as £750 of the piano purchasing loan was still outstanding. Further advice to be sought on this matter from a solicitor.

Miss Musgrave offered to purchase the piano from the club for the amount outstanding on the loan thus enabling the club to repay this in full. Miss Musgrave would then hold the piano in trust for the sole use of the club.

Agreement had been established with the CA executive prior to the purchase of the piano that it should remain the property of the Music Club as an exception from the CA rules.

As a direct result of this, an Extraordinary Committee Meeting of the Music Club was called for 5th February 1978 to review the situation.

Minutes of Extra-Ordinary Committee Meeting
Held on 5th, February '78

Mrs Greatrex out of the country, all other committee members present,

Purpose of meeting – To review the club's financial situation in response to the CA's demand that club funds be submitted to the CA to form part of a central fund. Furthermore, to consider any action necessary to protect the interests of Music Club members.

Financial Situation – Mr Hall reported that the CA did require the club's cash to be submitted, not merely a statement of the accounts.

Mr Kirkwood reported that the club's debts did not at present outweigh its assets. However, £600.00 previously paid into the Halifax Building Society was held in receipt of ticket sales for the June Concert (Menuhin recital). In order to protect the interests of the purchaser, Mr Kirkwood proposed that this money be withdrawn and individual sums labelled ready for immediate return if the committee considered this necessary. This proposal was carried unanimously – Mrs Terry and Mr Kirkwood to prepare same.

Mr Kirkwood offered to prepare a graph showing the club's financial outgoings, which increase as the season progresses. This he would present to the CA Executive together with a copy of last year's accounts and the figures at present.

This, he hoped, would demonstrate the difficulties the club would encounter if not in control of its own finances. He would also point out that the £150 left in the account was already committed mainly to expenses regarding the Old Time Music Hall.

The committee agreed unanimously to this course of action.

Piano – Miss Musgrave reported that she had consulted a solicitor regarding transfer of ownership of the piano. He was preparing a document stating that the ownership of the piano would be transferred from the club to Miss Musgrave on receipt of £750 (amount of NFMS loan still outstanding). Miss Musgrave in return would hold the piano in trust for the club and keep it available for the club's use at all times.

Committee agreed unanimously that ownership of the piano should be transferred, precise terms of repayment to be considered at a later date.

At a committee meeting held on 28th February 1978, David Kirkwood (chairman) reported on the CA council meeting held earlier that evening:

He had been unable to reach any agreement with the council regarding financial arrangements between the CA and the Music Club.

The council insisted that all sections pay their funds into the CA's central fund. Applications for funds would then have to be made by the sections treasurer or her representative at monthly meetings of the Finance Committee.

The committee felt that this arrangement would be totally impractical due to the long term commitments and large sums involved in organising a season's concerts.

Attempts to form a CA Fundraising Committee had failed for lack of volunteers. Mr K had proposed at the meeting that each section should offer an idea for as fund raising event. This had been received favourably.

Having reviewed the CA membership rules, Mr Hall proposed the Music Club change its status from Section to Affiliated Group. This being in accordance with the statement that members of national bodies (e.g. NFMS) are constituent bodies and as such can be affiliated to the CA.

Proposal seconded by Mr Harrop and agreed unanimously.

Mr Kirkwood proposed that the club offer to run one event entirely for the benefit of the CA, probably the Quiz/Wine and Cheese evening.

This proposal was accepted.

Mr Kirkwood to communicate with the CA executive on both matters.

At an extraordinary committee meeting held on 10th March 1978, David Kirkwood reported that:

... the CA had refused the club's application to become an affiliated group rather than a section. A copy of the letter had been supplied to committee members.

The committee then discussed the advantages and disadvantages of CA membership and once again concluded that the new financial arrangements were impractical.

Mr Kirkwood proposed the following resolution:

With the greatest possible respect to all those concerned, the Committee of Ongar Music Club is not optimistic about the ability of the Community Association to run the Music Club's affairs better than they are run at present. Therefore the proposals put forward in the Community Association's letter of 8th March leaves the Music Club with no alternative but to adopt the other proposal suggested in that same letter and to withdraw from the Association entirely.

We take this course of action with great regret, as we had hoped that 'affiliation' would have enabled us to retain some direct connection with the Community Association in the future. This is formal notification of the Music Club's decision to withdraw.

This resolution was agreed unanimously by all committee members.

Mr Kirkwood to inform CA immediately.

There being no further business the meeting closed at 11.30 pm.

Miss Musgrave was thanked for her hospitality.

The subsequent committee meeting on 9th April 1978 indicated that all members had been notified of the action and motives with regard to the CA membership, and no unfavourable reactions had been received.

There was also clear uncertainty as to whether existing bookings in the Budworth Hall would stand following the recent decision to withdraw from CA membership.

David Kirkwood reminded the committee that he would be unable to stand as chairman for the following season in accordance with the agreed rules of the club. They should therefore be thinking of a replacement. He also suggested that thought be given to new or improved concert facilities, as money may be available from various sources to connect with, improve or build a suitable hall.

During the period of unrest with the CA, the club's piano had been moved temporarily for storage at Fyfield Boarding School, from where it was removed when needed. One such occasion was to Ongar Comprehensive School for the special evening with Yehudi Menuhin on 8th June. This is noted in the minutes of 2nd May 1978, which also record that Mr Menuhin would be presented with three or four bottles of claret to the value of £50 as a token of the club's appreciation. Also noted is the possibility of a memorial concert for the late Hugh Terry, which Mrs Terry was to discuss with the Rotary Club before a final decision was made about moving the idea forward.

It is interesting to read in the same minutes that at an extraordinary CA council meeting, the "executive council had been ousted following a vote of no confidence at the meeting". The committee discussed the possibility of the club becoming a member section again and supporting the new CA executive. No decision was reached but an informal meeting would be arranged with CA representatives to discuss the matter.

The meeting on 30th April 1978 reported that all arrangements had been finalised for the Menuhin recital and that 'Mr Hall' had arranged twelve bottles of wine to be presented to Mr Menuhin at the reception following the concert. The committee agreed that Miss Musgrave should be repaid her loan of £750 for the piano, plus interest in the form of a £15 garden token. It was also confirmed that Allan Schiller had agreed to give a Chopin recital for the club, and that the eminent percussionist

James Blades [1] was willing to play for the club. The meeting also agreed on committee positions for the 1978-79 season as follows:

Chairman	– Mr John Harrop
Secretary	– Mrs Joyce Perry
Treasurer	– Mr David Kirkwood
Membership Secretary	– Mrs Sylvia Terry
Publicity Officer	– Mr Barrie Hall

Mr Kirkwood and Miss Musgrave reported on an informal meeting with the CA chairman and warden. Mr Barnes had expressed interest in the Music Club becoming a member section once again and was willing to try and find a solution to the problems at present barring membership. Agreement was reached that a CA representative should meet with the complete Music Club committee for further discussion. The committee agreed that the club's interest should be protected in writing if it were to rejoin the CA. A further meeting was held on 5th June, following which agreement was reached on a way forward, and the Music Club rejoined the CA as a Member Section.

As greatly anticipated, the concert three days later, on 8th June, was a huge success and the highlight of that season. The 'President's Evening' with Yehudi Menuhin and The Juviller Trio (all former pupils of the

The souvenir programme produced for Yehudi Menuhin's 'President's Evening' on 8th June 1978

---

[1] Apart from his wider fame, James Blades was responsible for striking the real gong (actually a Tam Tam) for introductions to films made by the Rank Organisation. The one seen on screen being made of papier-mâché.

Yehudi Menuhin School at Stoke d'Abernon) was a triumph and the hall of Ongar Comprehensive School was packed. Apart from the obvious delight of having such an eminent musician perform for the club, the occasion had also been in aid of the club's piano fund, and the result was that the instrument was finally paid for.

1978–1979

It's interesting to note that following the 1978 AGM (15th September) the formality of the record-keeping becomes a little less formal with occasional reference to committee members by their first name only, although it would be some years before this practice became commonplace. The AGM also ratified the new officers, as proposed by the committee.

There had been a request to members for extra help, and the new committee read as follows:

Chairman	– Mr John Harrop
Secretary	– Mrs Joyce Perry
Treasurer	– Mr David Kirkwood
Membership Secretary	– Mrs Sylvia Terry
Publicity Officer	– Mr Barrie Hall
Social secretaries	– Miss Phoebe Musgrave
	Mrs Betty Greatrex
Committee Members	– Mr Kenneth Bird
	Mr Peter Lewis

An autograph given to founder club member, Sylvia Terry

Following acceptance of the new committee members, David Kirkwood welcomed the new chairman and asked him to chair the meeting. John Harrop thanked the former chairman for his hard work in founding and supporting the club and said that he hoped to continue his good work. It was noted that the idea for a choral society in Ongar, mooted in the previous year's minutes, had now come to fruition and it needed more male members – 'twas ever thus.

It had been agreed that for the concert on 17th November 1978, the club would open the bar which would be run by two of the CA's bar committee. The bar receipts amounted to £18, and it was observed that if other sections opened the bar in this way, the CA could have a steady income. The bar was to become something of a stumbling block for the club in the future.

An interesting note in the minutes for a meeting held on 9th January 1979 came from Geoffrey Timms, who broached the idea of a competitive music festival in the area to be organised by the Music Club. This was discussed briefly, and it was decided to talk about it in detail at a later date after Geoffrey and John Harrop had done a quick feasibility study. It was recorded that the idea was a 'most acceptable one'. This idea would ultimately prove to be a milestone in the development and status of Ongar Music Club.

By the meeting on 6th March 1979, the domestic situation seemed much more stable. There was a healthy bank balance of around £950 (although there were liabilities to be taken into account), and the concert series was progressing smoothly and with a good audience response. By now, most concerts were taking place in the Budworth Hall, and use was being made of the bar facilities, both during the intervals and after concerts.

A rather nice anecdote from this meeting came from Phoebe Musgrave under the heading of 'Money Raising'. She was particularly anxious that the club should be thinking of money-making activities and suggested a 'paté and plonk' at her house. She also agreed to approach Sylvia Hatfield about the possibility of using her garden for a summer evening concert in early or mid-June. The 'Paté and Plonk' lunch raised the surprising (for the time) sum of £77.75.

In fact, there were various diverse ideas for fundraising along the way, which included not just coffee mornings but also social evenings, cheese and wine parties with entertainment, soup and savoury lunches, farmhouse teas, garden performances and 'Sherry Mornings'.

There was subsequent discussion (meeting 6th March 1979) of a Music Festival for young players administered by local music teachers but under the club's auspices. Geoffrey Timms was to investigate whether there was sufficient interest in local schools.

David Kirkwood announced at the April meeting that he was shortly leaving the district and would therefore be stepping down as treasurer. This came as something of a blow as it was David who had been instrumental in establishing the Music Club and had steered it through a number of challenging periods to its current position of stability and growth. At his request, Peter Lewis agreed to step into the treasurer's role with immediate effect.

At the following meeting, John Harrop had received a letter from the CA asking for further help with fundraising. After some discussion, it was decided to ask him to draft a letter in reply, reminding them of the help the club had given in the past and of their own financial commitments.

David Kirkwood's last meeting was on 2nd July 1979, and John Harrop expressed his appreciation to David for all he had given and been to the club since its inception. David subsequently wrote to the club to express his and his wife Margaret's appreciation of the farewell gift – a painting of Ongar High Street done by Alan Chaplin. This is recorded in the minutes dated 31st July, which also notes discussion about the vexed issue of ticket prices. It was agreed that these would be:

> Season ticket – £10 (including CA membership)
> OAP – £7.50 (including CA membership)
> Membership Ticket – £3 (including CA membership)
> OAP Concert Ticket – £1.85 (including CA membership
> Members to receive a reduction of 20p on each concert

It was of particular interest to note a section in these minutes headed 'Ongar Anti-Airport Group'. I was due to give the traditional recital following the club's September AGM that year, and it was suggested that I could be asked to play one of my pieces to the accompaniment of the recorded sound of a jet aircraft!

1979–1980

At the 1979 AGM, the chairman was able to report yet another successful year. The club boasted a hundred and fifteen members, including sixty-one season ticket holders. There had been eleven concerts and a variety of social functions. Relations with the CA were good; the Budworth Hall was used for most concerts, and during the year, the club had donated a record player to be raffled for CA funds. The average audience was between seventy and eighty, although the maximum of three hundred had been reached (in the Ongar Comprehensive School hall) for the piano recital by Denis Matthews. The chairman also announced the resignation of David Kirkwood; he reiterated how much he would be missed and expressed how much the club was indebted to him. He also presented the audited accounts showing a balance of £452.48. The committee was re-elected 'en masse' with Mr Frank Spinks filling the vacancy created by David Kirkwood's departure.

The meeting on 7th November 1979 noted that James Blades had agreed to a reduced fee of £100 and that a recital by Allan Schiller had been attended by a healthy one hundred and twenty people. Steven Isserlis had written asking for a contribution of £18 towards his pianist's expenses in travelling from Edinburgh – another world compared with contemporary rail fares. It was also agreed to send a donation of £5 to the memorial fund for Arthur Bennett, a founder committee member, who had been tragically killed during that week.

The following meeting on 28th November 1979 involved planning for the forthcoming Victorian Evening (14th December), as well as another of the regular series of children's concerts on 20th January in which Colin Handley was coming to talk about, and play, some unusual wind instruments. After the interval, there was to be a showing of the film

'Peter and the Wolf'. These children's concerts were now a regular feature of the club's programme of events, and future events included other instrumental demonstrations and film presentations, including 'The Carnival of the Animals'. Many of these occasions included a children's painting competition which was judged by local artist Alan Chaplin who personally offered an extra prize for the youngest competitor. The main prizes were usually vouchers for WH Smith.

Early in 1980, Barrie Hall had been negotiating with the manager of the Midland Bank in Ongar regarding a sponsorship plan. It was the bank's 10th Anniversary in the autumn and it was suggested that the club might invite Sir Peter Pears to entertain the club, with his fee and expenses (£250 + VAT) being paid by the Midland Bank and the proceeds being donated to the CA building fund. Ultimately a date was fixed for 31st of October. It was also noted early in 1980 that the Budworth Hall had also been booked for all the club's concerts up to the end of the 1981 season.

1980–1981

As might be expected, Sir Peter Pears brought a capacity audience of two hundred and forty, and it was a splendid occasion. According to the minutes, the reception afterwards at Blake Hall was "in grand style and made a fitting end to a very pleasant evening".

The issue of the club's piano arose again at the meeting on 13th May 1981 when it was acknowledged that the instrument was becoming

elderly and in need of "repair in various particulars". Barrie Hall suggested that the club should be thinking seriously of trading it in for a reconditioned Steinway. The committee agreed to give some thought to the idea. In addition, John Harrop would consult the club's regular piano tuner and technician Mr Kear, regarding the making of a trolley to fit the present piano and which could be adapted for use with a Steinway B grand, if purchased. At the following meeting on 3rd June, Barrie Hall reported that he had contacted John Lill, who had agreed to inaugurate a new Steinway if and when purchased. It was also agreed to look into the possibility of using the Budworth Hall's Concert Room for events rather than the Ballroom as it was much cheaper to hire.

ONGAR MUSIC CLUB

President: Yehudi Menuhin K.B.E.

1980-81 SEASON

Friday,31st October 1980

ONGAR COMPREHENSIVE SCHOOL

8.00p.m.

An
evening with

S I R   P E T E R   P E A R S

Ongar Music Club is proud to present this function in association with Midland Bank Ltd., celebrating ten years of service to Ongar

On 14th July, Barrie reported receiving a letter from Steinway with details of prices for new and reconditioned pianos. He also drew attention to the private sales of good pianos. There was a great deal of discussion as to whether they could raise the money required for such a big project or whether it would be more prudent to hire a good piano when required. Either way, the existing piano would need a major overhaul before long, which would be very expensive.

1981–1982

That year's AGM was held on 18th of September. In his last report as chairman before his term completed, John Harrop spoke of another successful year, with the highlights undoubtedly being the evenings with Sir Peter Pears and Denis Matthews. Kenneth Bird proposed amendments to the club's Constitution:

Rule 1 to read:
The title shall be Ongar Music Club, hereinafter referred to as 'the club'.

Rule 4 to read:

The management of the club shall be directed by a committee consisting of an Hon. President, a Chairman and up to nine club members elected at the Annual General Meeting in accordance with Rule 7. The Federal Representative of the National Federation of Music Societies, for the time being shall also be, ex-officio, a member of the committee.

The Committee shall, at its discretion, appoint such honorary officers as Vice-Chairman, Secretary, Membership Secretary, Publicity Officer, Social Secretary etc. and such sub-committees as, in its opinion, the interests of the club require. All honorary officers shall hold office until the Annual General Meeting of the Club. The office of chairman shall be tenable for a period of not more than three consecutive years.

The Club may, at its discretion, nominate as Honorary Vice-President for Life, one or more of its members who have rendered outstanding service for the Club.

Five members of the committee may constitute a quorum at any meeting, and whoever shall attend in case of a General Meeting.

It was at this meeting that Barrie Hall would take over as chairman of Ongar Music Club. At the subsequent committee meeting held on 23rd September, arrangements for the new committee were put in place:

Chairman	– Barrie Hall
Vice-Chairman	– Geoffrey Timms
Secretary	– Daphne Tinsey
Membership Secretary	– Sylvia Terry
Social Secretaries	– Phoebe Musgrave
	– Betty Greatrex
Treasurer	– Archie Norrie
Publicity	– Barrie Hall
John Harrop	
Kenneth Bird	
Peter Lewis	

Routine jobs were allocated as follows:

Barrie	– to collect keys to Door, Kitchen, Office, Piano, Meeting soloists etc. and organising posters
Geoffrey	– Music, Tape-recorder & all musical equipment

John   – To work with Geoffrey. Programme printing etc,
            arrange piano tuning. Assist with rehearsals.
Kenneth – Hall, chairs, curtains, blinds, props, stage,
            stands, lighting
Peter   – To work with Kenneth on hall, raffle, and coffee
Sylvia   – All ticket selling and dealing with Highway
            Travel (which sold concert tickets).

The 4th November meeting mentions a suggestion from Betty Greatrex that an outing be arranged in the New Year to visit the 'new' Barbican. Sylvia Terry reported that there were currently seventy-five members. Geoffrey Timms again suggested the idea of a 'Young Musicians Contest' with 'good prizes', and it was agreed to discuss this at a later date. Geoffrey also reported that for the children's concert on 7th February (1982) he was hoping to arrange for 'The Gnaff Ensemble' to come at a fee of around £60+VAT. The *internationally unknown* Gnaff Ensemble consisted of six musicians – Bramwell Tovey, Paul Hart, Christopher Stearn, Russell Jordan, Harold Sim and myself. All highly expert in their own musical fields, they had met as members of the Redbridge Youth Orchestra and regularly came together to bring their own special brand of musical humour to unsuspecting audiences across the southeast. The afternoon was a terrific success, not least because the Gnaffs had decided to present the world premiere of the hitherto unknown Ongar Conga. Traditionally, this involved a raucous procession out of the main doors of the Ballroom, crossing Banson's Lane, around the car park, and back in the rear doors of the hall – much to the delight of all concerned. This proved to be a highly popular item in the programme, although that may also have been its last performance. It was subsequently agreed that the admission charge had been too low for what was a capacity audience.

The suggestion of a competition arose again in April 1982 when it was reported that Barrie Hall had approached International Distillers, who were prepared to put up a large sum of money, but for an international contest. Geoffrey Timms suggested perhaps the ITV programmes could be contacted for help – the contest would be discussed again. Sometime prior to that meeting, Phoebe Musgrave, a founder committee member, had

ONGAR MUSIC CLUB
President: Yehudi Menuhin KBE

Sunday 7 February 1982 at 3am prompt

The Budworth Hall - Ongar
(just opposite 'The Cock' Tavern)
-Dress: optional but preferable-

L A F F   W I T H   G N A F F

(or The Gnaff Ensemble's Country Show)

POSSIBLE ORDER OF EVENTS

1. "THE SWAN"   arr. Saint-Saëns (1835-1921)
   Soloist: Miss Catherine Giles

2. GRAND PRELUDE IN D double flat Minor   Fred. Chopin (1810-)
   Soloist: Mr. Roderick Elms

3. GNAFFINSTRUMENTEN
   Featuring Mr. Paul Hart and Mr. Christopher Stearn

4. GNAFF VOCAL FINALE
   Mr. Bramwell Tovey and the entire company

:::::::: INTERVAL ::::::::

5. UNBEKNOWN TO ALBINONI   arr. W.A. Mozart (1756-1791)
   Soloists: Mr. Bramwell Tovey and Mr. Christopher Stearn

6. THE YOUNG GNAEF'S GUIDE TO THE ORCHESTRA
                                   Erique von Bateau (1721-1670)

        (i)   Gnaff Opening

        (ii)   Tuba Gnaffs

        (iii) Gnaff Piano

        (iv)   Fairground Gnaffs

        (v)   Gnaffrobats

        (vi)   Percussion Gnaffs

        (vii) Gnaff Ballet

        (viii) Young Gnaffs (Doghouse)

        (ix)   Gnaffs' Cat

        (x)   Fine Ale

The audience is requested not to snore except in the key or related keys
of the works being performed at the time.

been taken into hospital, and she sadly passed away prior to the following meeting on 26th May. I have a great personal memory of Phoebe; as on the occasion of my first recital for the club in December 1975, I was suffering from severe neck pain and Phoebe, a physiotherapist by profession was able to give me some relief by massage prior to the performance.

At that same meeting in May, came the first mention of the club's book and record stall, which ran for many years on concert days. This idea came from Barrie Hall, who suggested a member of the committee could act as the librarian. Peter Lewis made the necessary stand for the books, and at a later meeting, Kenneth Bird agreed to act as the librarian when the lending library started that September.

Meanwhile, plans had been developing for the new young musician's competition. Sylvia Terry suggested (meeting 28th July) that the club should award the winner with a silver cup, and it should be known as the Phoebe Musgrave Cup. The committee all agreed, and Mr Triggs (silversmith) be asked the price of such a cup.

1982–1983

The 1982 AGM was held on 17th September and was chaired by Barrie Hall. Sylvia Terry, as membership secretary, announced that there were forty-four season ticket holders and thirty-two regular members. The average concert audience was eighty. The new price for the 1982–83 season (eight concerts) was £14.00 and £12.00 for senior citizens. Social Secretary Betty Greatrex spoke of the sad loss of founder club member Phoebe Musgrave. She also introduced Margaretta Walker-Arnott, who had agreed to be co-opted onto the committee. It was hoped to introduce some outings into this season, the first being on 23rd October to The Maltings, Snape. Kenneth Bird made reference to the 'handsome' new cabinet holding the books for the new Lending Library, and Geoffrey Timms (Vice-Chairman and Music Adviser) gave 'vague warning' of the impending arrival in Ongar of the Gnaff Ensemble on 8th July. The audited accounts for the year ending 31st August 1982 were presented to the meeting.

At the following committee meeting (19th October 1982), it was reported that the club had taken receipt of a solid silver rose bowl cup to be approved by the committee – the cost being £57.50. This would be used for the Young Musicians Competition now being planned. It was agreed that it was most suitable and should be known as the 'Phoebe Musgrave Trophy'. The committee would also investigate the cost of medallions for the competition winners to keep. At the following meeting in December (8th) it was reported that Mr Triggs suggested no engraving on the cup itself as it would devalue it. Rather, the cup should have a stand with a small shield for names to be added. It was also agreed that the committee members would contribute towards the cost of the cup. Barrie Hall reported that he hoped to hear further from International Distillers as to whether they might now be willing to sponsor the young musician's competition – he hoped it might be £500.

Domestically, a trolley had been ordered and would shortly be fitted to the club's piano, making its movements both easier and safer, and the chairman had been able to purchase fourteen records at £1.00 each to be used as raffle prizes. Such activities were ongoing in the background, with many raffle prizes being given from quite large concerns in the form of record players, televisions and the like.

At the first meeting of 1983 (9th February), Barrie Hall reported that the idea for sponsorship of the new competition by International Distillers had failed to come to fruition. It was agreed to form a subcommittee to carry forward the planning of the new competition (for 1984), and this would consist of Barrie, Geoffrey, Peter and Sylvia. Various other firms were suggested for investigation regarding possible sponsorship, and Barrie would investigate making an appeal on Essex Radio. This Barrie did, although none of the committee heard it. Never one to miss an opportunity to publicise the club, Barrie had also included a brief history of Ongar Music Club by way of background for listeners and potential publicity for the club's activities.

By now, the café at the front of the Budworth Hall had been developed under the name of 'The Taste Bud' and was doing well. There had also been ongoing discussions about the renovation of the club's piano, and the NFMS had agreed to pay half of the cost, interest-free, over five years. By March 1983 it had been agreed to get advice from Mr Kear regarding the necessary work to both the mechanism and the bodywork. It was later suggested that additional quotes be obtained from the piano firms Chappell and Knight.

1983–1984

The 1983 AGM was held on 30th September at which Sylvia Terry noted that the average concert attendance was then around eighty – the three favourite evenings during the previous year having been Dame Eva Turner, the Christmas concert and the Dave Shepherd concert. A very successful outing had also taken place to hear the Essex Youth Orchestra play at the Thaxted Festival.

A crucial decision came at the committee meeting on 28th September 1983, when it was agreed that Barrie Hall would contact John Lill to ask whether he would help with the young musician's contest – perhaps have a John Lill Award and combine it with the Phoebe Musgrave Cup. Maybe John could appeal on Essex Radio or have a fundraising event. Barrie Hall later reported (18th January 1984) that in December, he had had a working lunch with John Lill, who was willing to help in connection with the 'young musician's contest'. He would give a free recital for the club in May and broadcast on Essex Radio, appealing for sponsorship. He also gave permission for his name to be used for newspaper promotion and on Essex Radio. The 'contest' would be known as the John Lill Award in conjunction with the 'Phoebe Musgrave Trophy' – all other details to be decided later.

At the meeting on 15th February 1984, Barrie Hall suggested that a new sub-committee be formed known as the Awards Committee, consisting of Geoffrey Timms, John Harrop, Peter Lewis and Sylvia Terry. The first meeting was arranged for the 29th February with details to be discussed including the age limit and the best way to find young musicians. Geoffrey Timms suggested contacting the Essex Educational Music Department for recommendations. A sum of £15 was granted for the cost of obtaining copies of the John Lill photograph.

It's interesting to note that at the same meeting, it was reported that the raffle held at concerts was becoming increasingly hard to promote. After consideration, it was concluded that there was no viable alternative. At 14th March meeting, the John Lill Award now had its own heading:

Barrie reported the John Lill Piano recital would be on Saturday May 12th, at the Comprehensive School, Ongar. It was agreed to hire a Steinway Piano for the recital, it will arrive on Friday May 11th, at the cost of approximately £250-£300.

John Harrop is to book the school for the recital. John brought to the notice of the Committee that a new Fire Rule has been installed by the County Council Committee regarding the seating arrangements at the school – only to be 250 seats, to provide more seats would involve the club in extra expenses. It is thought a Fire Officer will check on the evening that all seating is in order.

It was decided the tickets should cost £5 each, and be numbered.

Geoffrey and the Sub-Committee have drawn up Conditions and Rules for the Entry Forms for the auditions regarding the Young Musicians Contest. Dates are to be confirmed with Budworth Hall.

The 1st Prize will be £350, and to retain the Phoebe Musgrave Trophy for one year.
The 2nd Prize will be £150.
Age limit 21 years, and the applicant must have an Essex postal address. No organists or singers to apply.

Geoffrey to arrange five people to judge the contest.

The chairman and committee expressed their thanks to Geoffrey and the sub-committee for all their hard work in preparing the Conditions etc.

It was later suggested that the 2nd prizewinner of the Young Musicians Contest should play at the AGM on 28th September.

In April, Geoffrey Timms reported that he had mailed a hundred and seventeen schools in Essex regarding the forthcoming 'Young Musicians Contest' and still had the colleges and public schools to write to. Meanwhile, John Harrop reported that the piano renovations had

begun and should be completed by the second week of May. However, the club's piano was not to be used for John Lill's recital in May for which a Steinway was being hired.

The Concert Room, Budworth Hall, Ongar (looking from the performing area)

Another innovation had previously arisen when discussing new avenues for generating income, additional to those already in place. Geoffrey Timms had said that he would investigate the requirements for running a Century Club and reported on this to the next meeting (9th May) – it would be for Music Club members only, with payment by Bankers Order. 50% of the money would be used for prizes and 50% for expenses and profit. It was decided to print a leaflet explaining the rules, placing it on chairs at the June event, asking the audience if they were interested and, if so, to write their name, address and phone number on the leaflet.

The John Lill Award recital was to be on 12th May at the Ongar Comprehensive School, and as expected, tickets were selling well. John Lill had consented to be the club's first patron and thanked the club for the honour. It was decided to give John a case of wine in appreciation of his generosity.

The concert returned a surplus of £695.22 and was agreed to have been an outstanding and very special evening. Geoffrey Timms reported that the competition entry forms were returning slowly but would likely all arrive in the last few days (this has been the case ever since). The Essex Young Musician of the Year (EYMY) competition was set for the weekend of 20th and 21st July, and more details would be reported at the next meeting on 10th July. Essex Radio agreed to sponsor the first prize of £350, and Kenneth Bird provided a cheque from his company Yule Catto & Co. (Revertex), for £250, being the second prize. Dr Christopher Green of Essex Radio was invited to be one of the judges, along with the conductor Bramwell Tovey, the violist John White, the pianist Eileen Broster and Geoffrey Timms, who acted as chairman of the judges (the competition is discussed fully in Chapter 7).

Meanwhile, plans were progressing for the new Century Club, and at the 25th September meeting (1984), Geoffrey Timms reported that it was hoped to start this new venture on 23rd November. It was previously noted from remarks which had been overheard that the audience might be getting a little tired of the concert raffle, although it did bring in a useful income. Therefore this new venture might prove to be a welcome alternative or additional method of bringing income to the club.

1984–1985

The plan for a Century Club was reported to the September AGM from which came a delightful anecdote from the pianist Peter Wallfisch, following his recital for the club on the recently renovated piano:

"A dear piano, good for a few more years yet".

At 19th October committee meeting it was decided to stop buying new books for the library as they were proving more expensive than anticipated, and the chairman had discovered a way of buying books at a discount. It was resolved to buy no more than three or four new books each season.

There had been ongoing discussions about producing a car sticker to advertise the activities of the Music Club, and final wording was to be produced for the next meeting. This was eventually agreed at the subsequent committee meeting on 19th October and the new car stickers were presented to the committee in December. The October meeting also agreed that the Century Club would now start on 1st December and if there were a hundred members, the monthly prizes would be £15 and £10, with six-monthly prizes of £100 and £50. It was also decided that all club members should be issued with a club card, and associate members would pay 25p to belong.

For the Allan Schiller recital on 26th October, it was decided not to hold the usual raffle but to ask everyone to join the new Century Club. Also, in October, Barrie Hall made the suggestion that more young people might be encouraged to join the club:

… if letters could be sent round to the schools offering children to come to concerts free of charge – it would enable them to see how Ongar Music Club worked, this was thought a very good idea.

The following month it was decided to investigate, in collaboration with the Budworth Hall restaurant, the possibility of a 'Meal-and-Music' ticket for concert nights. Meanwhile, the raffle continued during concert evenings with a seemingly never-ending supply of prizes. These were largely donated by committee members, their families, and friends. In December, as was customary when planning for the festive season, small gifts were purchased to be given to third parties who had been particularly supportive of the club – a bottle of whisky to each of the local newspapers, as well as Highway Travel which helped considerably by selling concert tickets.

Early in 1985 came the proposal for a Grand Draw, with prizes to be given out at the next AGM. The six prizes are noted as being: a television set, a silver vegetable stand, a lighter and stand, a case of wine and a bottle of champagne. It had been decided to have five hundred lottery books to be sold at £1 a book. The draw proved to be a great success, and it was reported in October that: "To date, the sum of £383.40 has been made. The good result is due to the hard work of some members of the committee".

For some years, there had been regular children's concerts with the proceeds frequently being sent to charities such as 'The School for the Deaf Children' in Woodford and 'The Sir Winston Churchill School for the Deaf'. However, at the May meeting, it was suggested that instead of the usual Children's Concert, there should be a 'Concert of Young Artistes' and this revised format was agreed. This being essentially a concert *by* children rather than one *for* them. It was also decided that at the next recital (Valerie Tryon, 7th June) they would not hold a raffle but sell tickets instead for a Grand Draw.

The committee had been stable for quite some time, but a blow came when the super-efficient and highly respected treasurer Janice Tompkins gave notice that she would be stepping down from the end of the 1984-85 season due to pressure of work. This came as a great shock to the

committee, and her duties were taken over by John Harrop.

A significant event in 1985 was the twinning of Ongar with the French town of Cerizay, and it was decided to organise a concert for the Twinning Association. This took place on 26th May at the Budworth Hall when the Stondon Singers gave a

1985

performance to a full hall. They were subsequently invited to perform for the club at its popular Christmas concert.

Domestically, a new cabaret sub-committee was formed to plan this popular and money-generating event, and invitations were issued to Dave Shepherd and 'The Blue Birds'. The Cabaret Evening on 3rd May was, as usual, a great success and hugely enjoyed. It was subsequently felt that there was scope for a further jazz-based evening later in the year, possibly a return visit from Dave Shepherd in December. The jazz and cabaret evenings had now become a regular part of the Music Club's yearly activities. An evening was being planned for May of the following year (1986) which would feature Ronnie Scott as well as the Rainbow Ballroom Orchestra – there would also be dancing. As always on such occasions, there was a very large attendance, and a surplus was made. In April of that year there had been a suggestion of a separate jazz organisation being introduced to Ongar, and this is discussed in the chapter on Ongar Jazz Club.

At a meeting in early May (1985), I was proposed and co-opted onto the Music Club's committee and was formally welcomed at the subsequent meeting on 28th May. Unfortunately, I was a rather infrequent attendee in those early years due to regular concert and recording commitments. Still, I was always kept very much in contact with what was being discussed and able to give my views when required.

The club outing to hear John Lill play in Thaxted that July had been a great success with twice as many people as in the previous year. Hopes were expressed that the club would arrange more such outings.

The highly successful second Essex Young Musician of the Year competition heralded the close of the tenth season of Ongar Music Club. There were ninety-one members, sixty-seven season ticket holders and a total bank balance of £629.36. The club had developed significantly from its early beginnings in people's homes and was bringing a wide diversity of music and associated social activity to a healthy membership. The committee of five had grown substantially, and a huge amount of effort was being put into nurturing and supporting the club and its activities. Nothing was taken for granted, and offers of help from outside the committee were frequently acknowledged by way of a small gift.

A fun poster devised for the 1984–1985 season.

3. 1985–1994 Seasons

With the AGM on 29th September 1985, Ongar Music Club moved into its second decade of concert giving. At this meeting, the members formally appointed me to the committee on which I was privileged to serve for thirty-five years. Memorably, at that meeting, committee member and chairman of the Community Association, Kenneth Bird, announced that there were now many sections of the CA, but the Music Club was a 'glittering' one – a heart-warming sentiment to share. Mention was also made of the forthcoming closure of Ongar Comprehensive School, a building which was used regularly by organisations in the district as well as by the Music Club for its larger events. Also, at this AGM, the auditor announced that the Century Club, which had started the previous year (December 1984), showed an anticipated profit of £623 in the year to November 1985. Up to that point, £393.70 had been paid over to Ongar Music Club with a further 'expectation' of £229.30.

It was noted in October that the piano[1] had been damaged and that the attention of a cabinet maker would be required. An investigation would be made into the insurance situation (via the CA) as well as possibly having the value of the piano reassessed. Such damage was, unfortunately, to become something of ongoing concern for those unable to respect the nature and value of such an instrument and piece of furniture.

Maybe a precursor of things to come, it was noted, following the Edwin Dodd evening on 7th March 1986, that the noise from the bar became very loud. A letter was sent to the chairman of the Budworth Hall committee seeking assurance that this would not happen again. However …

By May, a further Grand Draw was being planned with another television set heading up the list of possible prizes. Other money-making ventures were also discussed, such as pens advertising the Music Club and the sale and loaning of records in the club's library.

---

[1] I've included quite a bit of discussion regarding the pianos owned by Ongar Music Club. I felt this necessary as a piano is crucial to the operation of such an organisation. Finding and maintaining a piano took up a great deal of the committee's time. This involved fund-raising, both general and with special events. There were also great club deliberations regarding where it could be housed, and therefore where the club would be based.

Geoffrey Timms had written to Sir Yehudi Menuhin, the club's president, offering congratulations on the occasion of his seventieth birthday on 22nd April. A most gracious reply was received.

```
MUSWELL HILL ROAD
HIGHGATE
LONDON  N6 5UG


                                30th April 1986


Dear Mr Timms,

        Many thanks for your good letter. I
am deeply touched that you remembered my
birthday.

        With all good wishes for the continued
success of the Ongar Music Club.

                        Yours sincerely,




                        Yehudi Menuhin


Geoffrey Timms, Esq
Chairman
Ongar Music Club
Chipping Ongar
Essex    CM5 9BJ
```

There was a meeting in late June regarding the possibility of a separate jazz club at the Budworth Hall. It was felt that it would be advantageous if the new jazz venture and the Music Club were to run in parallel, using the same system of membership – a first jazz evening was subsequently arranged for July. The Music Club committee agreed to give the new jazz section[1] a loan of £25 to assist with their startup costs, such as for printing and advertising. It was also agreed that money for the section would be held by the Music Club but within a separate bank account. The concert was very successful, and everyone was highly

[1] When it first started, the new group was formed as a section of the Music Club and was variously described as the Jazz Section, Jazz Group and Jazz Club.

optimistic about the future of the new venture. In recognition of the Music Club's support, the Jazz Section's committee suggested that they could, in return, do something to help the Music Club, such as help in arranging the annual cabaret, the established jazz evening, or maybe introducing people to the Century Club. Further jazz evenings were planned for 2nd January and 27th March 1987. From this point, the activities of the Jazz Section regularly figured on the agendas of Music Club committee meetings. The first concert in July 1986 presented 'The Eastern All Stars' and was declared "enjoyable, interesting and, above all, successful". There was a large audience, and many expressed interest in future such jazz events. As stated elsewhere, the new Jazz Section was very appreciative of the help given by members of the Music Club committee, particularly Peter, John and Sylvia – see Chapter 10.

During the year, there was ongoing discussion regarding unauthorised use of, and further damage to, the club's piano – many ways were investigated to try to avoid the situation arising again. Although the key was kept by the hall staff, there were occasions when the lid of the piano had simply been forced open, causing significant damage. Some of these unofficial uses were even highlighted in the advertising material posted by various groups – one being the 'Ladies Over-50 Keep-fit' group who had not sought permission.

The Essex Young Musician of the Year was an ongoing point for discussion, both for ways of improving the competition and also for generating financial support. The Midland Bank had offered to continue with support in the sum of £75. It was also suggested that committee members sound out possible patrons who might be willing to put up, say, £10 per annum in support. There was some discussion about holding the competition biennially as it would lighten the financial load and maybe also allow more talent to develop between events – this never went further although it was to be suggested again in 1994. Meanwhile, Essex Radio had been in touch, expressing interest in the competition. This was a greatly welcome development and it was agreed that a meeting should be planned with the radio station before too long.

1986–1987

The club's financial position was now quite healthy, but as always, the treasurer John Harrop regularly cautioned against complacency. The Grand Draw idea had been a great success with takings of £529.58 and expenses of £150.50, leaving a profit of £379.08. Once again, this draw took place at the AGM at which, as was traditional in those days, each committee member with a position of responsibility would stand and offer a brief report of what they had done during the year – this practice was not always welcomed by the more retiring committee members. Also, Barrie would suggest a bottle of whisky as an additional 'thank you' for the club's auditor. In fact, it might be said that Barrie had something of a penchant for offering bottles of whisky in such situations.

An interesting note in the October minutes states that, in future, smoking would not be allowed during recitals. Also, that there was again a problem with noise coming from the bar during recitals, and this would be taken up again with the relevant people. By this time, membership of the Century Club stood at a hundred and eight and had a healthy balance of £1,299, with £640 having been paid to the general account. By December of that year, together with income from concerts and other sources, the club's financial resources

---

FUTURE EVENTS

(all at the Budworth Hall. 8.00 pm start)

Friday, 21st November 1986

AN EVENING WITH JOHN AMIS

The well-known member of the 'Face the Music' panel's visit to the Club promises a fantastic evening. Get your ticket now (£4 non-members; £3.50 members) they are selling like hot cakes! Season ticketholders have priority in the event of a sell-out.

Friday, 5th December 1986

THE DAVE SHEPHERD QUINTET

The popular annual visit of this group will draw an additional clientele this year – members of the newly formed Jazz section of the Club.

This is NOT a Season ticket concert, so early application for tickets is advised (£4 non-members; £3.50 members)

Friday, 19th December 1986

ANNUAL CAROL CONCERT

with the Stondon Singers and, of course, the Choirboy of the Year

Again NOT a season ticket concert. The ticket price (£3.50 non-members £3 members) includes mince pies and a festive drink.

Tickets for all events are obtainable from Mrs Terry

stood at £3,184 – a great testament to the hard work and dedication of the committee and the eighty-three members.

Sadly, club founder member Betty Greatrex passed away early in October and chairman Geoffrey Timms paid tribute to her in the subsequent meeting. There were ongoing concerns about the selection of a chairman for the next season when Geoffrey Timms would have completed his three-year term. There was some reluctance to bring in someone from outside, and most of the committee had either served at least one term or were reluctant to stand. I had been asked many times, but due to regular commitment to play for Radio 2's 'Friday Night is Music Night', and the fact that the regular club concert night was a Friday and traditionally introduced by the chairman, it never seemed appropriate to accept this valued invitation.

It was decided to distribute forms at the forthcoming jazz event, inviting those present to subscribe to the Century Club. As an additional means of raising revenue and always mindful of the need to raise funds, a new 'patronage' scheme had been launched to encourage support of the competition by members and local businesses. By the beginning of 1987, this was showing great promise, with a total of around £300 having already been pledged. The jazz concert held on 2nd January had been 'an outstanding success' with the hall filled to capacity and many people without advance tickets had been turned away. Many felt that the hall was overcrowded and it was agreed that in future, ticket sales would be limited to a hundred and forty. The possibility of acquiring smaller tables was even suggested. It was also reported that Humphrey Lyttleton had agreed to be the President of Ongar Jazz Club.

Study groups had been arranged in preparation for the talk in April to be given by Denis Matthews on Mozart piano concerti. These were variously held in the homes of Geoffrey Timms, Barrie Hall and John Harrop, being led by the hosts. Writing to Barrie Hall in late March, Denis Matthews had provided some personal notes on the concerti to be discussed – these make fascinating reading.

As for Mozart concertos it is hard to choose a 'top twelve' but here are my thoughts:

K271 in E flat - the first great concerto, inspired
  by a visiting pianist to Salzburg, Mlle Jeunehomme;
  full of profound surprises and jeux d'esprits, e.g.
  entry of solo in answer to the orchestra's very
  first phrase, and introduction of slow minuet halfway
  through finale. Minor-key slow movement with tragic
  recapitulation of 'consoling' second group and
  eloquent original cadenza.

K449 in E flat - first of six concertos written in
  the 'annus mirabilis' of 1784, though still scored
  for strings and optional wind, like the previous
  delightful group of three K413-5, of which K414 in
  A is the most well-known and warm-hearted. K449 is
  remarkable for its long-breathed slow movement theme
  and the varied returns of the finale's rondo subject.

K450 in B flat - important as first concerto with
  essential wind-parts, reflecting prevalence of good
  players in Vienna (as opposed to Salzburg!). NB the
  marvellous Quintet K452 for piano and wind dates from
  this time. Virtuosic 'hunting' 6-8 finale with
  cross-rhythms and much hand-crossing.

K453 in G - again wonderful wind-writing and light
  transparent textures. Slow movement unique in
  withholding real answer to opening phrase until the
  coda. Final variations look forward to Papageno,
  clinched by witty opera buffa ending, reminding one
  that 'Figaro' was soon to come too.

K459 in F - 'monothematic' domination of favourite
  opening dotted rhythm. But the finale is the tour de
  force in its alternation of comic opera or 'galant'
  and 'learned' styles, e.g. unexpected contrapuntal
  first entry of strings.

K466 in D minor - the first minor-key concerto, with
  subdued agitated opening much admired by the 19th
  century, which neglected most of the others. Much
  'ironic' use of the major key and eloquent new theme
  given to soloist alone. No original cadenzas, but
  Beethoven's, though anachronistic, are too good to
  miss. More conventional mood of Romance offset by
  G minor episode; and surprising 'happy ending' to
  finale with witty new asides in horns and trumpets

K467 in C - forget 'Elvira Madigan' and the popular
  derangements of the slow movement; again unique in
  its constant triplet accompaniment, its serenity offset
  by remarkable 'clouded' dissonances. Also note amazing
  dissonances in 1st-mvt passage-work (second-subject are
  and resourceful treatment of opening figure of rondo.

K482 in E flat - wonderful wind-writing throughout, with
clarinets for the first time in the concertos. Notice
that recap in 1st mvt recalls material of orchestral
opening. Slow mvt astounding in mixture of variations
and episodes with delayed wind-entry; subduing of full
orchestral forces by quiet eloquence of piano in final
variation anticipates Andante of Beethoven no 4! Like
K271 the revels of the finale are interrupted by a slow
minuet-like episode. As with other later concertos
written for himself Mozart left many solo passages in
sketch and almost certainly amplified them.

K488 in A - the 'popular' A major, also with clarinets
but without trumpets and drums. Surprisingly the solo
is content to follow the orchestra's discourse, and it
left for the orchestra to offer the 'new' theme in
mid-movement. Profound F sharp minor Adagio, with coda
again left in sketch (though many pianists leave it as
such). Finale abounds in opera buffa themes.

K491 in C minor - arguably the greatest, and with the
richest scoring, clarinets and oboes, which alternate
in the slow movement episodes or 'serenades'. The drama
of the 1st mvt is amazing and the whole work influenced
Beethoven, who particularly admired the haunting wind
phrase in the coda of the finale. This 'Neapolitan'
harmony (D flat in relation to C) had characterised
the marchlike variation-theme of the finale. The MS
(in the RCM) shows the haste in which the solo part was
squeezed into the existing barlines of the score.

K503 in C - one of the more neglected great concertos,
with a certain austerity belonging to the world of oper
seria; but grandly architectural in the outer movements.
Note gentle and tentative first solo entry, and magic
new 'solo' second subject; also domination of 1st mvt
development by march from opening tutti. The rather
formal finale is relieved by the F major middle episode
and the long almost Brahmsian preparations for the
rondo-returns.

K595 in B flat - the intervening concerto, K537 in D
('Coronation'), had been more neutral - a travelling
work, hence with 'safe' and unsoloistic wind-writing;
but back in Vienna Mozart wrote K595 in his last year
(1791) in which the wind again have independence. In
the light of the D minor or C minor - or K503 - the
music is intimate and restrained, the simplicity
deceptively profound. The 2nd mvt has the spiritual
depth of much of 'The Magic Flute'; and even the carefree
rondo is subject to minor-key pathos later. Is it in
fact carefree? It derived from a song, 'Longing for
Spring', almost as though Mozart knew that 1791 was to
be his last.

Just some random thoughts which I hope may be helpful? I hope
we'll meet before long. Much love to Jean meanwhile.

Yours ever

Denis

In April, it was confirmed that BBC Essex would feature items about the competition in their lunchtime programme. They also indicated that they would broadcast a recording of the final, making a payment of £40 to each finalist. By late April, there were some twenty-one offers of support, excluding that promised by the Harlow Chemical Company – a total of £810 had been pledged to the competition.

A note in the minutes for 28th April may have been a portent of things to come:

> Profound discontent was expressed over the attitude of certain members of the Community Association in respect of Music Club and bar activities at Budworth Hall. It is most important that the club remains alert to any possible threat to its continued use of, and access to, the premises. As many as possible of the club's members should be encouraged to attend the CA AGM in September in order that our views can be clearly expressed. John [Harrop] reported that approximately one hundred of the eight hundred total CA membership are Music Club members, and this alone should ensure that the club receives a fair hearing.

This friction between the pro-bar faction and others continued for quite some time. Various proposals were put forward, including the relocation of the bar to upstairs. However, the situation was ultimately to lead to a change of policy by the Music Club. There had also been ongoing concerns about the state of repair of the club's piano, which would either need a major overhaul or replacement. This was the subject of much debate in the September meeting. Replacement would be a major financial commitment, and it was probable that the club would have to shoulder the burden alone. There was also concern about the ongoing issue of the piano's mistreatment; there having been several occasions in recent years when the instrument had been forced open, presumably for illicit use during other functions. Suggestions were made for some form of boxing or maybe a cupboard – perhaps relocating the piano upstairs and away from the bar and other users. However, that would also involve a steep set of stairs, and at the time, a room in a rather drab decorative state. In addition, a public entertainment licence would be required for the room to facilitate the selling of tickets. It was agreed that in the short term, an expert should be brought in to examine the current piano at a fee not exceeding £100.

A regular feature of the club's calendar for many years was the cabaret. This was usually held in late Spring and would normally include a fish and chip supper together with interludes of musical entertainment of a lighter nature. Members of the committee would supply table provisions such as grapes, cheese, celery, salt, vinegar and cutlery, as well as raffle prizes. These usually included many 'bottles' as well as chocolates and other consumables, and Jean Hall routinely provided the floral decorations for the tables. This was a very popular event, and the one in 1987 was noted as being oversubscribed. There would be the usual raffle, and the whole evening could usually be relied on to give a useful boost to the club's finances. A slightly unusual departure for the Music Club came in June, when the Jazz Club had organised an outing on a steamer on the River Medway, with music provided by Digby Fairweather and band. Members of the Music Club were invited, and despite indifferent weather, this was a great success.

Following the 1987 EYMY competition, it was felt that due to the increased stature of the competition, the prize money might be increased and the possibility of a winner's recital in London's Wigmore Hall would be investigated. These ideas would also require increased sponsorship and patronage. Following that meeting, I wrote to the hall, enquiring about possible dates for early in 1990 – see Chapter 7. Meanwhile, a letter had been received from John Lill indicating that he planned to attend the following year's competition, and also offering help in a more general way, suggesting that he might be able to give a recital to generate financial support for the event. It was subsequently agreed that £550 from club funds would be allocated for prize money at the next competition.

1987–1988
The 1987 AGM reaffirmed that following the recording of the EYMY competition final that year, BBC Essex would be broadcasting excerpts around Christmas. This had been a greatly anticipated development

which was not only welcome for the candidates but was also good publicity for the competition and the club more widely. The Century Club was continuing to flourish, and there was a generally healthy financial situation. Peter Lewis reported that the Jazz Club was now firmly established and that Humphrey Lyttleton had agreed to be the club's president.

By October, a technician from Steinway & Sons had inspected the piano and concluded that no amount of restoration would produce a first-class instrument. He suggested that somewhere in the region of £3,500 would be required to finance repairs and bring the piano to a reasonable standard. It was thought that the club should consider what it could afford before deciding on its way forward. All fund-raising ideas were considered, including a piano recital by John Lill, a jazz evening, expansion of the Century Club, the holding of a Grand Draw, and the seeking of sponsorship from the Ford Foundation and other institutions. It was eventually concluded that the maximum expenditure which should be considered for a replacement piano was around £8,000 – the inevitable piano sub-committee was formed. The first meeting of this committee agreed that a piano could be purchased up to a value of £13,000. This would mean the club finding around £10,000 after allowing for a club discount. The whole venture would rest on the club acquiring an interest-free loan, and an application was made to Eastern Arts. In the months that followed, various discussions took place to help boost the piano fund and these included committee members offering further study evenings in their homes. The amount of time and dedication offered by members to support the club was quite remarkable, and it entered 1988 with total assets of around £5,651.

There had been ongoing discussions about the piano situation. By March 1988, it was agreed that the purchase of a replacement instrument could not be considered for another two to three years. A colleague of mine, David Flanders, a Steinway technician who lived in North Weald, was therefore asked to inspect the current piano with a view to preparing details of the restorative work necessary in order of priority. He advised the committee that if sold to trade sources, the current instrument would probably only realise around £400. In April, he also reported to the committee that he was currently refurbishing a Bechstein instrument which would be sold for £4,000 on completion. It was agreed that this would be inspected in due course. He added that the instrument under restoration was nearly ninety years old, and it might not be available 'for a long time'.

Meanwhile, the piano fund progressed, and a jazz concert, held in support of the fund on 25th March that year, raised more than £1,000. In June, David Flanders reported that the Bechstein instrument should be ready in September. It was agreed to inspect it as soon as possible, and also another instrument which was currently owned by a school in Waltham Forest and due for complete refurbishment. In the meantime, the treasurer would approach the NFMS regarding the possibility of a small loan. It was subsequently noted in September that the Bechstein instrument currently undergoing refurbishment would not now be ready until Christmas at the earliest and that the price would be in the region of £4,000 plus VAT. However, the final cost would likely be in the region of £5,000 as the instrument would also need to be polished. Meanwhile, the Waltham Forest instrument had been deemed not worthy of consideration, and therefore, the club's focus was on the Bechstein instrument under restoration.

By now, the children's concerts had been rebranded as Young Music Makers (YMM) – a name which continued for the duration of these events. In April it was agreed to arrange for the production of special YMM badges at a cost of 25 pence each and these were distributed during the following concert, providing additional awareness of Ongar Music Club, as well as a novelty appreciated by the young people. Sometime earlier, there was mention of a member selling their late husband's viola in aid of club funds. In April, it was agreed that the club would purchase the instrument for resale. This would incur no expense for the club, and the subsequent proceeds would be donated to club funds.

Over the years, there have been highs and lows in respect of audience figures, and there never seemed to be any obvious reason for this. During 1988, concern was expressed about an apparent drop in concert attendance, and the treasurer offered various suggestions to help the finances. These included engaging less 'expensive' artistes and a members' circular with details of forthcoming recitals, emphasising the importance of regular support for club events to ensure its future security. It was also agreed that ticket prices would increase by 50 pence for the 1988–89 season, with the membership fee rising to £2.00 annually.

The season headed towards its final event and the competition on 7th July, which John Lill had indicated that he would be attending – seventeen entries had been received. The 1985 winner Alison Baker (piano) had offered a small trophy to the competition and suggested the inscription 'John Lill Award – Runner Up. The Alison Baker Trophy'. In the July meeting, it was reported that Barrie Hall had received a 'very minor' complaint from the Brentwood Gazette – photographers had been requested to wait until the interval before being admitted to performances to take photographs, except in cases where this would not cause undue disruption to the performance. This had sometimes caused delays to their tight schedules, and it was agreed that in future, photographers would be admitted when they arrived to avoid missed photo opportunities.

1988–1989

In September, it was reported that Arthur Pittock was retiring as Outdoor Activities Organiser, and it was agreed that Jean Hall, Barrie's wife, would take over these duties. The club was now planning for the arrival of the refurbished Bechstein from David Flanders. However, there were ongoing discussions about the finish of the casework (polish or polyester) and also the small matter of how the instrument would be stored. Chairman Barrie Hall had also received a letter from the warden of the Budworth Hall advising him that the CA had recently acquired a grand piano from the closing Ongar Comprehensive School. This was to be placed in the upstairs Concert Room and the club was invited to make use of it. October also saw the welcome of Jean Hall onto the committee.

Geoffrey Timms had been advised in early November that the 'new' Bechstein might be available in time for the scheduled piano recital by David Silkoff on 18th of that month. However, it was decided that considerable thought was still needed in respect of matters surrounding storage, security, finance, insurance and maintenance. Delivery of the Bechstein was therefore deferred until a suitable time could be established. There was also discussion about the existing instrument – an offer of £500 had been received from the principal of the Walthamstow Technical College. Unfortunately, the wheels of the piano had been removed sometime previously, and messages were therefore dispatched in all directions to locate them!

John Lill had generously agreed to inaugurate the club's new Bechstein with a complimentary recital, and this took place on Friday 31st March of the following year. Ticket prices were fixed at £10 for the front area of the hall, with £7.50 for the middle area and £5 for the rear two or three rows.

As a complement to the club's ongoing efforts to raise money for its own activities, it also received requests from other organisations for financial help. Occasionally, impossible requests were received from individuals, which could rarely be acceded to for purely practical reasons. One such request came in December 1988 from a young lady asking for financial assistance in the purchase of a new harpsichord.

By mid-January, the Bechstein was in place in the Budworth Hall and being protected by two covers on loan to the club while a suitable new cover was sourced. The new instrument had been tuned and insured.

The Ballroom, Budworth Hall, Ongar

It was agreed that, in principle, the new piano would not be loaned out to other groups on a hire basis. On occasions, and in response to special requests, the use of the piano by other groups would be given careful consideration. If sanctioned, a discretionary charge of £20 would be made. However, the agreed NFMS loan of £2,000 had yet to be received. Geoffrey Timms was afforded a vote of thanks for his considerable efforts in locating a buyer for the club's old piano. At the January meeting, it was also recorded, with great sadness, that the Loughton Music Society had been forced to close.

It had been hoped to have a hundred and ninety people seated in the Ballroom of the Budworth Hall for John Lill's recital, and by mid-February, all tickets had been sold. That seems a remarkable number in view of previous correspondence and would likely not be considered today due to changing fire regulations. One hundred and forty chairs were loaned by Ongar Comprehensive School to assist with this large but welcome number, and the Ballroom's gallery was cleared 'of all visible debris'. Barrie Hall suggested that all the gentlemen in the audience should wear dinner suits for the occasion. A souvenir programme would be produced and sold for 50 pence. The preparations are noted in the March minutes:

> Barrie, Peter, Geoffrey and Kenneth will fulfil the role of stewards during the evening. Each will be issued with a seating plan, and all reserved/allocated seats will be labelled accordingly.
>
> Peter will attend to the spotlighting during the evening of 30 March, if convenient to the hall authorities.
>
> Sylvia and Valerie will attend the main door and conduct ticket inspections etc. Barrie will act as gate guard during the recital and will prevent unwelcome intrusions.
>
> Following the conclusion of the recital, a case of claret will be presented to John Lill and a basket of flowers to Jackie. Daphne will arrange provision of the latter. Following careful and considered examination, the proposal to acquire a flower display for suspension from the Ballroom gallery was shelved. A reception will be held by kind permission of Janice and Geoffrey Tompkins, post-Budworth Hall clean-up operations.

The same meeting also notes a query from Kenneth Bird as to whether the Jazz Club was happy with the existing arrangement whereby it remained as part of the Music Club – the first of several such queries to be raised over the years. It appeared that the Jazz Club was, at that time, completely happy with the arrangement.

Despite all the effort expended on the 1989 cabaret, attendance had been surprisingly disappointing, and Barrie Hall (chairman) expressed 'profound disquiet' in respect of the financial result. He concluded that the level of support recorded should bring into question the whole future of this long-standing and usually popular event. As contracts had already been dispatched to the Rainbow Dance Orchestra and the soprano Jane Webster, it was initially decided that the following year's cabaret should proceed as planned. This decision was made on the basis that if the 1990 attendance remained at a low level, the event would be deleted from the planning of future seasons. However, following further discussion, it was decided that the cabaret had likely 'run its course' and that the benefits of cancellation outweighed any penalties. The artistes were therefore cancelled but Jane Webster was offered a recital slot during the 1990–91 season. However, by September, this decision was reversed yet again – the revised plan being for pianist Keith Nicholls to appear with the band; Jane Webster and her pianist Nicholas Bosworth occupying the central slot. In fact, the cabaret was held once more (in 1990), and although it was much better attended, it had been resolved that the jazz committee would organise such future occasions.

In June, the Young Music Makers event had been notable for the staging of something of an orchestra, this having been assembled from those participating. This was a welcome addition to the occasion and due, in no small measure, to the efforts of my good friend Mrs Janet Roberts, a cellist living in Ongar at the time. Also in June was a talk/ lecture by Dr Arthur Jacobs, whom I well remember from my student days at the Royal Academy of Music. This was scheduled to take place in the upstairs Concert Room and was something of an experiment to see whether greater use could be made of this room for club events – especially as it was cheaper to hire.

At the June meeting, it was reported that a letter had been received from the organisers of the London International String Quartet Competition offering the club a winner's recital in April of 1991, and at no cost. This venture went ahead and was to run for several years, with the winner of the competition's third prize performing for the club.

1989–1990

Ahead of the September AGM, chairman Barrie Hall announced that, rather than asking individual committee members to talk about their roles, he would summarise all functions of the committee during his chairman's presentation, the only exceptions being the treasurer and jazz section representative. This had been discussed at a previous meeting when some members of the committee had indicated that they did not wish to speak and "would not do so". That discussion is described as a "'lengthy, and often heated debate"!

It was also noted that despite the great success of the competition in 1988, the evening final had yet again started late due to the length of the semifinal. It was agreed that in 1989, the competition would be held over two days. As it would not be realistic to convene a full panel across both days, a panel of 'local' judges would be arranged for the purposes of adjudicating the preliminary round.

By October, and following ongoing discussions, a formal booking agreement had been received from the Wigmore Hall, confirming the first of the club's Essex Young Musician of the Year winner's recitals to be presented in London. This was a big moment for the club and the competition, and something which, for several years, brought an extra level of kudos to the award. The hall had requested six A2 posters for display, together with a thousand handbills to the same design. For a fee of £280, they would also include details of the recital in their regular press advertisements. Barrie Hall had also written to the leading music critics of all the national newspapers in an effort to obtain maximum publicity. Rehearsals would take place in both the morning and afternoon of the concert day, and members of the committee would be on hand on a shift basis.

Another celebrity evening took place in November when the club presented 'An Evening with Dame Janet Baker'. This proved to be a

ONGAR MUSIC CLUB
—o—

17TH NOVEMBER 1989

DAME JANET BAKER

Budworth Hall - 8.00 p.m.
£4.50 OAP £4.00
(MEMBERS 50P

1989

wonderful insight into the life and career of a distinguished and greatly loved singer, presented to a capacity audience.

Midst all this organisation and preparation, a Dave Shepherd jazz evening had been held on 1st December with another planned with Humphrey Lyttleton for 5th January (1990). Also, the annual Christmas concert would take place on 22nd December – never a dull moment. The first Wigmore Hall recital on 8th January was a huge success with a very good audience. The evening was shared between three past winners – Alison Baker, Helen Knief and Jane Webster. More details of this can be found in Chapter 7.

The evening with Michael Berkeley on 16th March had again brought to the fore the issue of noise from the bar adjacent to the Budworth Hall's Ballroom. The presentation had been seriously marred by such intrusions, and appeals for quiet had been met with verbal abuse from both the bar staff and patrons. To combat this ever-present and worsening situation, Barrie Hall suggested that:

> ... active consideration be afforded to the possibility of identifying a suitable alternative venue.

Immediate suggestions were Great Stony School and the former Ongar Comprehensive School (by then the Adult Education Campus) – Barrie would investigate costs. There was a council meeting of the Community Association in mid-April to discuss outline plans for changes to the hall, and this brought a little hope for the bar and noise situation. However, it turned out that the proposals would not afford any significant benefits to the Music Club's situation. Meanwhile, investigations had taken place – a hall at Great Stony School had been offered but would be problematic due to the lack of any practical access for a piano. However, investigation of the Adult Education Campus proved to be much more fruitful, and it was proposed that the club transfer its association from the Budworth Hall to this new location with effect from September 1990. John Harrop was commissioned to make enquiries of the county authorities as to hire charges.

An in-depth discussion about moving the club's base was held in the meeting on 25th April:

> Barrie reported that investigations into the possibility of transferring the club's activities to the Adult Education Centre had proved extremely fruitful. With the assistance of Ron Barnes, it had been established that the old school hall was available for hire at almost the same cost as the Ballroom in the Budworth Hall. A long discussion then followed on the perceived merits of establishing the Adult Education Centre as a new base, and the following points were distilled from same.
>
> If a move were to take place, the number of chairs available would need to be ascertained. Screening may be required for some recitals to produce a more intimate atmosphere [this hall was substantially larger than the Ballroom at the Budworth Hall], and the inclusion of incidental costs such as heating in the hire fee would be confirmed. Bar licences would be required for a number of events, and their provision will be investigated.
>
> Barrie confirmed that all the above queries could be answered easily if and when firm bookings were made with the Education Authority. The chairman then formally proposed that the club transfer its association from the Budworth Hall to the Adult Education Centre with effect from September 1990. The motion was seconded by Jean and carried unanimously. Barrie reported that both Geoffrey and Peter had already declared their verbal agreement to the idea.
>
> A long discussion followed on the legal position with regard to club assets. It was agreed that a constitution would be drawn up by Mr Devonald [solicitor] and Barrie, and that steps be taken to ensure removal of the piano from the Budworth Hall at the earliest opportunity post the Essex Young Musician of the Year competition. Barrie will advise the committee of developments as they occur. A newsletter will be promulgated to the membership, outlining details of the move, in early September.

Not long after this meeting, Barrie Hall visited the former comprehensive school and met Mr Mike Fleming, the caretaker – someone crucial to any such venture. He had proved to be most helpful and offered to help in any way possible. Making such a decision to move its base would also affect the club's relationship with the Community Association. It would cease to be a member, which would also necessitate a change to the Music Club's constitution. A revised constitution was drafted and presented to an Extraordinary General Meeting of the club for approval – it could not wait until the regular September AGM for reasons of planning. The committee's recommendation was approved and formally accepted. The new constitution, signed by all members of the committee, was duly presented to the membership some weeks later, together with the AGM notification. The response from the membership towards the change of venue was very encouraging despite the longer journey for some.

Plans swung into action for the move to the new premises, and Geoffrey Timms reported to the September meeting that he and Barrie Hall had been busy painting parts of the hall. Peter Lewis had also been busy erecting new floodlights and spotlights – these and a portable control panel had been purchased at the cost of £816. It was noted that two hundred and fifty chairs were available, as well as thirty tables, although forty-five tables would be required for jazz evenings. Unfortunately, the county authorities weren't prepared to clean the hall's curtains, so Jean Hall, Sylvia Terry, Patti Nicholson and Valerie Chetham set about cleaning and restoring them as far as was possible. The move involved the club in considerable expense, and the treasurer John Harrop, not known for displays of enthusiasm when it came to spending the club's money, fully endorsed the decisions to spruce up the old hall – making it a more appropriate and welcoming venue for the club's forthcoming concert season. However, he cautioned that those funds would need to be replenished ...

Never one to be quiet for long, Barrie had also been busy giving a broadcast for Essex Radio in support of the Essex Young Musician of the Year competition with a view to heightening awareness and also attracting sponsorship. Three firm enquiries offering assistance were received, although one subsequently withdrew, leaving Travis Perkins and the Essex Chronicle Group (ECG) – the latter ultimately entering into an agreement with the club. Discussions with the ECG followed, and the agreement was formally acknowledged in a meeting on 20th June 1990 at which Mr Peter Smith, representing the Essex Chronicle Group, was present and said he "looked forward to a long and happy association with the club".

1990–1991

The details of the new Essex Young Musician of the Year sponsorship agreement with the Essex Chronicle Group was formally announced to the membership at the AGM on 28th September that year – this followed the first competition to be run under the new partnership with the ECG back in July. This news was greeted with great enthusiasm. The next meeting gave rise to a number of suggestions regarding the setting up of future events in the new premises (AEC), such as positioning for the table where Sylvia Terry sold tickets. Also, a request from Valerie Chetham that money for tea and coffee be taken at the point of sale.

A note in the minutes of those particular proceedings records a typically wry request from Barrie Hall that:

> ... it was always his intention to see the season started in the new hall and then to ask the committee's indulgence. He is seventy this month, and wishing to live a little longer, asks to be absolved in future from heavy lifting whilst remaining perfectly willing to arrange seating, put up the posters, and anything else; but not lifting stacks of chairs or the grand piano.

Sylvia Terry thought that maybe the club could work towards being able to offer a little extra money to the caretakers to do some of these more onerous tasks.

As the club headed towards the close of the year, the committee was looking forward to the new partnership with the Essex Chronicle Group which had already offered to help with the cost of a new winner's cup – it was anticipated that it would also help with the printing requirements for the competition. Preparations were also well underway for the second Wigmore Hall recital, scheduled for 25th March 1991. There was understandably an atmosphere of great positivity

Sylvia Terry, founder member of Ongar Music Club

amongst the members as we approached the end of the year. Therefore a 'bombshell' in December from Geoffrey Timms' came as a great shock – he would likely be moving to Wales in the Spring. However, as might have been anticipated, Geoffrey had thought this decision through carefully and with the club's interests very much in mind.

Apart from what might perhaps unkindly be described as more routine events, the early weeks of 1991 were focussed on two major recitals – John Lill on 15th March and the Wigmore Hall EYMY winner's recital on 25th March. John had very kindly declined the offer of a Steinway on this occasion as a financial saving for the club. All the usual arrangements were in hand for seating, flowers, door-manning, raffle, library, refreshments, and of course, the obligatory post-concert party, to be hosted by Jean and Barrie Hall. It was also agreed that the Century Club draw be brought forward a couple of months to coincide with this high profile event.

Tickets for the Wigmore Hall recital had been slow to sell, and everyone was encouraged to do what they could in this regard. Geoffrey Timms and John Harrop would be on duty all day; flowers for the performers, as well as a page-turner, would be provided by the hall. As previously, the gentlemen of the committee were requested to wear dinner suits. It was agreed that this was an outstanding musical evening – Anthony Marwood (the first winner of the competition in 1984) and his pianist William Howard had delivered a first-rate performance to an appreciative audience. It was agreed that the Wigmore Hall series was certainly worth pursuing but maybe with more than one performer. In practice, it was suggested that future such occasions would involve two past winners – one in each half.

It had been decided that the 1991 competition would occupy two days to avoid the ongoing issues of the main day running late due to the number of applicants in the semifinal. A preliminary day was planned for Sunday 7th July in the club's new home at the Adult Education Campus, with the main competition on 13th July in the Shire Hall, Chelmsford. The new arrangements worked well, and the new setting for the final competition day was greatly appreciated.

After the competition, it was agreed that the entry fee would rise to £15 from 1992, and replica miniature first prize trophies would be minted at the cost of £25 in order that the competition winners would have a permanent memento of their achievement. It was also agreed that in future, a page-turner would be provided on permanent standby.

1991–1992

In September, it was reported that the Essex Chronicle Group had expressed a wish to establish a separate competition for players aged under eighteen and attending school in Essex. The company was willing to put forward £400 to fund such a contest. The idea was agreed and a date set for 22nd February 1992, with the occasion being largely organised by Geoffrey Timms and John Harrop.

The Century Club was still a great success and a substantial contributor to the club's funds, as noted by Geoffrey Timms in the October meeting. With initially 118 members, there were by then 133, with an income that year of £600, of which £300 needed to be paid out in prizes. The minutes of that meeting also contain a wonderful line regarding the change of chairmanship for the following season:

> The committee, at the chairman's suggestion, and to her surprise, agreed that Jean would be Chairman-designate, to take office from September 1992.

This did not result in any difficulties, and Jean was to become a highly respected chairman in due course (the club never formally used the word 'chair', and it's a word I've never personally cared for in such a setting). At the same meeting, Geoffrey Timms presented a proof of the brochure for the 'Brentwood and Ongar Gazette (Essex Chronicle Group) Awards' that would shortly be circulated to all schools.

By February 1992, there were sixteen entrants for the first Essex Schools Musician of the Year competition – piano, winds, strings and a vocalist. It was agreed that the event on 22nd February would start at 2.00 pm with a final round starting at 7.30 pm. Pianists could try the instrument at any time between 1.00 pm and 1.50 pm. Interval refreshments would be provided to the competitors at a charge of 25 pence, and each would be given one complimentary ticket for the

evening final in the hope that they would stay
to hear other performances if they themselves
were not successful in reaching the final. The
new competition was felt to have been a great
success with a generally high standard of
performance.

Dr Geoffrey and & Mrs Janice Tompkins, 1998

Social events were a regular feature of the
Ongar Music Club calendar and a welcome
boost to the finances. One such occasion
was planned for the evening of 13th June at
the home of Dr Geoffrey and Janice Tompkins.
Geoffrey worked as a GP in Plaistow in East London. He lived with
his wife Janice in Fyfield, and they were both enthusiastic members
of the local wine club – having their own small vineyard. They were
founder members of the Ongar Singers and also joined the Ongar Music
Hall. This particular social event was on something of a grander scale
than many of its predecessors. Therefore, this social evening came
up for discussion at every committee meeting from March onwards.
For that particular occasion, a bar licence was sought, as tickets were
being sold. A designated person would be responsible for 'catering and
victualling', and plans were to be drawn up for a 'wet weather routine'.
There would be 'taped music', and the jazz committee would also be
advised of the event as soon as possible. A sub-committee would be
organised. It was subsequently announced that a tombola would be
set up with prizes donated by the committee and club members, and a
food sub-committee would 'convene soonest'. The early June meeting
reported that the steering group and the food sub-committee had both
met, and all arrangements were well in hand. Invitations to attend on
a complimentary basis were to be issued to Essex Chronicle Group
and Raggett, Tiffen and Harries – these organisations had both been
extremely generous in their support of the Music Club's activities and,
in particular, the competition. As might be expected, this event was a
tremendous success, and it was suggested that a similar style of event
might conclude future seasons.

1992–1993

The new season started with the AGM, held rather later than usual, on 2nd October. Retiring chairman, Dr Geoffrey Tompkins paid tribute to the committee's hard work and pointed out that the success of the club depended upon a vigorous and active committee, each bringing their individual strengths to bear in their work for the club. In ending his term of office, he felt sure that Jean Hall, the first lady chairman, would bring a further period full of enthusiasm and activity – he was not wrong! He also mentioned that the duties of the secretary would be taken over by Barrie Hall, who was stepping down as Vice-Chairman.

As the year came to a close, the Essex Chronicle Group had indicated their willingness to financially support the club again in 1993 for the Essex Young Musician of the Year competition as well as the Essex Schools Musician award. In addition, to further enhance the EYMY, it was suggested that all Essex mayors be invited to the final held that year in Chelmsford. The ECG also gave their blessing to Chelmsford Music Society, offering an engagement to the winner of the EYMY as well as offering support for a further Wigmore Hall recital. Geoffrey Timms subsequently had lunch with representatives of both the ECG and Chelmsford Music Society, who confirmed that they would like to open their season with the winner of the EYMY competition. This information would be included in the competition brochure as being part of the prize. It was also agreed that the club would pay £50 towards the costs of an accompanist where necessary. Chelmsford Music Society later also offered a recital to a previous competition winner, Gregory Walmsley, and his pianist.

ongar music club

A COMPETITION TO FIND THE
ESSEX SCHOOLS MUSICIAN
OF THE YEAR

SPONSORED BY
BRENTWOOD & ONGAR GAZETTE
(ESSEX CHRONICLE SERIES)

PROGRAMME   25p

Essex Schools Musician of the Year • 20th February 1993

During the last few months of 1992, doubts had been sown about the long term future of the hall in the Adult Education Campus and the campus as a whole. Although at that time the future was not clear, the club had been given dates up to the end of 1995 in order to show commitment. However, contingency plans had already begun, and other venues in the area were being investigated.

As usual, the year concluded with the traditional Christmas concert – Christmas tree, lights, the Stondon Singers, handbell ringers, choirboy, punch, and two or three dozen mince pies being required from each committee member. The presents around the Christmas tree would

---

**THE
BRENTWOOD & ONGAR GAZETTE (ESSEX CHRONICLE SERIES)
AWARDS**

This competition is organised to encourage advanced musicians of school age who attend Essex schools and was held for the first time in February 1992. The performances in general were impressive, the finalists achieving encouragingly high standards. The winner, Anthony Woollard (cello) from Brentwood School, and the runner-up, Pippa Stewart (flute) from Chelmsford County High School for Girls both played with great distinction. Anthony, as part of his prize, was excused the preliminary round of the competition for the John Lill Awards held in Chelmsford last July. He took full advantage of this opportunity and won a place in the Final.

After such a successful inauguration which involved candidates and schools from all parts of the county, this event takes its rightful place alongside the parent competition for the John Lill Awards for the Essex Young Musician of the Year.

-------o0o-------

PRIZES

Sponsored by Brentwood & Ongar Gazette
(Essex Chronicle Group)

1st Prize: (a) £100;
(b) an award of £100 to the music department of the candidate's school;
(c) the Ongar Music Club Trophy to retain for one year;
(d) a place in the semifinal of the Essex Young Musician of the Year competition.

2nd Prize: (a) £75;
(b) an award of £75 to the music department of the candidate's school;
(c) the Alison Baker Trophy to retain for one year.

---

again be designated for Norway House – a home in nearby North Weald for vulnerable and homeless people. There would also be a decorated bucket for those wishing to make a cash contribution. It was decided that a compère would greatly enhance the enjoyment of the evening, and Howard Nicholson, chairman of the jazz section, was thought to be the ideal candidate – he did a magnificent job.

Geoffrey Timms was again in overdrive as the club entered 1993. There was the second Essex Schools Musician competition on 20th February and the Wigmore Hall recital on 5th March (there was some panic over the latter, which is discussed in Chapter 7). The Essex Schools Musician competition was another successful occasion, although with fewer entrants than previously. Geoffrey Timms subsequently noted various ideas for the following year, such as the possibility of organising the afternoon round by instrumental group, with perhaps a small prize for the winner in each group who would then go through to the final. Meanwhile, in April, the Essex Chronicle Group had reiterated that they liked the Wigmore Hall experience as a part of the competition and agreed to increase their sponsorship by 3% (roughly £100) for the following year.

An ongoing concern for the club was the Adult Education Campus' long-term future, although it was reported in April that the club should be safe until 1996. Naturally, there was a good deal of comment about this in the local press where it was noted that the District Council considered that it would be "a deprivation to abandon the facility". On a more positive note, in June, there was great celebration when it was announced in the Queen's Birthday Honours that Sir Yehudi Menuhin had been made a Baron (a rank of Life Peer) and was now Lord Yehudi Menuhin OM, KBE.

1993–1994

Ongar Music Club has a tradition that members who have given long and distinguished service to the club, are awarded a gold life-membership card by the club. Barrie Hall presented this award to Geoffrey Timms at a social occasion prior to Geoffrey's retirement to North Wales in 1993.

By the AGM of that year, Geoffrey had moved to Wales and although no longer on the club's committee, he continued to serve as

Geoffrey Timms (left) being presented with his gold life-membership card by Barrie Hall, prior to his retirement to Wales in 1993

administrator of the Essex Young Musician of the Year competition with the same responsibilities as previously. The other jobs of fund-raising and sponsorship, crucial to the competition, would be carried out, as they always had been, by other members of the committee. Geoffrey's focus had always been on the core organisation of the competition itself, with oversight of the other supporting areas. His role of running the Century Club had been taken over by Don Anderson, and the Young Music Makers by Catherine Jennings, who was elected to the committee at the 1993 AGM. Geoffrey's departure was acknowledged at the AGM by chairman Jean Hall, when thanks were also recorded to Daphne Tinsey, who, with Hilda Barker, had for many years provided, and continued to provide, floral decorations for the performing area on concert evenings. She also acknowledged John Harrop, the club's long-standing treasurer, and Sylvia Terry, who had been in charge of the club's membership arrangements and, like Geoffrey Timms, had been a committee member since the club's inception in 1975.

The club's name was put on the rota for a stall in Manor Square on Saturday 27th November, displaying the major prizes for the Grand Draw and selling tickets together with leaflet distribution. Volunteers would be sought to officiate for an hour on the stall. Some sort of musical entertainment was also suggested for the stall. Other publicity options were considered, such as a table at a future car boot sale to be held by the White Bear pub in Stanford Rivers. Ideas also included a musical quiz as part of a feature on the club to be promoted by the Guardian and Gazette – this might attract new members. The committee was asked to jot down possible questions.

A discussion arose regarding the forthcoming Essex Schools Musician of the Year competition, being held on 19th March (1994). Catherine Jennings thought that there should be more recognition of teachers given in the programme. Also, it was pointed out that whereas the school which the winner attended received an award of £100 (together with a contribution from James Dace), the school might actually have nothing to do with teaching the successful performer to play. It was decided to revert to the Essex Chronicle Group to clarify these points for future years. It was also felt that it would be very interesting to know to what use the

Wigmore Hall, 5th March 1993 • Pictured (l-r) Harry Levy (Managing Director, Essex Chronicle Series), Gregory Walmsley *cello* (Essex Young Musician of the Year 1989) with Anna Guijarro *piano*, Don Alberto Aza, (Spanish Ambassador to the Court of St James), Alison Baker *piano* (Essex Young Musician of the Year 1985), Geoffrey Timms (Administrator, Essex Young Musician of the Year)

1993

schools put the money. As Geoffrey Timms was planning to attend the competition, it was felt that these matters should be left for discussion and decision-making between him and the Essex Chronicle, with no committee involvement. The 9th March meeting recorded that John Lill's fiftieth birthday would fall during the following week and it was agreed that the club would send him a bottle of Veuve Clicquot along with a suitable card. The Essex Schools Musician competition ran successfully in March and, as recorded in the minutes:

> ... proving that the organisation can be handled from Wales. Geoffrey Timms' preparations were, as ever, immaculate.

This, of course, was well before the advent of widespread domestic email and other technological innovations, which we now rely on as a matter of course. The same minutes recorded that another Grand Draw was planned, which was to be drawn at the forthcoming Gilbert and Sullivan evening in May. Once again, the club had taken a stall in the High Street for publicity purposes, manned by members of the committee – another booking having been made for Saturday 9th April 1995.

In April, something of a watershed arose for the relationship between the club and the Essex Chronicle Group, and this is discussed fully in Chapter 7. Despite the uncertainty, planning continued for the 1994 competition, to be held again at Chelmsford's Shire Hall. This planning proceeded with support from the ECG, as promised for that year. On the opposite page is an interesting and informative note from the 15th June committee meeting detailing aspects of the organisation.

Like its younger sibling, the competition had once again been administered most successfully from Wales by Geoffrey Timms. As might be anticipated, the competition progressed smoothly despite a last-minute issue with access for the piano hired from James Dace & Son due to another activity taking place in the hall. There was also an issue with there being no stage lighting, and an application was later submitted for a refund for the amount paid for this.

By now, the relationship with the Essex Chronicle Group had ended and the early September meeting was largely devoted to ways of moving

<u>Future Events</u> EYMC - 25 and 26 June.

Saturday: John Harrop noted that the Preliminaries would have to begin at 1.30, not 2.0 as previously advertised, in order to accommodate one performer whose accompanist had to perform elsewhere later that day. Roderick Elms had received various long faxes from Geoffrey Timms, and confirmed that there would be 16 performers in the preliminaries; 4 singers, 2 woodwind, 3 cellists, 2 brass players, 2 violinists, and 3 pianists. Four other competitors were already qualified for the Semi-Finals. Sylvia Terry agreed to see to refreshments for the candidates and adjudicators. Ushers to be Peter Jackson and/or Janet Pope. John Harrop to confirm piano tuning arrangements. Carpet to be provided for platform for cellists, and chairs set out at 11.00 am (Geoff Tompkins and John Harrop). At least two music stands should be available and it was believed the Chairman at present had the OMC music stand, and John would bring piano stool.

Sunday Geoffrey Timms had telephoned John Harrop just prior to the meeting to say that Dace's had phoned to say the Shire Hall were unable to accept delivery of the piano on Saturday, due to a Wedding Reception and evening function taking place. It was hoped Dace's would be able to provide a delivery team for Sunday; if not, a Steinway would have to be hired, at considerably greater cost, but a piano must be there, at all costs. Adjudicators would be Geoffrey Timms, Michael Boyle, Roderick Elms, Simon Joly, Barrie Hall, Nona Liddell and Graham Trew. Adèle was unable to help until the evening; Patti to collect Valerie and Sylvia at 10.30am Sunday and drive to Tesco to buy supplies, and arrive at Shire Hall by 11.30. Catering would include tea/coffee/orange and biscuits for competitors;

Semi-finals - tea/biscuits for audience at 4.0pm

Supper for adjudicators and OMC - 6.15/6.30pm - cater for up to 20 people

Interval - tea/biscuits for audience

Bucks fizz for Gazette people & panel (Barrie Hall to arrange)

Geoffrey Timms would announce results of Semi-Finals; details of competitors in final would be in programme.

Staffing: Sylvia Terry on door - programmes priced at 50p

Janet Pope, Peter Jackson and Catherine Jennings - Ushers

Valerie, Patti and Adèle - catering

Patti to make up four posies for table.

forward with the two competitions. One immediate consequence was the withdrawal of the Essex Schools Musician competition but with the agreement to add an extra prize for the under-eighteens in the EYMY competition. It was also agreed that a small 'think tank' be established for the sole purpose of providing suggestions for the 'vigorous promotion' of the club's activities. This would consist of Janet Pope, Peter Jackson and the chairman.

Also in September, the chairman, Jean Hall, sent out a newsletter in which she mentioned that Sylvia Terry was to step down from committee duties. Sylvia was one of the five founder members of the club and served on the committee since the club's inception in 1975. Jean noted that Sylvia had:

> ... served the club diligently for twenty years, and the committee will miss her cool common sense.

A presentation was made to Sylvia at the harp recital by Susan Blair on 25th November. Whilst researching this history, it's been a pleasure to note the presence of one or two of my friends and colleagues who have given recitals for the club. I've known Sue for many years, and I was delighted to note, in the assessment of her recital, that she "had greatly impressed with her charm and musicianship".

The chairman's newsletter mentioned that as the club was a charity, members could reclaim income tax on any financial gifts. This meant that for every £15 covenanted, the club would receive £20. She aptly pointed out that "concert-giving is an expensive business".

1994–1995

The September AGM noted the loss of Sylvia Terry from the committee and formally appointed Janet Pope and Peter Jackson, who had been co-opted to the committee sometime earlier. It was also mentioned that the Essex Chronicle Group was 'moving on'. The proceeds of the Grand Draw that year had been disappointing, and even income from the Century Club had declined. It was a matter of great urgency to revitalise the club's finances. There were now two Peters on the committee, and they were rather amusingly referred to in the minutes as Peter I (Peter Jackson) and Peter II (Peter Strickland).

By October, the chairman had received three promises of sponsorship for the EYMY competition. These were from Raggett, Tiffen & Harries, Davisons and Rhône Poulenc. Also noted in October was the forthcoming centenary of Ongar Parish Council and the fact that a fifteen-day event was being organised in celebration of this. There had been a preliminary approach for some contribution to the occasion by the Music Club. It appeared that it might be able to offer a Young Music Makers presentation along with one of the regular evening events – the latter possibly being

ONGAR MUSIC CLUB

(Founded 1975)

President   YEHUDI MENUHIN   KBE

COMMITTEE

Chairman:
David Kirkwood Esq.
Secretary: Mrs. Jean Wilson   *Treasurer:* Mrs. Betty Greatrex
Membership:
Mrs. Sylvia Terry
Services: Miss Phoebe Musgrave
Artistic Adviser: Geoffrey Timms Esq.
Publicity: Barrie Hall Esq.
Mrs. Joyce Perry   John Harrop Esq.

The front cover of the press-cuttings book kept by Barrie Hall.

of a more prestigious recital as money might be forthcoming from Parish Council funds. It subsequently came to light that the budget for the whole event was just £1,000, so the club would be lucky if it received £100 towards the cost of any celebratory presentation.

In November came the news that Geoffrey Timms may not be able to continue to administer the competition beyond June 1995. It was very much hoped that he might be able to reconsider, but if not, Jean Hall pointed out that her term as chairman would cease in 1995, and she would be in a position to take over this responsibility, if necessary. The November meeting also noted that Nicola Harries (who worked as a solicitor in Ongar and whose firm Raggett, Tiffen and Harries had generously supported the competition in recent years) had agreed to serve on the committee – this news was warmly welcomed. In December, she launched straight in when the issue of obtaining a licence to facilitate the selling of wine during concert intervals was raised by committee member Peter Strickland. The person receiving the licence would need to attend court to answer questions, and Nicola, therefore, volunteered to apply for the licence on behalf of the club. It was later noted that Peter II should be the one to arrange for the provision of wines, glasses and helpers, once again on the principle that "He who hath the vision getteth the job"! It was hoped that this venture might help to bring in some additional and welcome income.

Reporting on the competition, the 12th December meeting records that Geoffrey Timms was having a new winner's cup made. It also notes that he was now happy with the brochure for the forthcoming competition, which was then being printed. A letter was read from John Lill in which he expressed his hope to be present at the competition in June.

Peter Strickland had also been busy producing a marketing review which he tabled in the meeting on 15th December. This identified community groups from which the club was most likely to draw an audience – music teachers, brass bands and other instrumental ensembles and choruses were noted – making it clear to these areas that the club offered live music-making of a very high standard. The immediate objectives were to streamline the club's activities, such as the printing of leaflets and posters. Also, to ensure that every committee member was clear about his or her particular area of responsibility.

The New Year started with the usual prolonged discussion about the Christmas concert, which frequently seemed to divide opinion about the desirability or otherwise of the various component parts – notably from those who really didn't appreciate the traditional role taken by a choirboy. Essex Chamber Orchestra was to give a concert on 14th January and, as may be expected, this took quite a bit more organisation than the more regular concerts, with the requirements for additional staging and seating for the performers. Committee members were asked to buy (or bake) sufficient cakes, paper cups and drinks, ensuring that they were at the hall in time. They were also to be in attendance to make the necessary sandwiches with ingredients bought by Barrie Hall. This he did on his way to the hall, along with tea, coffee, sugar and milk. On other matters, the new competition brochure had been printed and John Lill had agreed to chair the adjudication panel. Preparations for the fourth EYMY winner's recital at the Wigmore Hall on 10th April were also well underway.

The February minutes indicate that the Essex Chamber Orchestra concert was a great success. They also demonstrate the considerable endeavours of the working party in relation to marketing the club's activities. In addition, it was noted that the Parish Council would contribute £250 towards the renovation of the stage in the Adult Education Campus, which, at the time, was being used for the club's events.

As previously mentioned, all events received an assessment at the following committee meeting. This was useful to keep in touch with how the season's programmes was received. It was also helpful so that a decision could be made as to whether the club would invite an artiste to return on a future occasion. These were always quite frank discussions, and it's fair to say that most comments were very positive. Considering that the club often engaged artistes without any personal knowledge, and frequently with limited information about what the nature of the evening might be, there was a remarkable level of appreciation shown by both the committee and membership. Like most of the arts, music is highly subjective, and you will never get total agreement from an audience regarding their personal enjoyment. In this respect, I think that Ongar Music Club has enjoyed outstanding success. There were very occasionally not-so-positive opinions shown by such responses as "Never again"! Others could be less direct but to very much the same effect:

> There were considered to have been no more than thirty-five minutes of second-rate music; thank goodness for the contribution of the pianist. The evening was not much fun and never really took off. The chairman reported a subsequent 'try on' regarding expenses, which were never agreed and will not be paid.

I rather liked the anecdote which described a concert as "Far more successful than hoped". There was also one other evening which was agreed to have been a 'dire event' with a certain committee member concluding, "We woz robbed"! The subsequent party at John Harrop's house was declared to have been the "musical highlight of the day". Not everything will be to everyone's musical taste, and I'm sure on these extremely rare occasions, the artistes did their very best. Most recitals progressed from planning to production without a hitch. Performers were booked, fees and arrival times were agreed upon. Food was organised, and transport from to and from Epping station provided, if required.

For most of the earlier years, it would be ascertained whether the performer would be able to stay for the traditional post-concert party, and some were offered overnight accommodation. Occasional problems arose due to travelling difficulties resulting from rail or road delays. A few artistes cancelled due to health or other difficulties, but that was extremely rare. Sometimes other aspects had to be navigated with diplomacy, such as the group for which it was reported that various [matrimonial] problems had arisen, which they were trying to sort out. Unfortunately, maybe due to the difficulties experienced by the group needing to change its makeup, this was subsequently reported by Barrie Hall in characteristically unequivocal terms as:

> One of the most disastrously boring concerts ever attended!
> The performers offstage afterwards had proved quite delightful, but their programme was uniformly dirge-like.

An experiment was planned to obtain a licence to facilitate the selling of wine during a concert interval. The first 'wine bar' experiment came during the recital given by the distinguished violinist Hugh Bean on 31st March, along with the pianist Shelagh Sutherland. The notes following this recital make mention of the great pleasure of hearing three violin and piano sonatas played in their entirety. They also note that Shelagh Sutherland's playing was "quite splendid".

The Wigmore Hall recital in April was given by the pianist Zoë Mather and the cellist Sarah Barnes. It is reported that they played splendidly and that the whole evening was given a huge lift by the presence of John Lill – it is reported that you could "feel the buzz" in the audience.

In June, due to the pressure of work, Patti Nicholson, a long term member of the committee, felt the need to resign from the committee. This meant the re-working of some of the duties she had carried out so well for the club over the years, not least that of designing handbills and posters. Later that month was the scheduled 1995 EYMY competition. In May, it had been reported that Chelmsford Music Society had unfortunately reneged on their agreement to offer a recital to the winner of the competition. John Harrop expressed the view that it was not worth 'wasting any more of the club's time' on the situation. Some of the committee wanted to invite other Music Clubs to the competition with a view to one of them offering a winner's recital – after all, this had been featured as a part of the prize. In fact, the chairman wrote to sixteen other Music Clubs regarding the recital, and by mid-June had received replies from Epping,

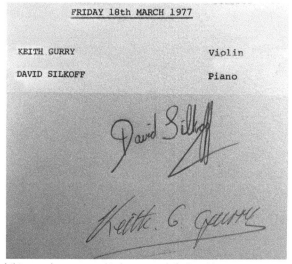

FRIDAY 18th MARCH 1977

KEITH GURRY — Violin

DAVID SILKOFF — Piano

Artistes were always encouraged to sign a programme for the archives

Theydon Bois and Brentwood. The competition that year recorded the largest entry in the competition's history, with twenty-eight soloists necessitating a 1:00 pm start for the Preliminary Round. It was felt that this might have represented the highest standard of entry to that point, and the whole occasion was lifted once more by the presence of John Lill.

The season proper ended with a social event on 8th July to mark the end of Jean Hall's term as chairman. Nicola Harries generously hosted this in her home and garden (the Concert Room of the Budworth Hall had been in reserve in case of inclement weather). More than thirty-five people attended and were treated to cream teas, 'appropriate beverages', and vocal entertainment.

At the September meeting, the treasurer, John Harrop, circulated the accounts, noting that the year's result was 'not bad' considering the club had lost £2,800 of sponsorship from the Essex Chronicle Group in respect of the competition. The usual arrangements were made for the forthcoming AGM – a bottle of wine for each of the performers (Edward and Philippa Bale), a bottle of whisky for the auditor, with wine or coffee for the audience – all of which would be provided free. As usual, Barrie was in charge of buying all the provisions.

Retiring chairman Jean Hall receiving a gift from John Harrop

1995

4. 1995 – 2004 Seasons

In the September 1995 AGM, the outgoing chairman, Jean Hall, drew attention to the new curtains in the hall of the Adult Education Campus, which Essex County Council had provided at a cost of £1,700. She reflected on a highly successful year with a fine Wigmore Hall recital shared by pianist Zoë Mather and cellist Sarah Barnes – a recital that saw the largest audience ever at one of these recitals, and which was greatly enhanced by the presence of John Lill. The chairman thanked her husband Barrie and the hard-working committee for all their support before she handed over to the incoming chairman, Janet Pope.

Howard Nicholson, chairman of the Jazz Club, had been hard at work refurbishing the poster display box located in the High Street, and that now looked splendid. He was sent a cheque for the materials along with the obligatory bottle of whisky. There was another poster display site in regular use outside the old Great Stony School that could be used on a first come, first served basis by arrangement with the caretaker. Both these displays were felt invaluable to the work of publicising the club's ongoing activities.

The October meeting reported that the membership for the previous year had been one hundred and twenty-one and that this year, there were currently ninety-five. Unfortunately, membership of the Century Club was down to ninety-eight, and some gentle coercion would be required. There had been a loss of £122 on the AGM, but that was average for the event as drinks were given to the audience without charge as a gesture for their support during the year. The chairman also read a letter from Geoffrey Timms in which, not unexpectedly, he confirmed that he would be unable to continue as administrator of the Essex Young Musician of the Year competition beyond that season. It was suggested that the chairman should write to him to say that he might like to stay in touch with the competition by remaining on the adjudication panel. Jean Hall would take over as administrator and she was already looking at alternative venues to the Wigmore Hall – the hall's new pricing structure making the venue unrealistic for the club to pursue again.

The November meeting was broadly given over to discussion of the Christmas concert, with various suggestions for a choir to sing with the Salvation Army band. The chairman also nominated a new charity for that year – Ongar Handicapped. Nicola Harries offered to ask her mother, Anne, whether she would provide two hundred mince pies. For many years, Anne Harries offered the most wonderful support of the club's gastronomic needs, not just for audiences but also during the competitions when she would provide a remarkable feast that was always warmly anticipated by the adjudicators. The meeting concluded with an invitation (from an unrecorded source) to attend an undertakers' concert – Barrie Hall said emphatically, "We won't be going!"

It became apparent in December that the club would shortly become liable for a public performing licence on Sundays, and this would affect the EYMY competition. There was really no way around this, although it was thought that the Young Music Makers might consider trying Saturday performances. Peter I (Peter Jackson) reported that the membership of the Century Club had picked up greatly, and had receipts of over £400. Peter was also warmly thanked for having arranged for his company Nortel to sponsor the competition's second prize of £300. The meeting was then asked to make selections from various suggestions for new livery to be included on the club's notepaper and other documents.

The ongoing encouragement to join the Century Club had clearly paid off, and by February 1996, membership stood at one hundred and twenty-four. There could now be larger prizes as a result. Meanwhile, Jean Hall had been investigating London venues for the competition winner's recital and had established that the Purcell Room on London's South bank could produce a profit of up to £500 as opposed to the Wigmore Hall's loss of £400, working with the same criteria.

Also, in February, the chairman Janet Pope mooted the idea of a social event to mark the club's twenty-first anniversary – food for thought. She had produced a rather interesting document detailing comparative figures for expenditure for artistes per concert, spanning the three years from 1994. Although this fluctuated slightly, it was fairly stable although it was noted that it was going down in the following year.

1994–1995: £363
1995–1996: £388
1996–1997: £318

Dr Janet Pope

I should add that when negotiating with artistes, I was always acutely aware that I was dealing with colleagues, and frequently, friends. Offering lower-than-normal fees always felt wrong, but I had no choice and always explained the reasons. Most were extremely understanding and said yes, for which I feel a great sense of gratitude, knowing that their performances were hugely appreciated by the club.

By March, the idea of a twenty-first celebration had fermented considerably, and a date was set for 13th July, to be held in the grounds of Nicola's home. It was agreed that live music would be preferable, and various suggestions were made. It was agreed that the event would start at 3:00 pm and that there would be a £3 charge. In the event, the live music option didn't work out but a great time was had by all.

The club had been notified of a special charity evening to be held at the Mansion House in London in celebration of the 80th birthday of the club's president, Lord Yehudi Menuhin. This was promoted in connection with the London International String Quartet Competition, and tickets for this dinner/concert were priced at £150 per head. In April, Jean and Barrie Hall had indicated their willingness to attend in support of the club and hoped that the club might contribute £100 towards the total cost of their tickets. In fact, the chairman and treasurer were adamant that the club should pay half the costs, which was much appreciated by the Halls.

By now, agreement had been given for the placement of a new club display board outside 'Essex House' in the High Street. This was in an excellent location and was hoped to be of great benefit. Coincidentally, the club also received a letter regarding the forthcoming centenary of this building, where the club started, when it was known as the 'Old

Library Building'. It was therefore hoped that the club might contribute to some sort of celebration. At that point, Barrie Hall proudly disclosed:

> ... that [one of] its first-ever public events had been a talk given by himself on the Promenade Concerts, as a result of which Jean and he had come upon the house they have lived in for the past twenty-one years. And then wondered why on earth he can't keep his mouth shut!

It was suggested that Barrie repeat his Proms talk on a date in early October, later confirmed as the 4th. This would be in the upstairs room of Essex House (the venue for his original talk and the former Arts Centre). Barrie had been invited to give his first talk as he had worked for many years as the publicity officer for Radio 3 and was therefore very much involved in the BBC Promenade Concerts – see Chapter 6. In 1981, he published an authoritative book on these concerts called *The Proms and the Men Who Made Them*.

The April meeting also noted that Valerie Chetham was to give up the catering at concerts after "long and faithful service", although she was willing to step in at any time in case of emergencies. Jean Hall reported that sponsorship of the Hugh Terry Prize (one of the under-19 prizes in the EYMY competition) had been obtained for three years from Rhône-Poulenc. This followed attendance by their representatives at the recital by Essex Young Musician of the Year, saxophonist James Scannell.

By May 1996, planning for that year's competition was progressing in earnest, with the dates set for the 29th and 30th June. In addition to the arrangements already made, Raggett, Tiffen and Harries had kindly agreed to sponsor the third prize and Valerie and George Chetham, the fourth prize. It was noted that with the recent change in the catering arrangements, Anne Harries "could probably cope on her own". Barrie Hall would provide the interval 'fizz' for the sponsors. The local MP Eric Pickles had stated his intention to attend the final and would be asked to present the awards. It was also noted that the Parish Council was planning another festival, coinciding with the opening of the new library. It was thought that the club might not wish to be involved on a second occasion.

Jean Hall noted that she had seen mention of the Brentwood Rotary Club's area music competition, with *Essex Chronicle* involvement and BBC Essex coverage. It was decided that the club would offer the winner of that competition immediate and free entry to the Essex Young Musician of the Year to subtly emphasise the seniority (and superiority) of the club's competition. It was noted that the press seemed to pick up favourably on this aspect in their reporting of the Brentwood competition. The June meeting concluded with the sad news of the closure of the Ongar Times.

By September, the chairman had written to both the Parish and District Councils to express the club's concern at the possible development of the Adult Education Campus and the consequential loss of the hall. She had received replies from both, and it was suggested that she also write to Essex County Council, which has the ultimate responsibility for the site. On a more positive note, it was reported that there had been no loss on the EYMY competition in June due to generous sponsorship.

1996–1997

In September, Peter Strickland stood down from the committee after many years of service. It was also noted that Barrie Hall had generously offered to supply some interval refreshment on the occasion of his talk at Essex House. This repeat talk was heralded a great success, being delivered to a packed room with several special guests.

By the October meeting, newspaper reports suggested that Essex County Council was likely to sell the Adult Education Campus site for development. The only hard news being that bookings are not being accepted beyond June 1997. This generated great concern, and serious discussion ensued about the implications for the loss of the present hall and current home of Ongar Music Club. Even if available and acoustically suitable, many school halls would have no storage for the club's piano. Possible options included Great Stony School, St James' Church Hall, High Ongar Village Hall and Elmbridge School. The chairman, together with Jean and Barrie Hall, pursued these as a matter of urgency. The vice-chairman (Jean Hall) also followed up on this concern with the council chairman Ron Barnes and Epping Forest District Council (EFDC), which had previously commented on the need for a hall in the Ongar area.

A subsequent meeting announced that the club had been told that there were no plans to demolish the hall and that its future was 'secure'. They were, apparently, prepared to take bookings on the rather extraordinary basis that "there is uncertainty over the future of the hall". It was therefore agreed to attempt to place bookings through to the end of the 1997–1998 season. This issue was discussed further at the next meeting, and it appeared that the only conclusion to be drawn was that there would be some form of development and that the club would be wise to have a contingency plan in place for the following season.

By the start of 1997, a block booking had been placed at the campus for 1997–1998, and no objections had been raised. Although it seemed best to carry on as we were until the future was more definite, it has to be said that there was an underlying sense of corporately bated breath! The 1996 Christmas concert had been a success – it had been well attended, and the request that the Salvation Army bandmaster should act as the Master of Ceremonies was well received. Also, a Christmas tree, having been provided by the Epping Forest District Council for a prior event, had been left behind for the club's use. It was agreed to ask the Salvation Army band to return for next Christmas and also to invite the Stondon Singers.

By February, Barrie Hall was getting very concerned about the uncertainty surrounding the forthcoming season and *insisted* that approaches be made to the administrators of other venues. Barrie and the chairman planned to set the ball rolling by having an informal chat with Ongar Primary School, which had indicated a willingness to help. A letter had been received from 'Theatre Resource' which was trying to organise support for the use of the Great Stony site, originally Great Stony School. However, it was felt that if there were any future in that proposal, availability would be longer-term than the club's immediate requirement. The February meeting mooted the idea of a 'super series' for the millennium and also resolved to investigate a possible banner across the High Street announcing the competition.

Never one to sit still for long, Barrie Hall had also been writing to many of the local papers and magazines with details of the EYMY competition, its winners and what they were then doing. This had the welcome result of articles being published in Essex Countryside and Arts East.

The committee heard in March that John Lill hoped to attend the final of the competition. MEP Hugh Kerr had also indicated his intention to be present and would present the prizes if John Lill didn't manage to be there. A discussion then took place about many of the halls in the area, some of which had already been visited. The outcome was:

> We assume that the school hall [Adult Education Campus] will be unavailable from the end of this season.
>
> • Ongar Music School is likely to move to Shelley Junior School, Chairman and Barrie Hall to visit Shelley School Hall.
>
> • The future of Great Stony Hall is under discussion but will not be available in the short term.
>
> • The Hall at Ongar Primary school might be suitable in extremis, but the layout is not good, and there are problems with the lighting: the school could house the piano.
>
> • The best venue so far is St. Martin's Church for our main concerts, with the upstairs room at the Budworth for YMM events and EYMY preliminaries. Chairman to contact [the Rector] about arrangements for the piano and the club's lighting.

Shelley School Hall and the Community Centre were both subsequently inspected, and it was concluded that the former had a 'dreadful echo' and the latter was far too small. The Rector was very helpful but needed agreement from the Parochial Church Council (PCC) – a reply was awaited. That said, whilst storing the club's lighting would not be a problem, there was no suitable place in the church to keep the piano. Another suggestion was that the club might sell the grand, buying an upright to keep in the church and hire a grand when required. A further issue arose regarding the selling of tickets – although it was understood other organisations had sold tickets for entry to the church, it appeared that they could not be sold for Music Club events. The church also confirmed that a piano could only be left in the church overnight.

The Great Stony site, although of interest, would likely not be a practical proposition for at least two years, although the club would continue to monitor progress. The chairman and Barrie Hall subsequently met with Derek Birch, chairman of the Community Association, and inspected the Concert Room upstairs at the Budworth Hall. While this hall would be too small for the annual carol concert and other larger occasions, it would work well for the majority of the club's events. The CA would allow the club to install its lighting in the room, although piano storage would be a problem. There was already a piano in the room (the aforementioned legacy from Ongar Comprehensive School). The preferred option would have been to store that instrument and relocate the club's Bechstein to the Concert Room. However, it was decided to fulfil a request to loan the piano to Shenfield High School, as this would allow its storage until such time as space could be provided at the Budworth Hall. Meanwhile, the Community Association's piano, already present, would be used, and an instrument hired for special occasions.

It was therefore agreed that the club would relocate its base to the Concert Room, moving its piano from the Adult Education Campus by

Halls in the Ongar Area	
Budworth	Bar noise but possibly suitable for EYMY
Great Stoney School	Layout of rooms off the hall makes it unusable
Ongar Primary School	Hall not ideal but piano accomodation
High Ongar School	Hall too small and odd shape
Shelley Primary School	to be visited
Elmbridge School	—— for sale
PNEU School	
St Martins Church	Possibility if piano can be housed, ideal for carols
St James Church Hall	—— Small not suitable
High Ongar Village Hall	—— not worth it.
Shelley Community Hall	—— Part of Shelley School.

Notes made of visits to halls in the Ongar area, 1997

the end of August at the latest – all costs to be borne by the Music Club. It was also agreed to attempt to book St Martin's Church for the Christmas carol concerts as it was now understood that whilst tickets could not be sold at the church door, they could be sold in the adjacent Church Rooms. How curious are our licensing laws? The Young Music Makers events would be in the Concert Room but would revert to Sundays as there had been concerns that audience numbers had suffered since moving to Saturdays. A Sunday licence would therefore be needed for the YMM events as well as the EYMY competition.

The Purcell Room recital on 2nd May had returned a fine performance but a disappointing attendance – the hall being about half full. Notwithstanding that fact, the loss was far smaller than had the recital been in the Wigmore Hall. There were around fifty members present. The violinist Sîan Phillip, who had shared the recital with cellist Rachel Barnes, performed a work by the actor Antony Hopkins who was present in the audience. By then, applications for the 1997 competition had started arriving, and agreement had been obtained for the High Street banner to be erected on 22nd or 23rd June.

In the event, John Lill was unable to be present at the competition due to another unavoidable engagement, and Geoffrey Timms chaired the adjudication panel. The prizes had all been covered by corporate or private sponsorship, with the first prize being sponsored by M&G Group, Chelmsford.

1997–1998

The whole issue regarding the uncertainty of the arrangements at the Adult Education Campus was explained to the members at the September AGM, along with the decision to move most of the club's performances back to the Budworth Hall, where it had been made most welcome by the Community Association which manages it.

The late September meeting recorded its thanks to Jean Hall for her fine organisation in her first year as competition administrator. There had been an unfortunate incident following the competition when one of the finalists (who did not win and apparently thought they should have done) decided to make a considerable fuss and spread several lies about what had been said by officials regarding the outcome and what it should have been. Sensibilities can run high on such occasions – the adjudicators frequently have difficult judgements to make, and by the very nature of music, individual reaction to, and assessment of, the performances is, to a large degree, subjective. No one does themselves any favours by behaving in such an immature way, and it certainly doesn't help their reputation going forward into the profession. Luckily this remains the only occasion on which there has been such a response in all the years since the competition started in 1984.

By October, the new arrangements in the Concert Room had been further consolidated with the arrival of crockery, which was located in a cupboard in the small kitchen, under lock and key. In future, tickets would be sold downstairs to avoid a crush on the stairs, and interval coffee would be served on tables at the back of the hall. Also, in October, it was reported that Geoffrey Timms was plagued with health problems that, so far, doctors had not been able to diagnose. Jean Hall offered to arrange for a gift which she would send, together with greetings from the committee. The October meeting also suggested that the Purcell Room be investigated for a London recital in the autumn of 1998. There was a subsequent delay in establishing this due to the possibility of the hall closing. In the event, this did not happen, and it was hoped that a recital could be held there in the spring of 1999.

The year came to an end with the traditional Christmas concert, held on that occasion in its new surroundings of St Martin's Church. There had been a degree of disappointment with audience numbers as well as aspects of the performance. Queries were raised as to whether parking had been a problem or whether the venue put people off. The Salvation Army band had been good but invisible (layout issues are frequently a problem in churches), and the choirgirl, excellent. The new ticketing arrangements worked well, with many being bought in advance, either from the club or Highway Travel in the High Street, which, for many

St Martin's Church, Ongar

years, supported the club by selling tickets for its events. Peter Lewis offered to take over punch-making duties on future occasions with help from Barrie Hall.

The following year started with discussions about the relationship between the Music Club and the Jazz Club. It was noted by Barrie Hall that Ongar Jazz Club:

1. Was created as part of the Music Club

2. Changed its name from Jazz Section to Jazz Club without reference.

3. Has no separate existence.

4. Is under Music Club Constitution.

5. Chairman and Treasurer of the Music Club are also chairman and treasurer of the Jazz Section.

6. Cannot separate except by permission of the main club of which it is a part.

7. Would then require to have its own constitution and chairman and other officers.

8. Would probably not be eligible for charitable status on its own and have to pay VAT and Income Tax.

9. Entitled to some - but by no means all - of the accumulated funds.

Another benefit from the Music Club was its charitable status which could result in the Jazz Club gaining tax relief on donations, although it appears that this was never taken up. This was not an entirely comfortable situation and one which was discussed periodically in Music Club committee meetings, eventually reaching a point in 2002 when the Music Club committee felt that it might be best if there were to be a complete break. There were further discussions with the Jazz Club, which unanimously decided to maintain the status quo!

Much of the February meeting was given over to discussions about the situation at the Budworth Hall – specifically, the Concert Room, which was not licensed. It came to light that in 1995, Epping Forest District Council had written to the CA to say that work would need to be carried out on the Concert Room before it could grant a public performance licence. Therefore, there was quite a degree of 'frustration' within the club that its bookings had been taken in the knowledge of this but without having been given due warning. The club was informed that they could hold events there providing that they were limited to the club's membership. On the other hand, the Ballroom was licensed, but at present, it had no piano and was located right next to the bar and still unacceptably noisy for concerts. It was agreed that whilst clarification was sought from the CA about the exact content and conditions of this letter from the EFDC, concerts would continue in the Concert Room, with any non-members attending being given honorary membership – thereby obeying the letter, if not the spirit of the law. By then, Sunday licences had been granted for the Young Music Makers and the Essex Young Musician of the Year and they were safe to proceed. Also, a garden party was to be planned for the outgoing chairman on 11th July, again to be held again in the garden of Nicola Harries.

By May, due to ongoing difficulties in getting a booking at the Purcell Room, it had been decided to book St James' Church, Piccadilly for the next London recital. This was to be on 12th March featuring pianist Joseph Tong and saxophonist James Scannell. The hire charge was £500 with an additional £206 for the use and tuning of the piano. The church would advertise the recital but had no box-office or press publicity arrangements, so these aspects would need to be done entirely by the club. There were three hundred seats available, and these would be sold at £8. Also, in May, long-term committee member Valerie Chetham stood down. She would continue to be a member of the club and would be willing to help with the refreshments for the competition. It was also reported that the Great Stony site was under development, and although the hall would be leased to Theatre Resources and available for hire, this would not be before January 1999. It was therefore thought sensible to plan the 1998–1999 season on the basis of performances at the Budworth Hall.

By June 1998, we had received twenty-one entries for the competition, including five previous finalists and three others who had been excused from the preliminaries. Unfortunately, no one had been found to sponsor the first prize, which would therefore be covered by the club. Nortel would be sponsoring the second prize for the third year running, although it was noted that they couldn't guarantee support for future years. The treasurer reported having received £582 from other sponsors. That year, the competition result was somewhat remarkable in that a thirteen-year-old violinist Tammy Se had entered for the first time and went right through from the preliminary round to win the competition.

The garden party went ahead in July but was the unfortunate victim of bad weather. Although some people didn't turn up, the rain failed to totally dampen the spirits of those present who were also treated to live music kindly organised by Stan Cornhill.

1998–1999

The September AGM reflected on the change of venue and also the fact that the club's Bechstein was currently on load to Shenfield High School due to the lack of somewhere to house it in the Budworth Hall. The Ibach grand in the Concert Room, belonging to the CA, was not really up to solo duties, and another instrument was hired when necessary. In November, the chairman (Jean Hall) pointed out that not only would the year 2,000 be the millennium but also the twenty-fifth anniversary of Ongar Music Club. She was actively thinking about suitable events. The London International String Quartet had once again offered a third-prizewinner's recital for the year but without sponsorship, meaning that such a recital would cost the club around £500. That said, the committee felt it desirable to maintain the connection with this prestigious competition. Nicola generously offered to make a special sponsorship provision. The latest EYMY winner Tammy Se would also be giving her winner's recital for the club in that memorable season.

As in the previous year, the annual Christmas concert was held in the delightful surroundings of St Martin's Church with "Mrs Harries kindly making all the mince pies again". Clearly, word had got out about the catering arrangements as the attendance at the 1998 Christmas concert was reported as "very satisfactory".

Early in 1999, the CA announced that it would be possible to house the club's Bechstein in the Concert Room, providing it could be stored in the alcove, together with the Community Association's piano. It was initially thought that the piano could be moved downstairs for the competition, but in practice, it was discovered that the cost of hiring a piano was less than moving the club's piano downstairs and back again. In the world of piano hire, it is always the transport that is the most expensive part of the operation, and in such a situation as this, it has to be done twice – it was only in the very early days that the piano had been known to be loaded onto a builders truck to be transported around Ongar! This welcome decision had come after much lobbying from chairman Jean Hall. The club had also indicated its commitment to staying at the Budworth Hall despite overtures received from Theatre Resources at Great Stony.

It was suggested that a two-piano recital might be mounted in the millennium season – with free use of the room and all proceeds donated to the CA. In March, the chairman reported that she had attended a meeting at Great Stony for those interested in using the new facility. Although the club was now firmly established in the Budworth Hall, it was felt that it would be useful to know the extent of the new facilities. When reading between the lines of the pricing structure, it became even more apparent that the club was not going to move again as the hire charge increased significantly after 9:00 pm.

Plans were progressing for that year's EYMY competition, and Nicola Harries had prevailed upon Barclays Bank to sponsor the first prize of £500 – the manager would be attending. As expected, Nortel had confirmed that this would be their last year sponsoring the second prize, and sponsorship was also to be found for the fourth prize.

The winner's recital had taken place at St James', Piccadilly on 12th March and the treasurer had expressed pleasure at the financial outcome – a loss of less than £62. Such pleasure was not expressed regarding the event itself, not because of the performances, which had been very fine, but due to the less than first-class piano which had not been properly tuned. The venue itself had been considered somewhat gloomy, echoey, and without a good ambience. Also, by the most unfortunate coincidence, those returning to the church after the rehearsal break were greeted by newspaper display boards announcing the death of the club's president, Lord Yehudi Menuhin – a minute's silence was observed before the start of the concert (this sad news was subsequently notified in a letter to the club by Lord Menuhin's son, Jeremy). Something of a final gesture of disappointment from the St James' recital came sometime later when an invoice for around £40 was received from the church for an additional

Lord Yehudi and Baroness Diana Menuhin • Gstaad c. 1997

payment due for the performing rights involved in a short piece of Szymanowski.

The chairman explained to those on the committee who did not know the history, why the Wigmore Hall was no longer practical – being far too expensive. She also reported that that the Purcell Room had refused a booking as it contained a piano recital which was deemed to clash with another scheduled recital fairly close to the proposed date.

The subsequent committee meeting also broached a fundamental question about the winner's recital – who benefits? The audience came mostly from Ongar and the surrounding area; some venues did not have the same prestige for this type of recital as the Wigmore Hall; newspapers no longer reviewed concerts routinely as in the past; and on the recent occasion, both soloists had played in London previously. The event took a considerable degree of organisation for, seemingly, not that much reward.

At the same meeting, the chairman announced draft plans for the next season, including a concert in Brentwood Cathedral by John Lill on 22nd March – either a recital or a concerto if a suitable orchestra could be found. It was noted that the venue cost £150 to hire as compared with St James', Piccadilly which cost £500. The 31st March had been put by for the two-piano recital previously noted.

The club was also delighted to hear that its patron John Lill had agreed to become its president. A final piece of news at that meeting, and one which was very welcome, was that the Community Association had agreed to erect a soundproof partition between the bar and the Ballroom.

All the usual preparations were being made for the competition – the banner to be erected by 6th June, newspapers requested to send photographers, Brian Lawrence to steward again, Catherine Jennings to page-turn, tea, squash, coffee and adjudicators' meals courtesy of Anne and Nicola Harries. The competition itself was thought to have been exceptional, even by previous standards, and the occasion was lifted further by the presence of its patron.

1999–2000

The AGM that year contained something of a novelty – the Magwitch Trio, engaged to perform after the interval and joined by members and ex-chairmen of the club for a performance of Haydn's 'Toy Symphony', conducted in very "trying circumstances" by John Harrop. John was commended, not only for keeping things together, but also for turning every mistake into a bit of fun appreciated by the enthusiastic audience. A particular pleasure was that the founding chairman David Kirkwood was present and played a toy. The evening was rounded off with a party hosted by Nicola Harries, by now well known for such occasions.

The usual events played out over the next couple of months with preparations for the Christmas concert at St Martin's Church, including the BBC Radio 2 Young Chorister of the Year accompanied by John Harrop, and bottles of festive cheer being dispatched in various directions. It was also announced that Janet Pope was being relocated by her firm to Southampton and would not be able to join the committee for some time.

I would imagine that most people reading this will remember where they were on the eve of the millennium. In my case, I had given two performances in London's Royal Albert Hall where the Green Room might reasonably have been described as 'party central'. I was now driving back home to visit my parents, taking in a sky lit with multicoloured flashes of early firework displays and the streets bustling with revellers, all with their own expectations and hopes for the new century, and for many, new beginnings.

For Ongar Music Club, there was also a great sense of anticipation and excitement. Many special events had been planned, not just to acknowledge the millennium, but also the club's own silver jubilee – the highlight of this celebration to be a recital by its president John Lill in Brentwood Cathedral. The secretary, Barrie Hall, carefully entered the year 2000 into the minutes as he recorded his wife Jean opening the first meeting of the New Year and millennium. There was general approval of the Christmas concert, although universal dislike of the nasty sound emanating from a small electronic keyboard which the choir brought with them. It was felt that there had been too many items, too many introductions, too much applause – in fact, it seems that the choir brought with them a great deal of seasonal excess. Publicity for John Lill's recital in March was well underway, a Steinway piano was to be hired, and a coach had been ordered to transport members of the club to the event, as for other club outings. Planning for the two-piano event at the end of March was also in full swing, with a list of groups and hall users being written to, advising them of the occasion in support of the Community Association. John Harrop had undertaken to arrange a piece for twelve hands as a grand finale – if he could find a suitable work. By the following month, the individual duos had been named, along with some of the works to be performed. Ongar shopkeepers would be approached for prizes, and there would be a grand raffle. It was also reported that Barclays Bank would not continue to support the first prize of the EYMY competition, but that was not, perhaps, unexpected. Banks are not known for their unfailing generosity – more sponsorship would be needed.

There was a good audience for John Lill's recital, which was overheard to be described as "magic from the very first note". The cathedral staff had been wonderfully supportive throughout, and there had been excellent press coverage. However, a rumour circulating in the days beforehand that the recital was sold out may not have been helpful. A Wednesday is not a regular concert night, and John Lill had played in Chelmsford only the previous November. There was also another major event in Brentwood the same night, and there were very few places in Brentwood willing to display posters. All in all, it was considered to have been a wonderful occasion, hugely appreciated and a proper celebration of the club's first twenty-five years.

President: John Lill, O.B.E.

ONGAR MUSIC CLUB

25th Anniversary Season

Celebrity Concert

BRENTWOOD CATHEDRAL
Wednesday, 22 March 2000

JOHN LILL

PROGRAMME   £1.00

Roderick Elms and Geoffrey Timms rehearsing for the two-piano marathon • 31st March 2000 • Concert Room, Budworth Hall, Ongar

A little over a week later, a completely different kind of piano-based event took place in Ongar. The two-piano recital had been given by six pianists, twelve hands, and the programme of diverse content and variety had been very well received. There were two nine-year-olds to represent the children's concerts, and the occasion closed with John Harrop's arrangement of 'The Dance of the Little Swans' to much audience amusement. There was great appreciation for the efforts of twelve hands trying to gain access to two keyboards – and without rehearsal. The shops in Ongar had been very generous with raffle prizes, and the club was able to give the Community Association a total of £560.

As a slight digression, it's interesting to note that during that year came the first mention of the club having some sort of presence on the internet by way of a website. Today, it's almost unthinkable not to do so, but then, such matters were in a state of relative infancy and certainly far less easy to organise than today. Mention had been made of perhaps taking some space on another local website such as that for St Martin's Church. In practice, it was quite a few years later that the club had its own dedicated presence on the 'web'.

PROGRAMME

Tarantella   Shostakovich
Fugue à la Gigue   Bach, arr. Duncan
Suite No.2 for two pianos Op.17   Rachmaninov
  (Introduction; Romance)
Geoffrey Timms & Roderick Elms

Caprice No.24   Paganini
Sarah Manning & Matthew Pengilly

Sonata in D (second movement)   Mozart
Spanish Dance   Moszkowski
The Skater's Waltz   Waldteufel
Catherine Jennings & Geoffrey Tompkins

The Arrival of the Queen of Sheba   Handel
Valerie Manning and Catherine Jennings

INTERVAL

Berceuse (Dolly Suite)   Fauré
Jean & Barrie Hall

Fantasy Suite No.1, Op.5 (Russian Easter)   Rachmaninov
John Harrop & Barrie Hall

Divertimento   Richard Rodney Bennett
    (Samba triste; Country Blues; Ragtime Waltz; Finale)
Tarantella Napolitana   Rossini, arr. Geehl
Jamaican Rumba   Arthur Benjamin
Geoffrey Timms & Roderick Elms

Dance of the Little Swans   Tchaikovsky, arr. Harrop
for six pianists, twelve hands

The programme for the two-piano marathon • 31st March 2000 • Concert Room, Budworth Hall, Ongar

Much of the April meeting was understandably spent in discussing the musical events of March. However, planning had not stood still – the third prizewinners of the International String Quartet Competition was due to play in Ongar the day after their win, this being part of the agreement with the competition. This meant that the performers and the programme were not known until the very last minute, putting the programme printing into top gear. In the event, the performers were the Con Tempo quartet from Romania, based at that time in England. It was reported that their performance was sensational and that they played superbly throughout. There was a meal held beforehand which was attended by the chairman and also the sponsor of the £4,000 prize. Ongar Music Club was, in fact, the only music club to benefit from such an arrangement with this competition. Of the six string quartet finalists, only the first three prizewinners were required to give a concert before returning home – one played at the Middle Temple, another at the Goring Hotel, and the third, for Ongar Music Club. This was solely due to the club's long association with Lord Yehudi Menuhin.

It had been mentioned that long-standing club member Dr Sylvia Hatfield and her husband Ted (also a doctor) were celebrating their diamond wedding anniversary in 2000, and it was felt that some sort of combined social occasion might be devised in celebration of that, as well as the club's own silver anniversary. Everyone was invited to give this suggestion their urgent consideration – Ongar Music Club has never been known to pass up the opportunity of a party.

It was discovered that the Ballroom of the Budworth Hall was available on 22nd July, and it was agreed to publicise this as a free coffee morning between times to be decided. It was also decided that there should be a substantial raffle. This proved to be a highly enjoyable event, and the Hatfields were presented with a garden table and chairs to which the club contributed.

There had been a good entry for the 2000 Essex Young Musician of the Year competition, but it had been one of those years where it had been extremely difficult to determine a winner due to the high standard of performance. The chairman remarked that it had been heartening to hear some competitors comment on the very friendly atmosphere during the competition, which was not something that they always experienced elsewhere.

2000–2001

The millennium AGM was held on 22nd September. The chairman, Jean Hall, opened the meeting by reporting that the club's president John Lill had been recovering from a mugging attack in Hampstead in which his hands were injured. His first performance since the incident was to be a performance of Beethoven's 'Emperor Concerto' with the Hallé a few day's later. Also, committee member and outings organiser Stan Cornhill was recovering from a serious illness and had made a special effort to attend the committee meeting earlier that month. She also mentioned Janet Pope's temporary removal from the committee due to work commitments in Southampton, and her hope to take early retirement in a couple of year's time which would allow her to rejoin. Jean also explained that the Century Club membership had fallen to ninety-eight, and therefore, the prize money would have to be slightly less than previously advised. Howard Nicholson, chairman of Ongar Jazz Club, mentioned that there had been a membership level in his section of a hundred and fifty with an average concert attendance of a hundred and twenty.

The millennium year ended with the usual Christmas concert at St Martin's Church which that year featured Harlow Brass and treble Oliver Lincoln, who came courtesy of David Rooke, the director of music at St Thomas' Church, Brentwood. All the usual accoutrements were in place, as well as an advertising banner displayed outside the office of Raggett, Tiffen and Harries in the High Street.

The appraisal of the Christmas concert noted that audience levels had dropped, rather as for the concert two years previously. There were proposals for trying to bolster attendance for next Christmas, including the engaging of an actor or a good speaker – some names were suggested. There was also the suggestion of having a compère throughout. A well-known local vocal soloist was also mentioned. It was also agreed that rather than accede to a suggestion for reducing the entrance charge from £8 to £5; concessions would be offered.

A coffee morning was planned in February, and flasks were requested – three coffee and one tea. Committee members were once again encouraged to bake cakes. By now, the club's library had been discontinued, and Howard Nicholson was to be asked whether he would kindly attend and act as auctioneer for the remaining books. In February, it was noted that Catherine Jennings was starting to put together the 2001–2002 season – a task she was undertaking for the first time. She pointed out that the level of fees was becoming a concern. These had to stay in the region of £400 per event, and even then, there would frequently be a loss – the losses being mitigated so far as possible by sponsorship, donations and fund-raising events. It should be recorded that in former years, some of the routine operating expenses were covered personally by members of the committee. As pointed out by the treasurer, these included newsletter costs, printing posters and programmes, interval tea, coffee, milk and biscuits, bouquets for artists, raffle prizes, small meals for performers, photocopies and the sending out of press releases. This generosity amounted to around £50 per concert, without which, many concerts would have shown a loss.

The 17th March saw the next in the series of London recitals for winners of the Essex Young Musician of the Year competition. Due to the charges of the Wigmore Hall, difficulties in getting a date at the Purcell Room, and no great incentive to return to St James' Church, Piccadilly, it had been decided to make a booking at St Giles' Church, Cripplegate in the Barbican. Despite the difficulty that some people had in finding the venue, it was agreed that this was a lovely setting, and both performers gave fine performances – cellist Anthony Woollard and violinist Tammy Se. It was felt that maybe the club could consider giving half-price entrance for students in future years to encourage their presence at the event. The chairman noted that St Giles had been a nice venue, but maybe without the cachet of a concert hall – she would investigate the Purcell Room for 2003. There was further discussion regarding the Christmas concert, and there should be a plea for a team of helpers for the occasion. Encouragingly, additional sponsorship had been received for the competition, with £100 coming from HSBC and £250 from Ford.

Over the many years since 1975, there has been no serious history of problems with fees or payments to artistes. However, in May, treasurer John Harrop reported that a recent performance group had, by their own admission, lost their cheque. This was subsequently stopped, and a new one raised, less the £8 bank charge for the cancellation – John took no prisoners when it came to the club's money. The treasurer was also able to report his financial statement to the June meeting, which included Stage 1 of the Gift Aid scheme. This should enable £0.28 in the pound to be refundable to the club from the Inland Revenue. There was also a likely shortage of 'backstage' support for the forthcoming EYMY competition on 1st July. Staffing this event has always been crucial, as the administrator needs to be able to concentrate on maintaining an overview of the day with knowledge and trust that the large number of necessary tasks are being carried out, as expected, and without distraction. The club has been lucky to have been so well supported in this regard over the years.

In September, great pleasure was expressed at the progress of the competition. Also, the treasurer noted an increase in surplus of some £1,400 over the previous year. The forthcoming season's brochures had been distributed, and special mention was made of committee member Brian Lawrence, who had made a great effort to distribute the brochures around the areas of Chelmsford, Springfield, Great Baddow and beyond.

2001–2002

The chairman explained to the 2001 AGM that Stan Cornhill had been forced to retire from the committee for health reasons. She also announced that Rosalie Ritson was willing to serve on the committee. Marie Korf MBE, a faithful member and generous supporter of Ongar Music Club, said that "she spoke on behalf of an audience well served in the provision of concerts", and she thanked the committee on their behalf for all their hard work in achieving success. The chairman noted in her report that the club was in a fortunate position, having had a highly successful season with a record number of members. The finances were strong, thanks to generous sponsorship from members and outside organisations. She noted that this was especially pleasing at a time when other music clubs, both nationally and locally, such as those in Woodford and Chelmsford, were being forced to close. None of our club's success would happen without the support of a very strong committee bringing their diverse skills to bear in their specific roles.

Feedback was positive for the recent Christmas concert – it was felt that the Salvation Army was "the best yet". There had been a good level of help in setting up the church, both before and afterwards. Unfortunately, the choir did not come supplied with a running order or words for the audience carols – the result of not having these was that too many programmes had to be given away. Although the church was noted as having been very cold, the audience warmed to the compère and the musical offerings. The meeting also heard that well-needed renovations were being made to the windows in the Budworth Hall's Ballroom and money raised by the two-piano marathon was being put towards this. The Community Association had also appointed a barman and was currently interviewing for the crucial position of caretaker. A particularly welcome announcement was that Ongar Parish Council had voted to give £200 towards the competition.

Always mindful of ways to support the club's finances, treasurer John Harrop explained a few aspects of his accounting to the March 2002 committee meeting. The auditor had recommended that the club's accounts have 'Independent Examination', as laid down by the Charity Commission – this also being less expensive than a full audit. John also suggested investigating a saving scheme for charity funds that offers higher rates of interest than building societies. This was agreed but "exercising great care". John also mentioned that now the club's books were back from the auditor, he could proceed with the Gift Aid scheme.

Finally, in his report, he cautioned that the Performing Rights Society (PRS) had changed their method of assessment, and in future, would require accurate audience numbers – PRS administers the rights in all music publicly performed in this country in order to ensure proper financial acknowledgement to its composers and publishers. The treasurer later reported that the Charity Commission also required a report from the club's trustees, which was to be signed by all of them.

Final preparations for that year's competition came with the knowledge that sponsorship had been obtained, which more than covered the prizes, leaving a small surplus towards the competition's running costs. The administrator had even received a post-dated cheque for the first prize in the following year. An appraisal of the competition was conducted in September, with considerable discussion about the time it had taken for the judges to reach their decision and the fact that the audience had become quite restless. It's a reality that sometimes, levels of performance are such that the judges can be drawn in equally strong but diverse directions for reasons that are not always easy to identify. Frequently it just comes down to a basic human response to the performance and musicianship displayed.

The administrator Jean Hall subsequently indicated her personal wish to institute a system of 'marking' whereby the judges would simply rank the performers out of ten, with the scores being added and a winner declared. That sounds so simple, but in practice, it can be somewhat soulless – a little discussion can frequently help you to gain another perspective on a performance. I'm not sure that this idea was ever really implemented. There was to be a rather half-hearted attempt in 2003, but in the event, we returned to discussion and instinct. The administrator had also indicated her wish to fill the adjudicating panel with past winners. This idea never came to fruition because, as was pointed out, the makeup of the panel has always been quite specifically arranged to have highly experienced representatives of the various instrumental and singing specialities. In addition, they should also be senior and respected members of the profession – frequently holding positions at a conservatoire where they would be known and respected by many of the applicants. This idea would be almost impractical to progress, and it was decided to find maybe one past winner to join the panel but not to make up a complete panel.

2002–2003

The 2002 AGM heard that the previous year had achieved a surplus of £2,000, but only because of sponsorship of £4,000 from members and friends. Picking up on a suggestion from a couple of years previously and relating to the use of the internet, it was suggested at the meeting that investigation be given to the possibility of emailing news to members – this would be investigated. Following discussion, the chairman then presented the usual summary of the previous year's activities, making special mention of the evening given by the famous Southend Girls Choir under the direction of Rosemary Pennington.

In January, it was noticed by chance in the local press, and somewhat surprisingly, that Ongar Council was to increase its donation to the EYMY competition to £250 – clearly a welcome discovery. The Christmas concert had been a great success with a much better level of practical help, including the choirboys moving the pews. By then, it had also been discovered that sixteen club members had email facilities and would now be sent news updates using that method.

There had been ongoing concerns about a new government bill that would change the licensing laws, having a financially crippling effect on concert promotion. The March committee meeting noted that the House of Lords rejected the bill, and the original proposals were ultimately waived in respect of churches and community associations. On a lighter note, and relating to a concert that featured a viola, the ever sharp tongue of Barrie Hall commented, "A viola always sounds like a viola". The poor viola players have a tradition of receiving 'fun' comments in the music profession. A lovely letter was then read by Jean Hall – this had been sent by Elspeth Taylor, who had won fourth prize in the competition two years previously. Such was the then chairman's opinion of her playing that she had offered the opening recital of the following season to Elspeth, who said:

'... that the prize, and the confidence shown in giving her the recital, 'kick-started' her into making the effort to achieve a 'First' at the Guildhall School of Music and Drama, after which she applied for, and was offered, the position of Principal Horn of the City of Birmingham Symphony Orchestra, where she now is [a position she still holds].

Brian Lawrence pointed out the generally drab and untidy state of the Concert Room, and it was agreed that the club should make an approach to the Community Association with a view to sprucing it up. Brian had already offered to get out his paint-pot! It was also hoped to make the balcony safe, and tenders were being sought for that work.

A further London recital was held on 14th May 2003, again at St Giles' Church, Cripplegate. This was given by oboist Janey Miller and guitarist Clive Carroll. On this occasion, there was not such a great audience although, as expected, the musical performances had been outstanding. A very similar discussion ensued, as had followed the event at St James' Church, Piccadilly – both soloists had already given London recitals, so was there any advantage for them? The club couldn't afford a hall with its own audience, such as the Wigmore Hall. Perhaps better use could be made of the expenditure, such as increasing the winner's prize, or the fee for the winner's recital for the club. It was agreed that Jean Hall should contact the most recent winner to explain that the London recital might now be abandoned. Barrie Hall did come up with the suggestion that maybe the club could promote a winner's recital at a respected venue in Essex and suggested Felsted or the Chelmsford festival. To my knowledge, this idea was never pursued.

Jean Hall also mentioned a conductor, Brian Priestman, who was apparently known worldwide. She had asked him to join the judging panel and to act as chairman. Jean was committed to employing her idea of marking, which Brian later assured the members of the panel that he had encountered everywhere. We were told that we would produce scorecards together with comments, but our comments would only be taken into account in the event of a tie. I still have a strong feeling that I would prefer any such arrangement to be the other way around. We did not employ that system again.

Since the club's inception, a regular programme of events had been planned, usually for the third Friday evening of each month during the usual school term time. The planning role was invariably undertaken by the current chairman of the club who would receive a great many brochures and requests for recital opportunities by post – these would be sifted through with care. I think it would be fair to say that of those submitted 'blind', very few actually went on to give a recital at Ongar – either due to it being style of concert that would probably not attract an audience or, most usually, due to the scale of fee being requested.

Many artistes were engaged through personal contact with a member of the committee. Sometimes, an artiste who had previously appeared would be invited to return or know someone appropriate to perform. There came a point in 2003 when there was difficulty in finding anyone willing to take over the role of chairman for the next season. I had never accepted the invitation to be chairman due to my own lack of availability in those years due to Friday concert work. However, it was suggested to me that if I would take on the role of concert planning, someone else might just be willing to take on the chairmanship. This idea was suggested to me over a very generous lunch in August 2003 at the home Jean and Barrie Hall – not the first time such tactics had been used. How could I refuse? I took over the planning the club's concerts from the 2004–2005 season and carried out this duty until the club ceased presenting regular concerts in 2016.

2003–2004

Much of the September AGM was taken up with a discussion about the June EYMY competition earlier that year. The title had been won by the impressive talent of the ten-year-old pianist Benjamin Grosvenor. This had been an extraordinary competition, and it should also be acknowledged that there was some quite remarkable playing from the other finalists. Benjamin Grosvenor has gone on to enjoy a glittering career, and he is now a hugely respected solo pianist on today's concert platform.

In October, Jean Hall announced that she had received a letter from the Tom Acton Memorial Trust, which had funds to offer an additional recital for the EYMY winner. This was to be held on 11th September (2005) in the chapel of Felsted School, being planned as an annual event.

The trust was formed in 1997 to raise money in support of young musicians in need. It commemorates Tom Acton, a brilliant young man who died in 1997, two months after his 21st birthday. He was educated in the cathedral school in Chelmsford, then Felsted School and subsequently at Exeter University. Tom Acton was passionate about music of all genres and was a keen amateur bassoonist.

In preparation for the Christmas concert, Peter Jackson was developing skills in preparing punch and mince pies, with help from Adèle Birch. Nicola Harries was buying the pies, and meanwhile, Barrie Hall was ordering the wine and glasses. There had been considerable difficulties in establishing a programme from the choir. However, it was eventually settled, and with considerable domestic help with door-manning, church-decorating and pew-moving, the evening went ahead as planned. Despite the careful planning, the audience was disappointing, and a change of venue was discussed for that year's concert.

With the treasurer's approval, an increase to £600 was made for the first prize of the EYMY competition, and the fee for the subsequent recital for the club was increased to £250. Nicola Harries then offered to sponsor the second prize of £300 and John Harrop, the third prize of £200. It was also confirmed that the London concert would be discontinued.

In February 2004, Jean Hall reported the successes of two past finalists of the EYMY competition – Benjamin Grosvenor had won the piano section of the BBC Young Musician Competition, and Suzanne Thorn was a finalist in the same competition. Benjamin Grosvenor currently had a Bösendorfer grand piano on loan to him until after the BBC competition, but he was not in a position to change his existing upright piano at the time. The meeting agreed that if needs be, the club would help by contributing £500 towards any costs in replacing his instrument.

John Lill was approached to see whether he might be willing to give a recital for the club in celebration of his 60th birthday. John responded with a typically warm and generous response, offering Friday 25th

February 2005 and declining a fee. John said, "your kindness and support I've always greatly treasured, and this will be a small token of my profound gratitude". Nicola Harries kindly offered to cover the piano hire and Barrie Hall, the cost of the hall.

September noted a smaller than usual number of entrants for the EYMY competition but with a good result. The winner, a thirteen-year-old violinist Victoria Goldsmith, was whisked off immediately following the competition final to stay the night in Mohammed al Fayed's private apartment in order to play for the opening of the Harrod's summer sale early the next morning. In the same meeting, the competition administrator, Jean Hall, read out a congratulatory letter from one of the panel of judges, Dame Thea King, in which she mentioned finding the club's competition "lighter and more informal than others, and therefore more enjoyable". Dame Thea was a remarkable lady who joined our adjudicating panel on a number of occasions. One year when the evening had run very late, meaning that she would not reach Epping station at a sensible time for a train back to London, I offered to drive her to Ilford mainline station, close to where I was living at the time. There were further difficulties when we reached the station (this was a Sunday), and I said that I would drive her back to central London. Thea wouldn't hear of it, and with a dogged determination not to put us out, she boarded a number 25 bus!

2004–2005

At the AGM, mention was made of Marie Korf MBE – a staunch supporter and benefactor of Ongar Music Club who had sadly passed away within sight of her hundredth birthday. Miss Korf bequeathed over £7,000 to the Music Club, which was used to fund the competition's first prize for many years. The club presented a memorial concert for her in November. The chairman also spoke of the recital by Patrick McCarthy, who had famously leapt from the audience during a live television Promenade Concert some years earlier in order to cover the solo role in Carmina Burana when Thomas Allen had fainted.

A situation arose in October whereby all three senior officers of the Community Association intended to resign. Roger Roles of the Rotary Club had spoken to club chairman John Harrop about the club's competition and other activities and indicated that he would provide administrative cover for the next twelve months. In fact, at the time of writing, Roger is still chairman of the CA and greatly supportive of the Music Club – attending the 'Soundbites!' events with his wife Mary.

On 19th November, the club was delighted to welcome Benjamin Grosvenor back to the Budworth Hall for his winner's recital in a full Ballroom – a terrific evening. In early December, the chairman met with a representative of Great Stony to discuss arrangements for the forthcoming piano recital to be given by John Lill on 25th February as part of his 60th birthday celebrations. It was agreed that committee members and their partners would be allowed to sit in the balcony, thereby allowing all one hundred and forty-one seats in the body of the hall to be available to the general public. It was suggested that a glass of wine be given to each audience member, and the cost of the wine and glass hire would be borne by the committee. Another note said that the requirement for a St John's Ambulance representative to be present does not apply if the club has a doctor in the audience – there usually was.

There was rejoicing at the January 2005 meeting with news that the club's president John Lill OBE had been made a CBE, and this seemed to add yet another dimension to his forthcoming recital and 60th birthday celebration in February – his own birthday honour perhaps. Final preparations were made during the next month, and John Harrop kindly offered to pay for the wine. A case of claret was provided by Janet Pope and Peter Jackson as a 'thank you' to our president. It was noted that with no washing-up facilities, that warmly-anticipated job would have to wait until after the recital. Adèle Birch had the rather good idea of selling programmes by circulating through the audience. It was felt that this would likely increase sales by personal contact and also give a chance to talk the audience members about the club, if appropriate. As anticipated, this was another wonderful evening by the club's president and warmly appreciated by a capacity audience.

With his finger ever on the pulse of music in the local area and beyond, Brian Lawrence regularly showed us leaflets and programmes from concerts he had attended. He would pass these around at committee meetings, and they could be very helpful to those preparing the club's recitals, keeping them in touch with other local artistes, or artistes who would consider playing for a club of limited means.

In April, a pianist had highlighted justified technical issues about the piano that were ultimately to lead to its complete restoration. Barrie Hall had also completed a questionnaire to 'Heritage, Arts and Sport' at Essex County Council, which offered monetary prizes in a draw. However, "he did not expect to hear much more, nor win a prize". Meanwhile, Jean Hall had been asked to broadcast on BBC Essex regarding the forthcoming Essex Young Musician of the Year competition on the 29th June. Ongar Music Club's thirtieth year concluded with a healthy membership of one hundred and six.

5. 2005 – 2020 Seasons

The 2005 AGM was held on 23rd September, and it was noted that Janet Pope was now able to make a very welcome return to the committee. It also recorded another new committee member, Joanna Smith – someone very well known to the club for her piano-playing and who, two years later, would become my wife. The post-AGM recital that year was given by Sophie Bieybuyck *soprano* (who would become Essex Young Musician of the Year in 2006) together with Joanna Smith *piano,* herself runner-up in the 1997 competition. By good fortune, this recital had been attended by a representative of the Brentwood Gazette, resulting in a glowing review.

In October, we heard that Benjamin Grosvenor had decided to buy the Bösendorfer grand piano that had been on loan to him. The club, therefore, made the previously agreed donation of £500 towards the cost. It was heartening to note Benjamin's progress which was regularly charted by newspapers and music journals alike, one of these being an article in the Guardian shortly before the November meeting.

It had also been decided to continue the long-standing tradition of a Christmas concert. For some years, audience levels had varied quite dramatically, and it had been felt that maybe, with other carol-based events taking place around the same time, the event had run its course. In 2005, the December event was a presentation by Hatstand Opera. Initially, there had been an agreement for four performers, although, in the end, there were just three. This plan was something of a gamble, the club having abandoned the Christmas concert, but frequently in the arts, you have to take a chance.

Forthcoming Events

25th October - Outing to Glyndebourne

Sold out, I'm afraid. Waiting list only – See Jean Hall

Friday 28 October at 8.0
Patricia Spero and Kate Cuzner (Harps & Flutes)

They will talk about and demonstrate harps and flutes through the ages, from medieval times, composers including Griot de Dijon and Alfonso el Sabio, to modern day composers Dussek, Debussy, William Alwyn. Expect an array of instruments and a lot of lovely music. **£10**

Friday 25 November at 8.0
Victoria and Inga Goldsmith (violin & piano)

Victoria was only 13 when she became the Essex Young Musician of 2004. Born in St. Petersburg, she studied there at 6 ½ years old, and later at the Yehudi Menuhin School. She has since played at many festivals here and abroad, and has recently returned from a recital in New York. With her mother she will play Corelli's La Folia. Paganini's La Campanella. Beethoven's first Romance, Prokofiev's second sonata, and a Rhapsody 'after Gershwin's Porgy & Bess'. **£10**

January 2006 opened with a two-piano recital by myself and Joanna Smith. This was to be the first of several such events, which were billed as 'Keyboard Konnections'. We were lucky that while concerts were being presented in the Concert Room, we were able to take advantage of both the club's Bechstein grand and the Ibach grand belonging to the Community Association. We were, therefore, able to play a variety of repertoire for two pianos and piano duet. Barrie Hall had specifically requested that we play Darius Milhaud's 'Scaramouche Suite' for two pianos, which we were delighted to include. We were touched to note the following comment in the minutes:

> Uninhibited by the presence of the duettists Joanna Smith and Roderick Elms, the committee congratulated them both on giving a superb evening's music.
>
> ... wonderful rapport and charisma between the players, a real 'entente cordiale'! They should be a feature of future seasons.

The committee was delighted to hear that we had recently become engaged.

Committee member, Catherine Jennings, made a fund-raising suggestion that if anyone had any surplus CDs, they might donate them to the club, and she would organise to sell them on club evenings – maybe £1 each or "bring one and take one". This venture was noted to have raised the sum of £15 on at least one occasion.

In May, Joanna and I were involved in another performance, but this time with our good friends (also engaged), horn players Stephen Bell and Charlotte Lines. This was billed as 'Mixed Doubles', and much fun was had by all, including a new piece that I wrote for the occasion 'Burlesca – Trio for Four', which featured two horns and piano duet.

The competition that year progressed as usual, although the preliminary round was held on the previous Sunday to avoid scheduling a Saturday – see Chapter 7. Final preparations were made at the June meeting held in the home of Brian Lawrence, who, as on many previous occasions, had produced a feast for our post-meeting delight, including scones, strawberries and fresh cream!

2006–2007

The chairman's report to the 2006 AGM noted a membership of one hundred and eight, and John Harrop paid tribute to the committed and painstaking work of Jean Hall as competition administrator. He also offered thanks to Catherine Jennings, who "tirelessly chivvies the music teachers to encourage their pupils to participate" in the Young Music Makers concerts.

It has always been a pleasure to hear news of former Essex Young Musicians of the Year. In October, the committee was delighted to hear that the 1986 winner Jane Webster was covering the role of Mother Superior in Andrew Lloyd Webber's production of the Sound of Music – this, in addition to many other more classically-orientated performances which included solo roles for the Royal Opera.

Past competition winners have frequently returned to Ongar for recitals. So it was in November when the club presented a further piano-duo recital but this time from Essex Young Musician of the Year 1996 Joseph Tong, together with his pianist wife, Waka Hasegawa. This fine recital followed another competition winner, oboist Suzanne Thorn, who had won the title in 2005. Another competition success came in December when we heard that EMI had awarded Benjamin Grosvenor a four-year contract for 'development' rather than just recording. Benjamin subsequently signed a contract with Decca in 2011.

The opening recital of 2007 was given by one of my 'oldest' friends, Helen Crayford. We first met as junior exhibitioners at the Guildhall School of Music and Drama, way back in the early sixties, and rekindled our friendship when our paths started to cross while working with the London orchestras. When we first met, Helen and I shared the same piano teacher, Cimbro Martin, but Helen also studied the trumpet, her party-piece being to play the trumpet whilst accompanying herself on the piano – as she did on this occasion, which "brought the house down".

A modestly declining trend in audience numbers was noted in 2007 with a slightly concerning deficit for the 2006–2007 season. At the June meeting, various options were considered for financial enhancement, including raising ticket prices, a big drive on sponsorship, and the setting up of a fund-raising committee. This was also the final planning meeting ahead of the 2007 EYMY competition, and it might be interesting to note some of the detail relating to the domestic planning, as recorded:

> There are 17 entrants. Judges are Stephen Bell, Colin Bradbury (replacing Thea King at short notice) and Roderick Elms for both days, plus on 1 July Jane Webster and Marianne Olyver.
>
> Catherine to find student as page-turner for both days (unpaid). Programmes, covering all stages, by Roderick and Joanna. Initial announcements to include location of exits, fire assembly point and reminder to turn off mobile phones, by Brian.
>
> 24th June
> No practice facilities will be available for the preliminaries
> Introductions – Brian
> Selling programmes- Rosalie
> Judges refreshments – Jean
> Competitors liaison – Janet/Peter
> Stewarding - John
>
> 1th July
> Ticket and programme sales – Adele (tbc), backup Janet
> Introductions – Brian for semis, Jean for final
> Judges refreshments in hall – Jean and Nicola
> Flowers – Catherine
> Judges meal – Anne Harries
> Evening audience refreshments (cold) – Nicola
> Stewards and competitor liaison – John and Peter
> Piano lid, stage re-arrangements – Janet (unless selling tickets)

2007–2008

The 2007 AGM marked the retirement of Adèle Birch from the committee after fifteen years of dedicated service. As usual, a Life Membership Gold Card was presented to her as well as to John Harrop, who was ending his term as chairman. As always at the AGM, committee responsibilities were agreed upon, these being as follows for that season:

Chairman   Nicola Harries
Vice-Chairman and Secretary   Janet Pope
Treasurer and Century Club   Peter Jackson
Music advisors and Events planners Roderick and Joanna Elms
EYMY and Outings   Jean Hall
Young Music Makers   Catherine Jennings
Membership secretary   John Harrop
Publicity   Barrie Hall
Sponsorship   Barbara Szymanek
Committee members Brian Lawrence and Rosalie Ritson

The meeting also recorded that the winner of the EYMY competition that year had been counter-tenor Timothy Wayne-Wright, who was, at the time, a lay clerk in the choir of St George's Chapel, Windsor. Shortly after winning the competition we were delighted to hear that he had become a member of the internationally renowned vocal group, The Kings Singers.

In September, I received an email from John Lill offering a recital for the club, maybe in 2009. This was obviously a very welcome suggestion, and it was agreed that the new chairman Nicola Harries would follow this up with John to establish a date.

The issue of the club's financial position was again discussed in December, with the treasurer noting a drop in membership in recent years. The income from the Century Club was also gradually declining, meaning that the prizes were at quite a low level, and they couldn't reasonably be reduced further. It was agreed that the Century Club would be wound up at the end of the season.

Towards the end of 2007, Barrie Hall had been undergoing a period of bad health, which meant that both he and Jean were unable to attend meetings – they were sorely missed. Janet Pope agreed to take the lead on the competition administration while Jean was otherwise occupied. As a precaution, it was agreed that Janet and Jean would talk through the essential details of the administration. I was asked to take over the appointment of the adjudication panel so that there was one less job for them to do.

During the competition final, there had been an occasional but ongoing concern about the delay in proceedings whilst the judges were making the necessary decisions, and this had sometimes been a source of some embarrassment. One idea to help with this problem arose during the March 2008 meeting, being that the previous year's winner, who ordinarily would be returning the winners cup, might give a 'mini recital' to cover this time. The idea would be explored further.

Although by April, Barrie Hall was enjoying much better health, he was suffering from increasing deafness. Therefore, he felt it impractical to attend committee meetings, although Jean would continue to do so. However, Barrie would be delighted to continue as publicity officer, although he felt he should resign from the committee. The committee's viewed this somewhat differently, and Barrie remained in his rightful place on the agenda alongside the names of the other committee members.

Also, in April, came further discussion about the finances. To break even, the club needed more members and larger audiences. For some time, we had been aware of similar issues with music clubs across the country, many of which had been forced to close. In many ways, Ongar Music Club had been fortunate in being able to find ways to maintain its programme of events. A big part of the problem was an increasing unwillingness of audience members to go out at night time, especially in the dark. Various possibilities were discussed, including introducing concerts earlier in the day or at weekends, but research at the time showed that for a variety of reasons, not least people at work or with family commitments, these ideas would not help the situation. It was therefore agreed that in order to go some way towards mitigating the immediate problem, the club would reduce the number of concerts, starting from the following season.

The committee's spirits were raised in June with an email from John Lill saying that he would be able to give the club a recital on 15th May 2009. This would take place at Great Stony, and John had suggested to me that we hire a piano which he had previously used for a recital in Southend – his idea being to save the considerable expense of hiring a Steinway. This gesture was greatly appreciated, and Nicola Harries indicated that her firm would cover the hire cost. John had already generously indicated that he would not be expecting a fee for the performance, which meant that all the recital's proceeds would benefit the club. Nicola further said that she would be delighted to host a reception in her home following the concert. The ticket prices were set at £20 including the party – £17 without.

In June, there was further discussion as to how we could prune the club's expenditure, and one way forward was to produce our own brochures rather than to engage a commercial printer. From the next season, I prepared the club's brochures with a six-page, bi-folded design – a few being printed in colour for the club's members and committee, and the rest being duplicated by Nicola Harries in black and white, for more general circulation to libraries and other appropriate outlets. Further suggestions were made for distribution, and as a result, some committee members travelled considerable distances to place them in appropriate outlets. It was also decided that we would try to obtain some recompense for the interval refreshments, which hitherto had been free. Rather than making a charge, it was decided to ask for donations – in part, to avoid holding up the queue. The season closed with a mixture of excitement and great determination for the future well-being of the club.

2008–2009

A pertinent comment was raised in the September AGM – concerts might well be better attended if the location was easier to access. Concerts were still being presented in the Concert Room, which is reached by a fairly narrow and twisty set of stairs that many people found challenging. This room had been the club's base since returning from the Adult Education Campus in 1997, in part because that is where the piano was located, but more fundamentally, due to the downstairs Ballroom being adjacent to the bar, which could be noisy – the Concert Room was also cheaper to hire. It was agreed that the committee would investigate alternative venues. A subsequent report indicated that High Ongar Village Hall had been contacted, and the charge was £12 per hour. However, the contact at the hall was noted as "not being very helpful, so the issue of piano storage was not raised".

The chairman's report that year concluded with the comment that the club had a "hard-working committee who are determined to continue to provide high-quality classical music for the people of Ongar to enjoy". It was announced that after many years of dedicated service, Jean Hall was standing down from the committee. We decided that Jean should choose a gift to mark the occasion – most likely earrings – and that these would be presented at John Lill's recital in the following June. It had also been mutually agreed that John Harrop would remain on the committee but would not be asked to exercise any special duties. Barbara Szymanek would be dealing with the mailing list and sponsorship matters.

Publicity, by way of reviews, has always been crucial to music clubs, both before concerts and afterwards. Therefore, it was a great sadness to learn that the Brentwood Gazette was closing its office with the consequence that its loyal arts reporter Mary Redman had lost her job. Mary had been very supportive of the club and always engaged herself and her readers with the annual competition in a very supportive way.

In March, we received a letter from Barrie Hall to say that he was no longer able to deal with the press publicity. Barrie had excelled in this role over so many years, this being one of his many areas of expertise. His support would be sorely missed, but the committee fully understood the reasons and was delighted to know that he would continue to maintain the press-cuttings book.

Some discussion took place regarding John Lill's forthcoming recital. The hire of Great Stony would be £175, towards which Jean and Barrie generously offered to contribute. A suitable gift for John Lill was agreed. Nicola was covering the piano hire, which was to be a Kawai – the instrument that John had previously played. A representative of Kawai had requested that the firm could mount a display during the concert and also have a free ticket. As the minutes record: "The first reasonable, the second definitely not"!

It was noted at the same meeting that I had been to North Wales to visit Geoffrey Timms whose wife Rosemary was suffering from Parkinson's Disease. Rosemary had been a great supporter of the club and especially Geoffrey, who by then was making three visits a day to the local hospital to tend to her needs. It was good to see him again and also his lovely home, high on a hillside outside the small village of Clocaenog, near Ruthin.

By early April, John Lill's recital was sold out except for two tickets held in case John needed any 'comps'. It was agreed to ask whether the balcony could be used as on the previous occasion. There were fifty-seven attending the reception for which a sensible cap of sixty had been placed.

Barbara Szymanek was also busy trying to establish sponsorship for the competition in June, contacting many local businesses and individuals. As usual, club members received a letter requesting support. Many members liked to help, if only in a small way. By May, she had obtained a grant of £300 from Ongar Town Council and was remaining optimistic about the other avenues contacted. Also, at the May meeting, I suggested that we consider a 'Conservatoire Series' as a theme for the next few years, inviting students from each of the London music colleges in turn, to give a recital. This worked very well with some fine performances, as might be expected. However, the underlying thought that this might help a little with the club's expenditure did not come to fruition. Most of the conservatoires seemed to run this sort of activity as something of a business – charging relatively high fees on behalf of the students, and putting a substantial facility fee on top for their administration. It would appear that the days when students would be eager and allowed to take on a Music Club engagement for a modest fee to gain performing experience were either gone or had had them taken away from them.

John Lill's recital on 15th June was a wonderful occasion which was enjoyed by a near-capacity audience. The staff at Great Stony had actually found us another twelve seats, although a few people didn't turn up due to the inclement weather. As planned, Jean Hall was presented with

Nicola Harries and John Lill at the post-recital reception • 15th June 2009 • Ongar

her earrings at the close of the interval. The post-recital reception was hugely enjoyed, and thanks were offered to Anne and Nicola Harries for their boundless hospitality.

There's one lovely anecdote recounted by Nicola Harries – in the excitement of the occasion, one thing which was overlooked was the provision of lighting for later in the evening when it would get dark. To quote Nicola:

> John, at his most gracious, said:
> "Not to worry, my dear, I played during the miners' strike and didn't need to see the keys".
> As the light gradually went, he played without any hesitation whatsoever.

In the June meeting, the treasurer noted that the £1,600 proceeds of John's recital would more than cover the losses of the season's concerts though maybe not the competition. Thanks were again expressed for the considerable generosity of committee members – Jean, Barrie, Nicola and also Janet and Peter, who provided a case of wine for John. The next event was the competition, for which sponsorship stood at £1,300.

In June, it was also agreed that for storage and other practical reasons, the bulk of the club's documents would be passed to the Essex County Record office in Chelmsford. There had been a good deal of paper collected since 1975. The meeting concluded with congratulations to my wife and me on the birth of our son Matthew earlier that month.

2009–2010

In September, the issue of the Concert Room accessibility was raised again, and the suggestion was made that a stairlift might be installed. This was thought unlikely as, at the time, the Budworth Hall was struggling financially. In October, the club heard that Hilda Barker, who had provided floral displays at the club's concerts for twenty-five years, had decided to step down from that responsibility. It was agreed to make an appropriate presentation to her at the forthcoming concert.

The 2009 Christmas concert was a "tight squeeze" in the Concert Room, with twenty in the Stondon Singers and the further twenty-one brass players of Brentwood Brass. It was mounted somewhat like a military operation with a one-way system for the audience's interval refreshments – in one door of the adjacent Green Room and out of the other. Meanwhile, the performers were being catered for in the Ballroom, which could not be used for this concert due to a prearranged party in the bar next door. It was felt that this might not have ended well.

The treasurer reported in early 2010 that we had received a refund of Gift Aid from HMRC amounting to more than £400. He also mentioned that all recitals that season (with the exception of the AGM) had so far shown a profit due to the lower artiste fees, which I had managed to negotiate. For some performers, it was simply not economical to come for a lower than usual fee. For most, if circumstances allowed it, they were happy to support the club. This news from the treasurer was clearly very welcome, and we were delighted that the new strategy was paying off. The season ended up showing a modest surplus. Unfortunately, the May two-piano recital by my wife and myself had made a small loss due to the need for tuning both pianos. I fear that this was self-inflicted – mea culpa!

2010–2011

Due to the ease of email communication and fewer concerts, it was decided that we would hold more occasional committee meetings – any urgent matters being discussed when necessary. In September, the idea of engaging Cantate Alumni for the Christmas concert was floated by Nicola Harries, whose daughter Amy sang with the group. Cantate Alumni is a group of singers who used to sing with the excellent vocal group Cantate, under their esteemed music director, Michael Kibblewhite. I used to work a great deal with Michael when he directed other vocal groups in London and the home counties, and it was a pleasure to meet up with him again when they visited Ongar. For a long time, he lived in the Essex village of Stebbing, not so far away. The first of the Christmas concerts by Cantata Alumni took place the following year and ran for four years, during which time they always performed to a packed Ballroom.

By October 2010, the committee had expanded to include long term club supporters Jean and Eric Crook, whose daughter Philippa is a violinist colleague. The committee had also recently discovered a number of local magazines and news sheets which were either new or about which it was unaware – this situation was immediately addressed, and they were contacted without delay.

The concern about the club's venue was ongoing and discussed further in the December meeting – research for an alternative continued. From audience feedback, it was clear that the steep stairs to the Concert Room were an ongoing issue that wouldn't get any better. Roger Roles, chairman of the Community Association, had suggested that we use the Ballroom, but the big problem was pointed out to him – that of the adjacent bar. It was suggested that maybe the bar night could be moved from Friday to Saturday, or maybe it could be closed altogether on a Friday evening. Roger was not keen on that idea, as I imagine the bar provided a welcome source of income. It had previously been established from the club's audience that moving our concerts to Saturday was not a viable option. It was agreed to conduct an experiment by holding the

Cantate Alumni with their music director, Michael Kibblewhite • Ballroom, Budworth Hall, Ongar

April concert (a guitar recital) in the Ballroom – a concert which didn't need a piano – that still being upstairs. The seating was to be arranged in a semicircle with the performer on the far side of the room.

Considering alternative venues, we were aware of the new 'Theatre Resource' facility scheduled to be opened on the Great Stony site in the Spring of 2011. It was thought that we should explore this, although there would undoubtedly still be a problem with piano storage. It was also felt that the venue would almost certainly be more expensive than the Budworth Hall. However, before we could arrange to view the new facility, we were told that the hire charge for the hall at Great Stony (now, somewhat obscurely called 'Zinc') was to be £200 for three hours. There would be an additional charge if a piano needed to be set up in the afternoon, so this idea was a non-starter. The meeting ended with a note that Barrie Hall had recently celebrated his ninetieth birthday – a card had been sent, duly signed by many members of the club.

Roger Montgomery's guitar recital in April was very well received, and the bar noise had not been too intrusive, although there had been noise from the corridor. There was a good audience of sixty, with many new faces. The Budworth Hall offered to reinstate the second pair of doors to the hall following the recital. These had been removed some years earlier, and it was felt that they would give an extra level of sound isolation from the corridor. Apart from the bar noise, another factor in using the Ballroom had been that of storing the club's piano. This had been due to the children's playgroup, which regularly met in there. However, by the end of 2010, this was no longer an issue.

By then, it had been agreed that the club's Bechstein should have a complete refurbishment. Therefore, it was decided that the piano should be removed from the Concert Room around the same time as the arrival of the hire instrument booked for the competition in the Ballroom – the piano hire company was also carrying out the refurbishment. It was decided that when the refurbishment was complete, hopefully by the start of the following season, the club's piano would be returned to the Ballroom where it would be used and the venue assessed for noise. If this was still problematic after refitting the second Ballroom doors, the piano would be moved back upstairs. Payment for the refurbishment had been secured by a very generous loan from committee member Janet Pope.

A rather lovely coincidence was noted for the club outing in April when a visit was made to hear the Royal Philharmonic Orchestra play in Chatham – one in which I happened to be playing. As always, by April, competition preparations were in full swing, with press releases being sent to all the Essex papers and magazines, the banner having been located and updated for that year's competition. Requests for sponsorship had been successful, and ultimately, there were fifteen entries.

2011–2012

As planned, the new season started in the Ballroom, with the new doors in place, and an option to place a heavy curtain in front of them, should it be felt necessary. Piano storage had been provided in the recess under the balcony by taking out some cupboards. New heavy drapes were purchased to cover the void, to which the club was quite reasonably invited to contribute. It was a privilege for my wife and I to inaugurate the refurbished piano, which we did at the traditional post-AGM recital. It was noted that several people attended that event, held in the Ballroom, who had not been able to manage the stairs to the Concert Room. It was

Peter Jackson with Roderick Elms and Joanna Smith, having inaugurated the club's refurbished Bechstein piano • 23rd September 2011 • Ongar

also pointed out that there was ramp access to the Ballroom via the rear doors from the road.

Peter Jackson took over as chairman from that season, allowing Nicola Harries a well-earned respite following six years in the role. As usual, the first meeting noted the committee members' specific duties. The minutes also record that some four hundred copies of the season's brochure had been sent out to members, the extended mailing list, and other locations.

The new arrangement for storing the club's piano in the Ballroom also meant that it could be used by others, with agreement. This included the Jazz Club, which has used it regularly. We took the decision to charge a nominal £100 for commercial use when a paying audience is present – this being considerably less than the cost of hiring an instrument from elsewhere. The club generally doesn't make a charge when the piano is used for rehearsal purposes by a community organisation. In this meeting, it was also noted that the annual Ongar Town Council event was again taking place in the following April. As mentioned previously, the club had regularly taken a stand at this event to facilitate awareness of its activities, and it was agreed that we would take one again in 2012.

The first Cantate Christmas concert took place on 23rd December to a packed hall and rasing nearly £900. This helped the club's finances considerably after paying the fees. From the start of 2012, there had been another small decline in audience numbers, and this was highlighted at the April concert in which the Aurora Ensemble appeared. Being a group of six, this was a more expensive evening, by design, but with only around thirty in the audience. This was a very special evening at a personal level as it included the first performance of my new piano and wind sextet 'Moody Moves'. Various other options were suggested to help with audiences, and publicity contacts were pursued to ensure that the club's details were being properly circulated. There was good news from Barbara Szymanek, who had received confirmation from Sainsbury's that they would give £500 in sponsorship for the competition that year. Barbara had also been investigating members who had not renewed their season tickets – the reasons included cost, illness, and already going to enough concerts.

In April, the hundredth birthday was announced of a very long-standing supporter of the club, Dr Sylvia Hatfield. Sadly, there was also a not-so-happy announcement – the passing, on 4th April, of long term committee member John Harrop, who had been in hospital for some time. He was almost a founder member of the club and had always offered sage advice as chairman, treasurer, and a multitalented musician. John had chosen a career in science, maintaining music as a hobby, saying that "he loved music too much to try and make a career of it". During his final degree, he was found revising for his chemistry exams from a book propped on the piano whilst simultaneously practising for his LRAM examination. Following time in research, John became a chemistry teacher at Ongar Comprehensive School. He also led musical appreciation classes in Ongar and played with the Pasadena Roof and Rainbow Dance orchestras. John was also musical director of both Loughton and Harlow operatic societies, and for many years, organist and choirmaster at St Martin's Church, Ongar. In April 1982, he performed Beethoven's fourth piano concerto for the club with the Harlow Symphony Orchestra. John left a very generous legacy toward the Essex Young Musician of the Year competition.

John Harrop, offstage at a performance by Ongar Music Hall for which he was Musical Director and Accompanist. c. 1983–1987

It was decided that an appropriate way to celebrate John Harrop's long and distinguished association with the club would be by way of a recital, and I was given the task of engaging Benjamin Grosvenor for the occasion. His agent was extremely helpful and we even managed to come to an understanding about the fee, in view of the special circumstances and Benjamin's prior relationship with the club.

2012–2013

The new season opened its AGM with the good news that the previous year had ended with a small financial surplus. At the same meeting, Nicola Harries was made a Life Member of Ongar Music Club in recognition of her long service. The treasurer reported that there had also been a refund of £1,339 from HMRC in respect of gift aid.

Benjamin Grosvenor's recital was set for the 1st February, and by early December, a hundred and twenty tickets had been sold – being the notified capacity of the Ballroom. It later transpired that we could actually have a hundred and sixty, although we eventually settled on a hundred and fifty to avoid overcrowding. It was a remarkable occasion, listening to this exceptional young pianist, almost ten years on from the first time we heard him in the competition at the age of ten. The evening also resulted in some new club members, and was a truly fitting tribute to one of the elder statesmen of Ongar Music Club.

In March, the new treasurer, Eric Crook, brought up the recurring issue of whether the Jazz Club wished to remain under the umbrella of the Music Club. As mentioned on many previous occasions, the Jazz Club had a separate bank account, separate insurance and generally operated independently. That apart, their presence did bring extra work for the treasurer in having to produce consolidated accounts for the Charity

Commission. The only advantage of their association with the Music Club seemed to be that of it enjoying charitable status in order to reclaim gift aid. Eric would investigate whether it actually did so.

It was subsequently learned that the Jazz Club did not reclaim gift aid, and it was decided that we should suggest to the Jazz Club that we prepare separate accounts from that season forward. If the two sections felt that they wanted to separate, then a formal resolution would be needed at an AGM – the Music Club's constitution describing the Jazz Club as a 'subsidiary entity'.

So far that season, audiences had not been too bad with some recitalists bringing their own friends in support. As with all concerts, there is a critical point of balance – one where a concert breaks even. It was unfortunate that the Music Club was then rotating somewhat around that fulcrum.

The April 2013 minutes gave fulsome acknowledgement of the recital by Benjamin Grosvenor. They also mentioned a recital by another young winner of the Essex Young Musician of the Year title (in 2012), Matthew Paris. Matthew played the double bass and is the son of Colin Paris, the co-principal double bass player in the London Symphony Orchestra, and grandson of Nat Paris, for many years a double bass player in the orchestra of the Royal Opera House, Covent Garden – a clear case of talent running in the family.

Following the concert, it was noted that the sound of the piano was not good due to the piano lid being fully down. There is an ongoing misconception about the position of the lid on a grand piano and one which we frequently have to address in the EYMY competition. The basic design of a grand piano is such that to obtain a balance of tone across its range,

Benjamin Grosvenor, Celebrity Recital • 1st February 2013 • Ongar the lid should not be fully closed. It's true that raising the lid, either fully or in part, does change the level of the sound. However, in a concert situation, and when played by a competent pianist, the use of a 'half-stick' for accompanimental roles should not create a problem of balance and will greatly enhance the quality of the piano's sound for the audience.

2013–2014

The September AGM noted that the following year would be the seventieth birthday of the club's president, John Lill. Part of the celebration included John performing the complete cycle of Beethoven's piano sonatas at London's Cadogan Hall, and a club outing was suggested.

It was also announced that Carole Brown was willing to join the committee, and also to take over the organisation of the Young Music Makers concerts from Catherine Jennings. Reporting on the EYMY competition, it was noted that there had been an unusually low entry but an extremely high standard of performance – the winner being another young performer, fourteen-year-old pianist Rebecca Leung.

The AGM also saw further discussion regarding the relationship between the music and jazz clubs. Eric Crook, the Music Club's treasurer, explained that from the Music Club's perspective, the Jazz Club was all but a separate entity, with its own bank account and committee. As things stood, the Music Club had to produce individual and consolidated accounts, which took quite a bit of time to prepare. These also needed to be passed to the independent examiner (formerly referred to as the auditor). Another disadvantage was that these combined accounts made the Music Club's finances look much healthier than they were due to the greater financial strength of the Jazz Club – this had always been the case. It was pointed out that this could make it more challenging to get sponsorship for Music Club events. The chairman again suggested that the two committees meet soon to iron out any difficulties or misunderstandings.

Following what had, at times, been a rather heated exchange in the AGM, this matter was discussed further in the October meeting when it was agreed that a meeting between representatives of both committees would be held on 6th November. It was also pointed out that as things stood, long term viability was likely to be greater for the Jazz Club than the Music Club. However, there was never any doubt about the future of the Essex Young Musician of the Year competition while it continued to thrive and provide such a great opportunity for young Essex musicians.

The November meeting concluded with retention of the status quo, although it had been agreed that the Jazz Club would help the Music Club by distributing flyers at its events as a gesture of support – one which might also encourage our audiences. There was also a discussion about the newly advised requirements for trustees that had been received from the Charity Commission. It was agreed that these would be the chairman, treasurer, secretary and two from the Jazz Club.

The first meeting of 2014 was in February when it was reported that fifteen club members had attended one of John Lill's Beethoven recitals at Cadogan Hall, which had been greatly enjoyed. It was also noted there had been a packed hall with a good many young people. Janet Pope had received a letter from Geoffrey Timms to say that he was very unwell, and although he was unable to write, he could type.

The meeting then proceeded to discuss the ongoing concern about audience numbers and the future. Whilst there had always been peaks and troughs in attendance, it was accepted that there was now a general downward trend, with fewer people coming to concerts. The club's finances were healthy, but the committee wanted to be realistic about presenting concerts to such small audiences. This situation could also be quite dispiriting for performers. When engaging artistes for recitals, I always felt the need to explain the modest fee and the fact that the audience would likely not be large. I feel a great sense of gratitude for the understanding and gracious support of my colleagues.

During committee discussions, it was suggested that the 2014–2015 season be considered the last in which we presented regular concerts in the way that we always had. Maybe have two or three big-name artistes and see how that worked for audiences. The Endellion String Quartet was already booked for October 2014, and any major decision would have to be brought before a general meeting. Whatever was decided as a minimum number of performances, we would continue with an AGM, a Christmas concert and the EYMY competition winner's recital. This agreement was reaffirmed at the subsequent meeting when additional suggestions were made for future recitals, if held – perhaps to engage more local artistes with their own following; and possibly consider a time other than a Friday night. That said, it was already known that the club's audience at the time would not usually be available during the day. Whatever the future held, it was decided to repay the loan for the piano refurbishment so generously made to the club by Janet Pope.

By way of encouragement, the April recital made a small surplus with a larger than usual audience of thirty-nine, plus six committee members. By that stage, the season was showing only a small loss of £80. Unfortunately, spirits were not so high at the May meeting, by which time we had learned the sad news that Barrie Hall had passed away, quite suddenly, on 7th May. Barrie had been a key figure in Ongar Music Club since 1976 when he first came to give a talk. His influence on the organisation and development of the club cannot be underestimated. There is a full tribute to Jean and Barrie Hall in Chapter 6.

2014–2015

Peter Jackson reported at the AGM in September (19th) that there were difficulties with the organisation of the Young Music Makers concerts. Catherine Jennings had stepped down the year before, following which Carole Brown had taken over. However, she, too, needed to step down. Barbara Szymanek had agreed to help and would organise one concert during the forthcoming season. Peter also spoke of the club's difficulties due to declining audience numbers and asked members to think carefully about how matters might be improved. Treasurer Eric Crook noted the repayment of the loan from

Barry Hall

Janet Pope in respect of the piano refurbishment. He also reported that there was an average attendance of forty at the club's concerts. That in itself was not so bad, but the adherent costs of artiste's fees, together with the cost of hiring the hall, had created financial challenges that could not be ignored.

The performance by the Endellion String Quartet on 17th October was a wonderful occasion. Although a more expensive venture, it did, as hoped, attract a larger and more diverse audience. As expected, the event made a loss, but there was an audience of sixty-nine, and the club benefitted from four new members. The October meeting brought a kind suggestion from committee members Eric and Jean Crook that they investigate, through their own connections, the possibility of the competition winner being offered a solo performance with the Essex Symphony Orchestra. The initial response from the orchestra was favourable, and the idea would be explored further at the orchestra's next planning meeting.

Planning had been underway for a concert in memory of Barrie Hall on 5th December. This involved many members of Barrie's family, together with several of his musical friends from Ongar Music Club, including Alisdair Hogarth, Marianne Olyver, Joanna Smith, Jane Webster and myself. Barrie was a great fan of Schubert, and so I made an arrangement of his song *Die Forelle* (The Trout) for Jane to sing, together with the assembled company – see Chapter 6. The concert was a remarkable occasion – a real celebration which was greatly enjoyed by performers and audience alike. The event raised £570 for the British Heart Foundation. The year came to a close with another appearance from Cantate Alumni to a full hall of family and friends, followed by a request from them that they return in 2015.

The following year opened with a Young Music Makers concert, a winner's recital by Rebecca Leung, and an unusual evening entitled 'Shakespeare in Song'. These events brought audiences of around forty-five – somewhat better than previously. In March, we heard from the Chelmsford firm of James Dace that they felt unable to continue supporting the EYMY competition with an annual £100 'under-19 prize' which they had given for many years. This prize then became the Geoffrey Timms prize, which he offered to sponsor. This felt very appropriate as Geoffrey had been the founding administrator of the competition and spent so much of his life working with young people in the field of music.

That year saw a very disappointing entry for the EYMY competition with just six entries – a level of support not experienced either before or after. Sometimes there is no accounting for these things, as is the case for audience numbers. We also had the curious case of one very young entrant whose mother wanted to enter her child twice, playing two different instruments. The administrator advised her not to do so as the applicant really was too young. Unfortunately, when the mother sent in the supporting documents, there were irregularities, and when these were pointed out, the mother withdrew the entry.

Notwithstanding the slight upsurge in audience numbers earlier in the season, the disappointing number of entries in the competition, together with previous concerns about audience levels, focussed the committee's thinking quite considerably over the summer months. Although it was known that far fewer young people were learning instruments, that would not, in itself, explain why there had been such a dramatic drop in entries for this particular year, and it was felt that this could well have been something of a fluke. However, after much soul-searching on these various issues, it was agreed at the June meeting that we should again bring up the issue of the club's future at the AGM and gain opinions as to whether the club should continue as it was.

2015–2016

At the AGM, Peter Jackson (chairman) explained the situation to the members present in unequivocal terms. Not just the reality of low audience support but also the lack of new blood to help on the committee. By then, both he and Janet Pope had an eighty-mile round trip to attend concerts or meetings. He also pointed out the age of some members of the committee, which made support challenging. He said that if members felt that they were able to join the committee, then existing members would be happy to help in any way they could. Failing any change in the prevailing situation, a motion might be brought at the 2016 AGM to dissolve the club. Doing so would bring considerations for the administration of the Essex Young Musician of the Year competition, not least the benefits it valued through the club's charity status. Whatever the future might hold for the club itself, it was decided not to rush into any decision regarding the future of the competition – waiting to see the level of support in 2016. If the support was good, the club would continue, but with the competition as its main event – maybe with the winner's recital and any other special occasions which might arise. If the competition entries were again low, then the club would close completely, including the competition.

All this provided much food for thought, and not a little anguish over the months that followed. Investigations were made as to precisely what processes we would need to adhere to if the club were to be dissolved, and I have to say, that from a purely personal point of view, this outcome was unthinkable to my wife and myself. However, we had to remain realistic.

Although subsequent recitals didn't have bad audiences, they were not felt to have provided evidence of any significant swing in the prevailing trend. However, the competition attracted fourteen entries, and the year ended with agreement that the club would continue, in the way previously suggested – it would promote the EYMY competition, the winner's recital and possibly an occasional, special recital. It would retain the name Ongar Music Club and sever its link with Ongar Jazz Club. The committee would be reduced to a bare minimum, with Janet Pope as chairman, Peter Jackson as treasurer, Nicola Harries as secretary – myself and Joanna Smith being the other members. All this would need a change to the constitution ahead of the AGM.

2016–2017

The greatly anticipated 2016 AGM was held on 7th October with the committee and some thirty members present. The proposals for the future of the club were presented to the meeting by Nicola Harries, who had overseen the necessary redrafting of the club's constitution:

The committee has decided to stop putting on regular concerts. There was sufficient interest in the Essex Young Musician competition this year to continue running it. This means that we need to amend the club's constitution to reflect these changes; also, some updating is required. The main changes are:

- Include the Essex Young Musician competition in the objectives
- Reduce the committee size to 6 with a minimum of 3
- The accounts are 'Independently Examined'
- References to the 'Century Club' and to 'Making Music' are deleted

Nicola noted that we intend to have a competition winner's recital and possibly other occasional concerts. We will continue with a membership basis; the annual subscription [£10] will give free entry to both days of the competition and reduced ticket prices for any concerts. The competition and any concerts would be publicised to members, local press, local posters and on the Club's website.

A motion to adopt the revised constitution was proposed by Ana Barber, seconded by Peter Lewis and accepted unanimously.

This came as a great relief for many of us – a way to progress, maintain the club's name, and buy some time to investigate whether other avenues might be discovered to help the club.

Ongar Music Club moved forward with a smaller committee and a different way of working. The year was scheduled to conclude with the 2015 Essex Youn g Musician of the Year winner's recital. Unfortunately, the artiste cancelled, and in their place, we were delighted to have a return visit from pianist Joseph Tong, Essex Young Musician of the Year 1996.

With this new strategy, 2017 was relatively quiet. However, the competition ran as usual and with a healthy number of applicants. We had a committee meeting in late July, in part to arrange for the AGM and also to deal with any domestic matters that had arisen. The chairman confirmed that, as agreed by the committee, she had gifted a substantial amount of archive material to the Essex Record Office. We also discussed a very helpful suggestion from Marie-Luise Heinecke of St John's Arts Centre in Old Harlow (ARC) that we allow it to present the competition winner's recital as part of their regular, and very popular, lunchtime recital series. It was agreed that this would be a good way forward, at least for the time being, and would guarantee a larger audience for this event and a substantially smaller loss for the club. It could also make a new audience aware of the club and the competition. Kayleigh McEvoy *soprano* (EYMY 2017) and 2018 Jamie Cochrane *piano* (EYMY 2018) gave their winner's recitals in Harlow in 2018 and 2019, respectively. At the time of writing, we still have to schedule a recital for the 2019 winner, baritone Michael Lafferty due to programming restrictions in 2020.

2017–2018

In her annual report to the September 2017 AGM, Janet Pope acknowledged the difficulties of the past year whilst recording the considerable success of the competition in July and the support of the committee in ensuring the ongoing well-being of the club. She also expressed her hope that all members would renew their membership at the new rate of £10, acknowledging the lower number of events now planned. The AGM concluded with the traditional recital by a competition finalist – Felicity Latham *flute* with Joanna Smith *piano*.

We were all very saddened to learn of the sudden passing of Jean Hall in December of 2017. As for many others, it is hard to quantify her contribution to the club, either directly or indirectly, in support of her husband, Barrie – see Chapter 6.

In May 2018, we had the first of the arranged recitals with ARC in Harlow, featuring the soprano Kayleigh McEvoy and this was followed by the EYMY competition in July, which again had a strong entry. There was no AGM in 2018 but this is allowed for in the constitution which currently gives a maximum period of eighteen months between such meetings.

2018–2019

The next AGM was held in April 2019, and by way of an experiment, this was held in the afternoon, during daylight hours. There were quite a few non-members present due to the song recital by Jessica Hope, (runner-up in the 2017 EYMY competition) planned to follow the meeting.

One might say that this meeting was something of a watershed for the club for it was then that Jane Webster not only joined the committee but rose spontaneously to the position of chairman. The new chairman outlined her idea to trial soirée type recitals with afternoon tea, rather than the traditional format of an evening concert. She planned to arrange the first such event in the near future, and if it proved successful, she would consider introducing these on a more regular basis. There would be discussion about whether there should be a charge for admission or a request for donations. A new invitee to the AGM, Margaret Payne, who was interested in joining the club, said that she thought this idea was attractive, and her fellow choir members might also be interested. She also offered her thanks from her choir for the use of the piano, confirming that if the piano were to be used for a ticketed concert, the club would charge a hire fee.

Gregory Walmsley

And so began a new era for Ongar Music Club and a completely new type of event – 'Soundbites!'. This format – an informal musical performance, coupled with afternoon tea, has been very popular, especially with those who dislike venturing out on dark evenings and those who enjoy cream teas. This new venture has done much to revitalise the club, which has a membership of around sixty at the time of writing. The first such event took place in June 2019, given by the cellist Gregory Walmsley (EYMY 1989).

The second of the EYMY winner's recitals to be held at ARC, Harlow, was held on 5th July and was given by the pianist Jamie Cochrane. Two days later was the annual competition – that year, held on just one day; a rather longer day than usual, and with the support of John Lill for the final round in the evening.

In August, I heard that my dear friend Geoffrey Timms was very unwell, and a visit was suggested. I travelled with my family to his home in Wales, and we shared a wonderful afternoon. He enjoyed re-living many happy memories of the club and its members, as well as a multitude of anecdotes from former years. He was delighted to hear of the recent upsurge in interest for Ongar Music Club, and I promised to do my best to help to support it. He smiled, and we said goodbye ... Geoffrey lost his struggle on 18th September.

Apart from being a fine musician, Geoffrey had exceptional organ-

Geoffrey Timms, studying a score in Beal School, Ilford

isational skills, frequently having a multitude of projects on the go – juggling large productions for his school in Ilford, and teaching privately, at school, and for the Redbridge Music Service on Saturday mornings. He would frequently be planning the Young Music Makers concerts alongside the Essex Young Musician of the Year competition, and while he was chairman, he would also be arranging the forthcoming season of concerts for the club.

In September, there was also great sadness for the club's chairman Jane Webster, who lost her father, Bert Webster. Together with his wife Betty, he had been a loyal supporter of the club since the eighties. Bert had been at the same school as Geoffrey Timms (Leyton County High), and they passed away on the same day.

2019–2021

September 2019 brought two 'Soundbites!' recitals, and others followed monthly until February 2020, when the pandemic brought most things to a halt. There had been a steady increase in membership from people who had not previously had any knowledge of Ongar Music Club, and who clearly enjoyed this new type of event. The membership grew steadily to just over fifty by the start of 2020. Other recitals had been scheduled, but sadly, these had to be postponed.

Unfortunately, 2019 also saw further changes to the administration of the club. Long term members Janet Pope and Peter Jackson had indicated that they would be stepping down from the committee – the chairman announced their departure at the AGM on 26th November. Breaking with tradition, warm tribute was paid to them from the floor of the meeting when past committee member Barbara Szymanek noted their exceptional dedication and generosity to the club over a great many years. During their time on the committee, they had served variously as chairman, treasurer, secretary and EYMY administrator.

In the meantime, Jane had elicited support from a family member David Hannibal who, with a background of financial experience, was willing to serve as treasurer. Despite living in Dorset, David attended his first committee meeting in early November 2019 when he introduced himself to the committee. Whilst his location precludes regular attendance, he has been able to provide support via email and 'Zoom' meetings. He was also able to attend committee meetings until the COVID-19 outbreak forced the club to meet 'online'.

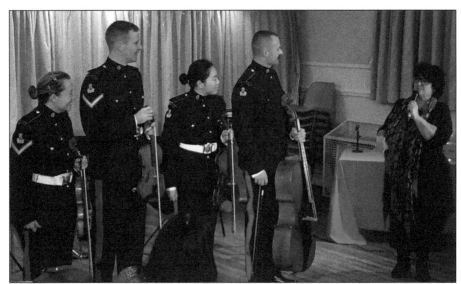

Chairman Jane Webster with the quartet from the Countess of Wessex's String Orchestra • 29th October 2019 • Budworth Hall, Ongar

At the November AGM, chairman Jane Webster presented the members with news of her plans for the club's future, which she was embracing with great personal zeal. She also reported that her singer friend Dominic Natoli was willing to serve on the committee – a most welcome suggestion. In fact, in February 2020, Dominic gave the club the last and greatly appreciated lunchtime event before the first lockdown in March. Unfortunately, following his recital, he decided he would be unable to continue as a committee member and resigned.

Earlier in the year, the club's secretary Nicola Harries had announced that she, too, was standing down from the committee. As with Janet and Peter, Nicola had been a pillar of the club for around thirty years and had similarly held all the main offices. She brought with her great legal expertise and business common sense, which was greatly valued by the members. Nicola also showed significant personal generosity to the club and was the club's unofficial 'hospitality manager', having organised so many wonderful events – frequently in her own home. Subsequently, Jane's near neighbour and good friend Carol Pummell joined the committee as secretary. Carol had been helping with the domestic arrangements for the new 'Soundbites!' events and therefore knew something of the club.

Therefore, the new committee was my wife Joanna and I, the chairman, treasurer and secretary. The first meeting was held on 9th March 2020 when a room was hired in Wanstead House in Redbridge. We covered a great deal of ground and got to know much more about each other. The committee also heard from Jane about her plans for the club. Following that meeting, my wife and I concluded that now was the time for us to also step down – I had served on the committee for thirty-five years and my wife Joanna for fifteen. However, it was agreed that I would continue to administer the competition with the usual support from the committee. My wife and I agreed to remain in our roles until the autumn, when it was hoped that new members would join the remaining three to make a viable committee. In practice, this happened in early October when Jane Webster had found two new potential committee members. These were Andy King, who had considerable experience as a military musician and was known to Jane. Also, Alisdair Hogarth, a past finalist of the EYMY competition and a highly respected pianist and accompanist.

Sadly, many of the club's plans had been put on hold in late March 2020 with the announcement of the national 'lockdown'. This situation brought a great deal of uncertainty for everyone, not just those of us involved in Ongar Music Club. Despite this putting a stop to the regular concerts, in no small measure due to our inability to use the Budworth Hall, we did proceed on the basis that the EYMY competition might just go ahead. I was something of a lone voice is trying to remain optimistic; after all, no one knew the reality of the situation at that time. However, after a period of great uncertainty, the position was clarified, and the 2020 competition had to be cancelled.

As with all charities, the Charity Commission requires that trustees be appointed. These had previously been members of the Music Club committee and two from the Jazz Club committee. However, those last two appointments had ceased with the separation of the Jazz Club, following the Music Club's reorganisation in 2016. Therefore, since early 2020, the trustees had been Jane Webster and me – this was not an ideal situation. Three new trustees were identified: Francesca Smith, a respected musician who is well qualified and experienced in business and charity-related matters; Mark Walmsley, a seasoned musician who now has considerable experience in marketing; and Jaymey McIvor, a local town councillor. Francesca was elected chairperson of the trustees. This was a particularly strong Board of Trustees with a broad range of skills and expertise to support the club. The proposals for these new appointments needed the sanction of the club's members, which would usually be done at an AGM or an EGM. In the prevailing circumstances, this was impossible, so Jane Webster and I used our powers as trustees to deem such a meeting unviable. Therefore, we notified all members of the plan to appoint the new trustees and asked them to ratify the new committee members – the new officials were all formally elected by

October of 2020. It's unfortunate that by the following July, for varying reasons, three of the five trustees had resigned.

Due to the greater expectations of the Charity Commission, policies had to be produced to protect the club's members. With the exception of two, these were completed and approved by the Board of Trustees on 20th April, with the remaining two being completed by the end of that month. These policies might well have been presented for adoption at the AGM held on 16th June, but due to procedural difficulties, this was not achieved.

As we head for October, it's positive to reflect that since July, following the challenges of the pandemic, concert-going has started to open up. The BBC Proms ran during August and September, and concerts organised by music clubs and other organisations are being presented again. The club still has a schedule of online recitals for the autumn, but I feel sure that it won't be long before Ongar Music Club feels able to join other organisations in moving back to some live music-making.

A Soundbites! concert, complete with cream tea and raffle • 2019 • Budworth Hall, Ongar

7. The Halls of Fyfield

It would not be an exaggeration to say that Barrie Hall and his wife Jean's arrival was something of a turning point for musical life in Ongar – both of them lived and breathed music. Barrie was born in Birmingham, where he had studied music at Birmingham University, and later at Exeter College, Oxford. After the war, he became manager of the City of Birmingham Symphony Orchestra, and later of the Royal Liverpool Philharmonic Orchestra. In 1957 he joined the BBC as 'Music Director of Publicity for Concerts and the Proms'. He became Chairman and Secretary of the Television and Radio Industries Club, Public Relations Officer to the Royal Academy of Music, and a Chevalier of the Winegrowers of Burgundy. Barrie travelled all over the world in his BBC role and enjoyed life-long friendships with the musicians whom he met and worked with. He also acted as an adjudicator for the Arts Council. Following his retirement from the BBC in 1980, he published a history of the Proms – 'The Proms and the Men Who Made Them'.

Jean Hall's love of music embraced a passion for singing, and for many years, she was a member of the Philharmonia Chorus. I remember playing in a number of concerts alongside this choir when Jean was singing – notably, two performances of Mozart's setting of the Requiem Mass conducted by one of her idols, Carlo Maria Guilini. Jean also had a great love of the English language and had studied English literature at Royal Holloway College. She had a remarkable facility for linguistic puzzles, notably the Telegraph crossword. Jean also worked for the BBC, for the 'Radio Times', where she became chief editor of the TV section. In 1961, she changed jobs, becoming Barrie's assistant. They shared a great love of music and became close friends. In 1974, they were married, and in 1975, following a period of extensive house-hunting in the home counties to the north of London, they eventually moved to Norwood End, near Fyfield.

Meanwhile, David Kirkwood, founder of Ongar Music Club, had written to the BBC early in 1975 to request that Ongar Music Club be

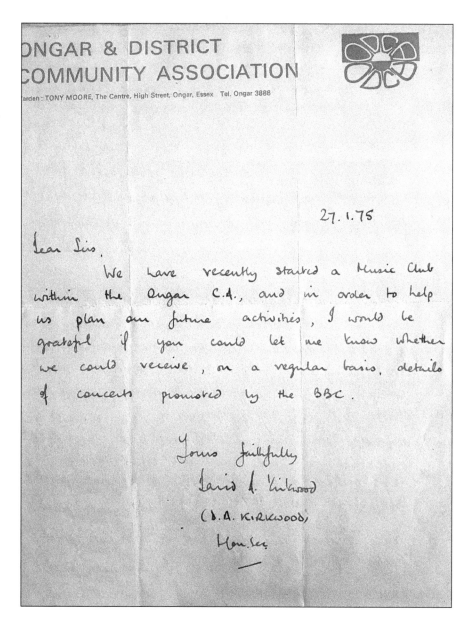

ONGAR & DISTRICT
COMMUNITY ASSOCIATION

Warden : TONY MOORE, The Centre, High Street, Ongar, Essex   Tel. Ongar 3888

27. 1. 75

Dear Sirs,

We have recently started a Music Club within the Ongar C.A., and in order to help us plan our future activities, I would be grateful if you could let me know whether we could receive, on a regular basis, details of concerts promoted by the BBC.

Yours faithfully,

David A. Kirkwood

(D. A. KIRKWOOD)

Hon. Sec.

sent details of concerts and other activities which might be of interest. Unwittingly, his letter (above) was to change the future course of the club, and in a most positive way.

Having navigated its way around a multiplicity of BBC corridors and desks, his letter found its way onto the desk of Barrie Hall in Broadcasting House, eliciting a typically effusive reply:

February 3rd, 1975

Dear Mr. Kirkwood,

Thankyou for your letter. There are perhaps two ways in which you can obtain advance notice of our public concerts. One is to receive leaflets when printed (I enclose the four covering this present season). If you want to receive these regularly each year, I can arrange this. The other is to have a copy of 'The Listener', wherein a schedule (quarterly at present) gives information, as you see from the most recent issue, also enclosed. BBC Ticket Unit will send you a list showing studio concerts to which an audience is admitted without charge.

Can I be of any assistance over speakers? I know presenters of music programmes to Clubs who charge high fees, low fees, and even no fees!

I am particularly interested, because Ongar is one of the areas in which we are looking for a house -- unsuccessfully up to now: we need a very large sitting-room for grand piano, hi-fi, and loud music making.

If you are going to take the Club on visits, block bookings, etc., you ought to come to the Proms Press Conference in June. Let me know your membership, and I might be able to persuade someone to talk about Proms to the Club.

I have been on the Music Club scene for many years, so don't hesitate to ask me if you think I can help. Ring me, if you like.

Yours sincerely,

Barrie Hall
Publicity Officer, Radio 3

Perhaps not surprisingly, this was to lead to an invitation for Barrie to visit Ongar and deliver a talk on the Proms, confirmed in a letter from the BBC in May 1975 and stating that as the club had no funds, "we shall be glad to waive the fee and expenses in this case". David Kirkwood's reply indicates a meeting at the Proms Press Conference that June which was to become the start of a long friendship – one which would be extremely fruitful for the fledgling music club.

Jean and Barrie had been looking for a new home for some time. They had bought a map "Thirty-five Miles Around London" and had drawn

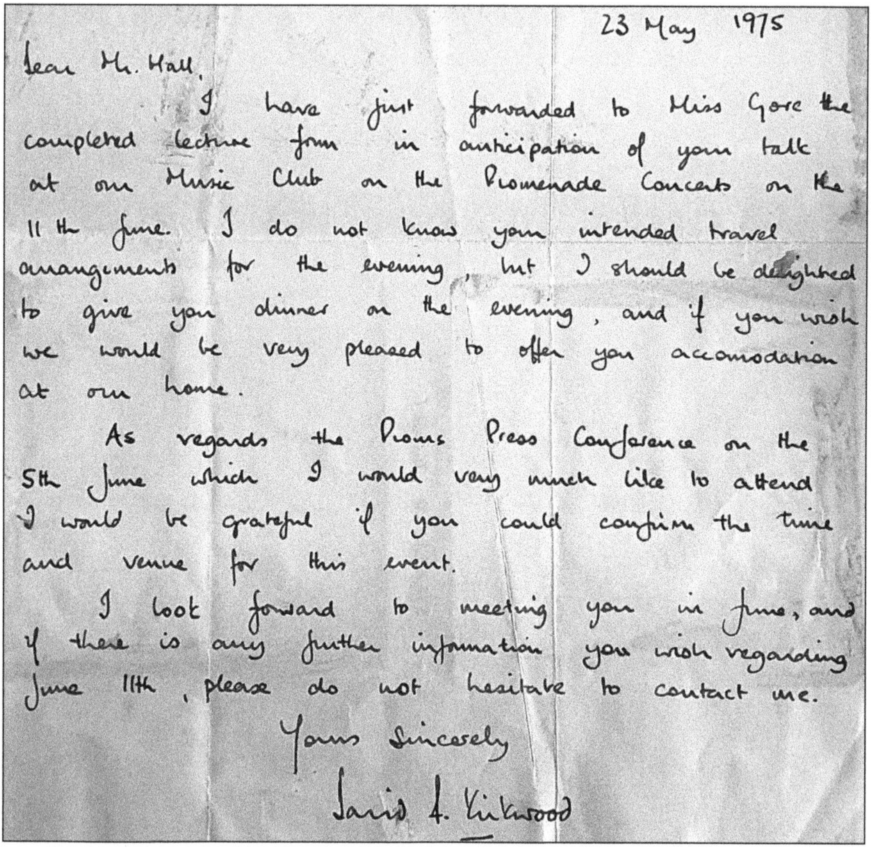

23 May 1975

Dear Mr. Hall,

I have just forwarded to Miss Gore the completed lecture form in anticipation of your talk at our Music Club on the Promenade Concerts on the 11th June. I do not know your intended travel arrangements for the evening, but I should be delighted to give you dinner on the evening, and if you wish we would be very pleased to offer you accommodation at our home.

As regards the Proms Press Conference on the 5th June which I would very much like to attend I would be grateful if you could confirm the time and venue for this event.

I look forward to meeting you in June, and if there is any further information you wish regarding June 11th, please do not hesitate to contact me.

Yours Sincerely

David A. Kirkwood

a semicircle north of Oxford Circus, inside which they hoped to find a house. Their search was eventually narrowed to the area between Chigwell and Ongar – Essex appealing greatly to them.

On 11th June, just a few days after the press conference, Barrie and Jean drove to Ongar to meet the Kirkwoods. As Barrie says in his diary, meeting in the surroundings of a press conference, they "had hardly had time for intelligent conversation". Over dinner, the question of houses arose again. Margaret Kirkwood (David's wife) worked in one of the local estate agent's offices and had heard of two cottages being developed in nearby Fyfield, just north of Ongar. On the following Saturday, Jean and Barrie returned to Ongar and looked at various properties, eventually settling on one of the two cottages at Norwood End, Fyfield. On their first visit, they discovered that one of the cottages had already been rebuilt and was about to be sold. However, the other was already under development, and it was this one that they bought.

Jean and Barrie moved into their new home in December 1975. By the time of his talk on the Proms in April 1976, they were both settled in their new home and Barrie was getting closely involved with the Music Club, joining the committee for the 1976-77 season. I think it would be

Jean and Barrie Hall

fair to say that within a relatively short period of time, Barrie became the powerhouse behind Ongar Music Club. He wouldn't accept any sloppiness, or presentation that was anything short of professional. Similarly, Jean brought her eagle-eyed editorial skills to everything that was printed – woe betide anyone who let pass documents with typos or grammatical errors. They meticulously kept scrapbooks with details, programmes and reviews of every concert and activity presented by the club.

Barrie's extensive circle of friends, gathered from his many years working for Radio 3, were to provide a nucleus for the many celebrity concerts to be presented by the club over the next few years. Many of these artistes appeared for little or no fee – a clear indication of their respect for Barrie. These included evenings with John Amis, Dame Janet Baker, Richard Baker, Antony Hopkins (who gave a BBC broadcast from the club), John Lill, Lord Yehudi Menuhin (who came with students from his specialist music school in Stoke d'Abernon in Surrey), Sir Peter Pears and Dame Eva Turner.

As noted elsewhere, Jean was also a member and chairman of the Music Club committee for a very long time, and for many years she administered the Essex Young Musician of the Year competition with great dedication. Like Barrie, she shared a great love of cooking and entertaining, and a meal with the Halls could be quite an extravagant affair. Many concerts would be rounded off by a social event, and in the early days, these would most usually be hosted by Jean and Barrie. Longtime committee member Peter Lewis recalls that "the committee often attended parties at Barrie and Jean's after a concert, which the performers usually attended, and they could go on until 2:00 am". Peter also recounts being at Barrie and Jean's one evening with his wife Jan, when "John Lill took his shoes off, knelt down, and then did the most hilarious impression of Toulouse Lautrec".

Jean joined the committee in September 1988 and was immediately awarded responsibility for organising the club's outings by the chairman – her husband, Barrie. In accepting this role, she suggested that a maximum of three outings a year was a reasonable target. Many of the outings were to opera performances, mostly at Glyndebourne, but they also included visits to many of the major concert halls, and of course, our own London recitals for the Essex Young Musician of the Year winners. From 1997, Jean was administrator of the competition, following in the esteemed footsteps of Geoffrey Timms. She continued in this role with supreme dedication until 2008.

Barrie was directly responsible for Yehudi Menuhin becoming president of the club, and later inviting John Lill to become president, as well as patron of the Essex Young Musician of the Year competition. Through this, John became a good friend to the club – making several visits to chair the panel of adjudicators for the Essex Young Musician of the Year competition, and also to give benefit recitals to support the competition as well as the Music Club's wider work.

Barrie passed away suddenly on 7th May 2014 at the age of 93, just a month before their 40th Wedding Anniversary, and Ongar Music Club organised a special celebratory concert in his memory on 5th December that year. This was a wonderful occasion, shared by Jean, and involving many of Barrie's extremely musical family. The performance also embraced close friends of the club together with former winners and finalists of the competition – the occasion raising money for the British Heart Foundation. In time-honoured fashion, there was a reception following in the concert, organised by Nicola Harries. Jean continued to support the club in so far as she could, and would occasionally come to concerts and the final round of the competition that she always greatly enjoyed. Jean passed away suddenly on 17th December 2017 in her early 80s.

Jean and Barrie shared a great sense of humour and great integrity. In the words of the club's president John Lill:

> ... their selfless application to the substantial demands of its [Ongar Music Club] organisation was extraordinary.

An extract from the souvenir programme ...

Tonight's Performance

Ongar Music Club is delighted to present this special evening in honour of one of its most distinguished and longest-serving members, Barrie Hall. Although the club's musical family was very important to Barrie, we also wanted this evening to reflect his personal family and we're delighted to welcome so many of its members to join in this musical celebration.

Also performing are the distinguished soprano Jane Webster (a regular jury member for Ongar Music Club's annual *Essex Young Musician of the Year* competition, onetime *Mother Bess,* and a former winner of the EYMY title in 1986), international violinist and regular EYMY jury member Marianne Olyver together with Nigel Yandell (Marianne's pianist partner in her duo *Postcards from Europe* and also a highly experienced performer and lecturer), the pianist Alistair Hogarth (a prize-winner in the 1996 EYMY and also artistic director of the highly acclaimed *Prince Consort* which recently celebrated its tenth anniversary with a recital from the Wigmore Hall, broadcast live on Radio 3) and the husband and wife pianist team Joanna Smith (also a prize-winner in the EYMY competition and a highly respected accompanist) and Roderick Elms – never a prize-winner in the competition although he did meet his greatest prize, Joanna, through his involvement as a jury member!

Ongar Music Club

Barrie Hall
A Musical Celebration

PROGRAMME

J.S. Bach (arr. Roderick Elms) Sinfonia (Cantata No. 29)
Mendelssohn Scherzo (from *A Midsummer Night's Dream*)

Joanna Smith and Roderick Elms *piano duet*

Thoinot Arbeau (1520-1595) Mattachins
(arr Edward Huws Jones)

Max Hall *violin*, Michael Hall *piano*

Vivaldi Concerto RV103 (2nd movement)

Emma Hall *flute* and Jeremy Hall *alto recorder;*
Michael Hall *harpsichord*

Schubert arr. Roderick Elms *Die Forelle* (The Trout) D550

Jane Webster *soprano*
Joanna Smith and Roderick Elms *piano duet*

Ennio Morricone Gabriel's Oboe

Twig Hall *oboe*, Andrew Haveron *piano*

James Hook Duettinos Opus 42 (selection)
Giovanni Giacomo Gastoldi Duet No.1 for soprano and alto recorders (1598)

Emma Hall *flute*, Jeremy Hall *alto recorder*

Vittorio Monti Czardas
Edward Elgar Serenade
Ernest Tomlinson Pourquoi pas?

Marianne Olyver *violin*, Nigel Yandell *piano*

Friday 5th December 2014
The Ballroom, Budworth Hall, Ongar

Interval

Mendelssohn	2 Songs without Words Op. 19
Kreisler/Rachmaninov	Liebesleid
Chopin	Three Waltzes: A flat, D flat and B minor
Vallier	Witches Dance

Alisdair Hogarth *piano*

Schumann	Frauenliebe und Leben, Opus 42
	i. Seit ich ihn gesehen
	ii. Er, Herrlichste von allen
	Dichterliebe , Ich grolle niche
Trad. Arr. Benjamin Britten	The Sally Gardens

Twig Hall *soprano*, Michael Hall *piano*

Eman Balzar (Erwin Schulhoff)	Susi (Fox Song)
Robert Dauber	Serenade
Trad.	Gypsy Carnival

Marianne Olyver *violin*, Nigel Yandell *piano*

Jean Baptiste Loeillet de Gant	Sonata in A minor, Op. 1, No. 1
	Adagio, Allegro, Adagio, Giga

Twig Hall *recorder*, Michael Hall *continuo*

Peter Warlock	*Two Cod Pieces* for piano duet
arr. Fred Tomlinson	i. Beethoven's Binge
	ii. The Old Codger

Joanna Smith and Roderick Elms *piano duet*

8. The Essex Young Musician of the Year

Ongar Music Club has always been passionate about fostering a love of music in the younger generation. The idea for an Essex Young Musician of the Year competition was perhaps a natural development from the early children's concerts, which later became the Young Music Makers series. The competition was established in 1984 at the suggestion of Geoffrey Timms, who administered it with extraordinary dedication and efficiency until a little after his retirement to North Wales in 1993.

In 1990, Barrie Hall produced a report on the competition, partly in the hope of encouraging greater interest as well as further financial support and sponsorship. An extract from his report provides a background to the birth of the competition. [1]

> Always looking for improvements, the Club's Committee, about eight years ago, took note of a suggestion by one of its five founder members, Geoffrey Timms, that a music competition might be a good idea.
>
> I had joined the Committee some years previously, and vigorously promoted and extended Club activities, using what expertise, contacts, or small influence I may have acquired during a lifetime in the professional music world (City of Birmingham Symphony Orchestra, Royal Liverpool Philharmonic, London Mozart Players, and twenty-four years at the BBC Music Division). I cautioned that the world needed another music competition like it needed a hole in the head.
>
> Yet the idea was basically a good one. To make it stick, exactly the right kind of competition had to be arrived at. Chipping Ongar is too small to house another Leeds Piano Contest. Nor is there enough money around for such undertakings.
>
> After a period of gestation I arrived at a solution I thought might just work. Some counties had a 'Musician of the Year' contest, or something similar. Essex did not. If we could give importance to a contest of manageable proportions, it might succeed. A possible way to do that soon followed. The distinguished international pianist John Lill OBE, born in Essex, had a country home in Matching close by Ongar. We often met for pub lunches or dinner at home. If he would allow us to link his name to such a contest, it might be an idea worth pursuing.

---

[1] Extract from a report on the Essex Young Musician of the year prepared by Vice-Chairman Barrie Hall ahead of negotiations in 1990 with the Essex Chronicle Group for the proposed competition sponsorship agreement.

John Lill and I met for a pub lunch, discussed the whole thing, and he readily agreed to everything. Not only that, he immediately offered the club a free recital to start us in funds. All this we accepted gratefully, and asked him to become the club's patron. (Our president had long been Yehudi Menuhin, who also gave a recital for us some years before.)

The format arrived at was:
The John Lill Awards for the Essex Young Musician of the Year presented by Ongar Music Club.

Once decided, the entire administration was handed over to Geoffrey Timms, on the principle that he who has the vision, gets the job. He has had a free hand to run the contest ever since, and done so impeccably.

For many years I worked alongside Geoffrey Timms in preparing the competition programmes, using what would now seem to be highly rudimentary desktop publishing software. Following Geoffrey's move to Wales, and the competition administration being taken on by Jean Hall, production of the competition programmes was adopted by longtime committee member and benefactor, John Harrop, until the task became too onerous, when it reverted to me.

First presented in the old Ongar Comprehensive School, the competition was initially open to anyone aged twenty-one or under and who had an Essex postal address. Brochures were prepared and distributed around the various music colleges, conservatoires and specialist music schools, as well as most of the secondary schools, music services and other music facilities in Essex. Applications were accepted from instrumentalists and singers – though rather curiously, singers were not admitted in the first year. Subsequently, the age limit became twenty-five or under, and the eligible territory extended to anyone who was either born in, lived in, or went to school in, Essex. Unfortunately, the competition has never been in a position to accept entries from organists due to the lack of a suitable instrument. However, there have been entries from an eclectic range of traditional orchestral instrumentalists as well as percussionists, recorder players, saxophonists and guitarists.

The competition has generally run across two days, close to the end of June or the beginning of July – the reason for this being that many potential applicants would be studying at one of the music conservatoires and therefore preparing for their end-of-year recitals. This would mean that those hoping to enter would not be having to prepare a recital programme at an inconvenient time in their studies.

The first competition was held on 20th and 21st July 1984 with the first round being held on the Friday evening from 5:00 pm to 10:00 pm, and the final round on the following evening – the competition was a huge success. Discussions ensued regarding the 1985 competition, and it was decided that singers would be allowed to enter. It was also agreed that the entry fee would be £10.00. Letters were written to many firms seeking sponsorship or simple donations, large or small, and money started to come in. Essex Radio responded, and although they were unable to help with sponsorship, they indicated their willingness to consider a broadcast of the winner. The Midland Bank was unable to help that year, but did so for subsequent competitions, along with Barclays Bank, Ford Motor Company, the Committee of General Practitioners of Essex, Harlow Chemical Company Ltd (Harco), May and Baker, Nortel, Ongar Sale Room, and many others. There were ongoing plans for fundraising, such as a Garden Party and an Auction. In 1985 it was decided to hold both rounds (semifinal and final) on the same day but on a Sunday (7th July) – this was done with an hour's break in between.

This pattern continued until the 1988 competition, which brought with it a substantially higher number of entries, resulting in a very late start to the evening final. It was therefore decided that there should be a preliminary round which would be held on the previous day. However, for practical reasons, the earliest that this could be implemented would be for the 1989 competition as this would need careful planning, both administratively and financially. Therefore, for the next year, a preliminary round was organised on the day before (Saturday afternoon) and the panel of adjudicators (smaller than for the final two rounds) would choose around nine or ten performers to go through to the semifinal round, which would be held on the following afternoon – the judges then choosing four performers to appear in the final round, held that same evening.

ONGAR MUSIC CLUB

President: Yehudi Menuhin, K.B.E.
Patron: John Lill, O.B.E.

1983/84 SEASON

Saturday, 21st July 1984

BUDWORTH HALL

THE JOHN LILL AWARD
*
A COMPETITION
TO FIND THE
ESSEX YOUNG MUSICIAN
OF THE YEAR
*
THE FINALS
*

Sponsored by ESSEX RADIO
Patron, REVERTEX

The Candidates

(in order of appearance)

Anthony Marwood (violin)

Marianne Malin (oboe)

Gregory Walmsley (cello)

Interval

(15 minutes)

Rosemarie Saunders (guitar)

Peter Sheppard (violin)

 President: John Lill, O.B.E.

ONGAR MUSIC CLUB

presents

JOHN LILL AWARD WINNERS

(Essex Young Musicians of 1997 and 1998)

ANTHONY WOOLLARD
(violoncello)

○ ○ ○ ○ ○ ○ ○ ○ ○ ○

TAMMY SE
(violin)

Saturday 17th March 2001 at 7.30 pm

St. Giles', Cripplegate

PROGRAMME £1.00

THE CANDIDATES

- •Rachel Barnes (19) bassoon
- Judith Black (24) soprano
- Helen Brockett (18) piano
- Timothy Brown (23) countertenor
- Gina Fergione (25) soprano
- Susan Fitzgerald (17) flute
- Philip Harper (21) tenor horn
- •Daisy Jopling (25) violin
- Lorraine Kelly (23) violin
- Lucy Manning (16) soprano
- Jonathan Newton (17) violin
- •Louisa Oakley (20) piano
- Warwick Potter (25) bassoon
- Joanna Smith (19) piano
- Kerry Sugden (23) piano
- Stephen Thompson (22) trombone
- Susan Tucker (24) 'cello
- ‡Ian Watson (17) freebass accordion
- Thomas Woods (21) cello
- Anthony Woollard (19) cello

• These candidates, as last year's finalists, proceed directly to the semifinal
‡ Ian Watson, as Essex Schools Young Musican of the Year (1994),
   also proceeds directly to the semifinal as part of his prize

Semifinalists for the 1994 Essex Young Musician of the Year competition

Holding the competition across two days always had the potential to create problems for some applicants in finding an accompanying pianist who was available for both days. Part of that difficulty being that the candidates had no way of knowing whether they would proceed to the semifinal round, meaning that their pianists had to commit to both days, and in many cases, be paid a retaining fee to ensure their availability. As a further experiment, the competition was held across two weekends in 1990, with the preliminary round on a Sunday and the main competition on the following Saturday – this changed again in 1992 when two consecutive Saturdays were tried!

However, a further change was necessitated in 1993 when sponsorship of the competition had been agreed with the Essex Chronicle Group. It was decided to hold the competition in the splendid surroundings of the Shire Hall, Chelmsford, and to revert to just one weekend, for both that year and 1994. Unfortunately, the new arrangement then ceased, and the competition reverted to Ongar and the Adult Education Campus for 1995 – see Chapter 3.

The competition ran for several years using this pattern of preliminaries on a Saturday afternoon, with the semifinal and final held on the following day. Ultimately, the availability of candidates on a Saturday became a defining issue, with the possibility of college commitments and the ever-present allure of paid performing engagements. Finally, the decision was made to move the preliminary round to the Sunday of the previous weekend, and this is how the competition ran from 2006 until 2018.

The competition's final adjudication has usually been a very cordial affair, although the decisions have frequently been close and could be challenging. Maybe it was for this reason that, while on the adjudicating panel, Barrie Hall was known to bring a small bottle of whisky with him that he insisted on opening once the decisions had been made – I think he looked upon it as something of a restorative! There have occasionally been expressions of surprise about our decisions, but that's the nature of performance. Music is a highly subjective art form – we can't all like

The Shire Hall, Chelmsford

the same genres, the same styles of performance, or even the same instruments – life would be very dull if we did.

Since the competition began, candidates have been required to play a ten-minute programme of contrasting pieces for the preliminary round. The semifinal required a fifteen-minute programme in which only one piece could be repeated from an earlier round. The final round was a twenty-five-minute recital with the same restriction. For many years now, and in all rounds, competitors have been requested to play at least one piece, or movement of a piece, from memory.

Members of the public are able to sit in on the competition, and the final round has always been a very special event – on a few occasions, we have been joined by the club's president John Lill who has chaired the panel of adjudicators. Candidates have always been asked to wear evening dress for the final round, but their interpretation of what that means has frequently been a source of fascination for the jury!

For many years the panel consisted of a mixture of club committee members together with external judges drawn from the music profession. In more recent years, as the status of the competition became more widely recognised, it was felt that a jury of professional musicians of standing would be more appropriate – for many years I have been charged with the duty of engaging colleagues for this duty. Over the years, those joining the adjudication panel have included many great names from the world of classical music, and these are detailed in Appendix B.

Funding and sponsorship have always been a priority for the competition with its relative high expenditure, not least for the prizes. Much of the ongoing work in this respect was undertaken by members of the committee, enabling the administrator to concentrate on the core organisation of the competition. For several years, Barrie Hall and Kenneth Bird were primarily responsible for achieving the necessary levels of sponsorship which came from diverse sources such as local businesses, large companies and individuals. There was also indirect patronage resulting from advertising within companies or shop fronts. Also, Essex Radio and subsequently BBC Essex both helped by way of on-air advertising, publicity for the competition, and the broadcasting of the finals. Sponsorship developed to the point that patronage was described as "being received at an encouraging rate". However, that wasn't always the case. In the early years of the competition, there was a tax advantage for companies supporting the arts, but unfortunately, that advantage was eventually to be taken away with very serious results for many arts organisations, not least, the London orchestras and other such icons of our artistic life.

In the following year (1985) the second winner of the Essex Young Musician of the Year title, Alison Baker, donated a small trophy was used to mark the 2nd prize in the Essex Schools Musician of the Year competition which ran from 1992 until 1994. The prize money increased periodically over the years until, in 2019, the competition took the bold step to increase the first prize to £1,000.

There was some discussion in 1986 about the virtue of presenting the competition biennially, partly to help the funding issue but also to allow more talent to develop. This idea was ultimately rejected, and the competition has run every year since 1884 with the exception of 2020 – a casualty of the COVID-19 pandemic. Initially, the Essex Young Musician of the Year was awarded a prize of £350 together with the 'Phoebe Musgrave Trophy', and they would be offered a recital for the club for a fee of £175. The second prize would be £150.

A bequest was made to the club by way of the sale of the viola belonging to the late husband of a friend of Geoffrey Timms. His friend requested that the money be used to boost the competition in her husband's name, and the second prize was subsequently named the 'Alan Matthews Award'. In 1987 it was announced by Geoffrey Timms and Sylvia Terry that there was to be a third prize – this being for the most promising competitor 'aged under 18 and who is not already a prizewinner'. This was to be known as the 'Hugh Terry Prize'. In 1988 there was an increase in the value of the first two prizes to £375 and £175 respectively.

For some years a winner's recital was organised in London. Initially, three winners shared the evening, but for the second recital there was just one performer. The organisers then settled on two winners for each recital. The first of these events was held on 8th January 1990 at the Wigmore Hall with performances by Alison Baker *piano* (1985), Helen Knief *viola* 1988 and Jane Webster *soprano* 1986. Subsequent recitals were held in the Wigmore Hall on 25th March 1991 (Anthony Marwood, 1984 *violin*); the 5th March 1993 (Gregory Walmsley, 1989 *cello* and Alison Baker, 1985 *piano*) and the 10th April 1995 (Zoë Mather, 1991 *piano* and Sarah Barnes, 1992 *cello*). Due to rising costs at the Wigmore Hall, it was decided to organise the next recital at the Purcell Room on London's South Bank on 2nd May 1997 (Rachel Barnes, 1994 *bassoon* and Siân Phillips, 1993 *violin*). It proved impossible to book the Purcell Room for 1997, and the recital was held in St James' Church, Piccadilly on 12th

Lessees: Westminster City Council

WIGMORE HALL

36 Wigmore Street, W.1   Manager: William Lyne, MBE

THREE
FIRST PRIZE
WINNERS

1985		1986	
ALISON BAKER		**JANE WEBSTER**	
(piano)		(soprano)	
'Les Adieux' Sonata	Beethoven	Music for a While	Purcell
Fantaisie F minor	Chopin	Under the Greenwood Tree	
		and Come Away Death	Arne
		Die Vogel	Schubert
1988		Das Verlassene Magdlein	Wolf
HELEN KNIEF		Dein Blaues Auge	Brahms
(viola)		Hat Gesagt	Strauss
		La Maja Dolorosa, La Maja de	
Sonata in E flat	Brahms	Goya, El Tra La La y	
Adagio	Kodaly	el Punteado	Granados
with WILLIAM HANCOX (piano)		'C' & Fetes Galantes	Poulenc
		with NICHOLAS BOSWORTH (piano)	

OF

THE
JOHN LILL
AWARDS

FOR THE ESSEX YOUNG MUSICIAN OF THE YEAR

PRESENTED BY ONGAR MUSIC CLUB

Monday 8th January 1990 at 7.30 pm

Tickets: £4; £5; £6; £7

All bookable in advance from Wigmore Hall Box Office 01-935 2141 and usual agencies. Postal applications should be accompanied by an s.a.e.
Box Office Hours Mon-Sat. 10am-8.30pm (days without concerts 10am-5pm). Sundays 45 minutes prior to performance. No advance bookings during half-hour prior to
performance. Telephone Bookings Mon-Sat. 10am-8.30pm. Credit Card Bookings Access, Visa, Amex, Diners.
No bookings after 6.30pm, or on Sundays, or from one hour prior to performance.

March (James Scannell, 1995 *clarinet/alto saxophone* and Joseph Tong, 1996 *piano*). Unfortunately, this venue was not felt to be so suitable for the club's purposes, and the next two recitals were held in St Giles' Church, Cripplegate. These were given on 17th March 2001 (Anthony Woollard, 1997 *cello* and Tammy Se, 1998 *violin*) and 14th May 2003 (Janey Miller, 2000 *oboe* and Clive Carroll, 1999 *guitar*).

The 'London' recitals reached the point when it was felt that the expense could not be justified. The audiences at venues other than the Wigmore Hall were essentially from Ongar or supporters of the artistes performing. In addition, there was no critical interest from newspapers or music magazines at these other venues. Although the Wigmore Hall was available and did have an appropriate following, it was felt to be not economically viable to return. The 14th May 2003 was, therefore, the last of these recitals to be held in London for competition winners.

The year 1990 had seen the start of an association with the Essex Chronicle Group. This followed an appeal by Barrie Hall on Essex Radio, resulting in a pledge to support the competition with the provision of £1,500 – this agreement being set out in a formal contract. An agreement had also been reached with Chelmsford Music Society that they would offer a recital to the winner of the competition though sadly, that agreement was not followed through. Also in 1990, discussions took place about the trophies. Mrs Matthews had been giving £100 per year towards the 'Matthews Prize' of £200 – the club making up the difference. Her contribution would cease following the 1990 competition, after which the name would also cease. Two smaller cups were also given in connection with the prizes. It was agreed that in the first instance, a more appropriate trophy be obtained for the first prize, and the Essex Chronicle offered to share the cost of this, engraved with the winner's name. Consideration was also given to a smaller cup being given to the winner as a permanent memento of their success when 'their year' had concluded. It was suggested that maybe the existing cups could be re-branded for other prizes.

This new arrangement with the Essex Chronicle Group was clearly advantageous to the competition, bringing a heightened level of publicity as well as funding. It had also facilitated the competition being held in the splendid surroundings of the Shire Hall.

For the first of those occasions, in 1993, and largely due to the competition's new and grand location, it was decided to revert to having both days of the competition across one weekend. This also facilitated keeping the whole competition in the same venue, which was clearly tidier, both for the domestic arrangements (such as piano hire) and also presentation and publicity. This arrangement continued until the 2006 competition when, for the same reasons as previously detailed relating to Saturdays, the competition reverted to being on two consecutive Sundays.

The competition had been highly successful in the Shire Hall, and the club was looking forward to repeating the venture in 1995. However,

St Giles' Church, Cripplegate, Barbican • Venue for the Essex Young Musician of the Year winners' recitals in 2001 and 2003

early in 1994, the club's chairman Jean Hall and treasurer John Harrop attended a meeting arranged by the then Managing Director and other officials of the Essex Chronicle Group, together with a representative of one of the Essex radio stations. At this meeting, they were presented with a memorandum regarding the future of the Essex Young Musician of the Year competition. This had clearly be prepared ahead of time and circulated to everyone except those from Ongar Music Club.

The document made various proposals, including that the management structure should change to one being based upon a charitable trust of around five members, with original trustees drawn from Ongar Music Club, Essex Chronicle Group and another Music Club in Essex – possibly Chelmsford or Southend – a further two trustees to be drawn from individuals with experience of working with young musicians. It was also suggested that a part-time organiser (paid an honorarium) would act as a clerk to the trustees, either from home or at the Essex Chronicle offices – that clerk to be accountable to the trustees for the overall coordination of the competition, based upon guidelines to be drawn up by the trustees. The clerk would liaise with appropriate organisations in relation to publicity, marketing, organisation of venues, adjudication panels and working with the candidates. Finally, the clerk would be responsible for developing a business plan for the competition ,which reflected the sources of income and trends of expenditure.

An immediate reply of 'yes' or 'no' was requested from the Music Club representatives. Not surprisingly, Jean Hall refused to give such a reply until the rest of the committee had been afforded the opportunity and courtesy of seeing this document. They would need to discuss it in detail to fully appreciate its implications.

Ahead of the next committee meeting, and not unexpectedly, the club's secretary Barrie Hall presented a detailed memorandum containing his own summary of the situation. In this, he felt that for the memorandum to be produced in this particular way rather suggested that someone wanted to take over the competition. Not surprisingly, he had his own ideas on who that might be. Barrie's conclusion from these events was that:

> The competition had prestige value and was, therefore, a great asset to the club, which should be retained at all costs. Having run unaided for seven of its eleven years, this simply meant that with the withdrawn sponsorship, the competition was simply going back to where it was in 1990.

At a meeting in early May, the Essex Chronicle Group's memorandum was discussed, and it was clear to everyone on the committee that the proposals in this document did indeed amount to a takeover bid for the club's competition. However, it was accepted that this was not necessarily by the ECG themselves as there were other interested parties who had also been active in supporting the competition with publicity in recent years. It was felt that the current funding situation should be secure for 1994/95 based on previous guarantees given to the chairman. Additionally, immediate registration of the competition's name was authorised with

Companies House at the cost of £50 – it appears that this didn't happen. The 'takeover' plan was therefore rejected, and an appropriate response was sent to the ECG.

By mid-June, further items of correspondence were exchanged, which included confirmation from the Essex Chronicle Group that funding for the 1994 competition was secure and that they would write further regarding funding for 1995 and the Wigmore Hall winners' recital. In the event, 1994 proved to be the last year of sponsorship from the Essex Chronicle Group and from that point, the competition was relocated to Ongar. It had been a productive four-year relationship which had facilitated a number of enhancements to the profile of the competition, but as Jean Hall tactfully said in her September newsletter to members:

> After four years of enormous generosity, they [ECG] have reviewed their sponsorship, as all large organisations do, and have decided to give it to some other worthy organisation.

Various new fundraising ideas were planned to help to make up the shortfall, and these included a new 'Friends of the Essex Young Musician' scheme by which those who covenanted £15 a year would have two free tickets for the competition final and also have their name in the programme. To further facilitate the competition, discussion took place that month (September 1994) about the frequency of the competition and also the prizes. It was again resolved to give 'serious consideration' to presenting the competition every two years (this was never implemented). It was also agreed that the number of eighteen-and-under prizes be increased to two. The entry fee was also to be increased to £20 (by 1994, it was £15). The competition would also return to the Adult Education Campus in Ongar, which was cheaper though (less glamorous) and also didn't involve piano hire, unlike the Shire Hall. It was also resolved that sponsors for individual prizes should be sought. Meanwhile, Geoffrey Timms was arranging for a new cup to be provided for the main prize, and there was general excitement that John Lill had indicated that he hoped to be present at the 1995 competition for which he would be invited to chair the panel of adjudicators.

The Chelmsford firm of James Dace & Son had supplied pianos for the competition when it was held in the Shire Hall and were keen to maintain an association with the competition. They indicated that they would continue to send out our flyers about the competition with their own mailings. In addition, they had previously offered £100-worth of vouchers to the competition, and this would be continued and be called 'The James Dace Prize' – being awarded as an eighteen-and-under prize. James Dace was also keen to offer a Bösendorfer grand piano for use in the competition (in Ongar) – free for 1995 only. This offer was declined because the club already had their Bechstein in place at the Adult Education Campus, which had been liked by many who had played it. As Barrie Hall observed in one of his wry and warmly-anticipated comments:

> Alison Baker [EYMY 1985] liked it and played well on it; any competitor who cannot, will not suddenly become a better performer for playing on the Bösendorfer [from James Dace & Son].

That same year the local MP, Eric Pickles, attended the competition and presented the prizes, by which time the money for the third and fourth

prizes had been guaranteed by external sponsorship. In fact, the level of commercial and private sponsorship for the competition had ensured that in 1995, there was no loss, despite fears following the withdrawal of support from the ECG.

It's interesting to remember one curious anecdote from the 1995 competition when a couple of competitors queried that they weren't given any food. It seems strange that there should be such expectations, and it was resolved that in future years it would be made clear to competitors that they would need to make their own culinary arrangements.

Efforts were frequently made to invite local dignitaries to the competition as this was felt to lift the occasion and also attracted a degree of press engagement. The then MEP, Hugh Kerr, attended the 1997 competition along with the chairman of the District Council, Ron Barnes. The 1997 competition was the last Ongar Music Club event to be held in the Adult Education Campus, which was to close for development. The competition,

EYMY 2009 finalists (l-r) Christopher Bearman, Matthew Lewis, Joanna Skillett *soprano* (winner) and Lindsey Isles • 5th July 2009 • Ongar

Matthew Lewis *trombone*, EYMY 2011 • 3rd July 2011

therefore, moved back to the Budworth Hall in Ongar, where it has remained.

As would be expected, sponsors have come and gone over the years. There were some regular sponsors such as Nortel, Ongar Sale Room, Raggett, Tiffen and Harries, and in 1999, Nicola Harries prevailed upon Barclay's Bank, which sponsored the first prize of £500. This was presented by John Lill, who had chaired the adjudication panel that year.

As noted elsewhere, with the end of 1990 had come the bombshell that Geoffrey Timms was planning to retire to North Wales in the following Spring, although he said that he would be willing to continue with the administration of the competition for as long as it was practical to do so. Eventually, he decided that the demands of life prevented him from continuing in the role of administrator, which was adopted by Jean Hall from the 1997 competition. She worked tirelessly and with remarkable enthusiasm until she, too, decided that it was time to hand over the responsibility. This she did following the 2008 competition when the role was adopted by Janet Pope, with whom I worked closely in preparing the necessary artwork – brochures, leaflets and programmes – as well as checking some of the musical aspects of the entries. Janet continued in this role until after the 2018 competition, at which point she felt that it was time to bow out. Although I had previously felt it impractical to take on this particular role due to the pressure of my own career, it seemed to be a natural process on this occasion, and therefore, at the time of writing, I am still the administrator, with the supporting roles being undertaken, as always, by the committee.

The 2019 competition saw something of an experiment with the competition's organisation, following the previous arrangement which had been adopted for some ten years. Mindful of costs, and also the difficulties experienced by some competitors in find an accompanying pianist who would be able to commit to two days, we decided to try holding the whole competition on just one day but starting mid-morning. The basic structure of the day worked very well, although we agreed that if we had a much larger entry, we would need to revert to a second day. The new club chairman Jane Webster decided to introduce a raffle as well as a lucky-number programme draw. We were very lucky that our president John Lill was able to join us.

Organising the competition is no mean task. Brochures are prepared and printed in January for distribution by early February, both by post as well as email, although this was just done by email in 2021. The competition also has a good presence on both Facebook and Twitter. Applications close on 31st May, following which begins the process of painstakingly

Finalists, Essex Young Musician of the Year 2018 • 1st July 2018 • Ballroom, Budworth Hall, Ongar
Vivien Wong piano, Alex Usher clarinet, Jamie Cochrane piano (winner), Ralph Thomas William counter-tenor, Rachel Bull cello

processing all the entries, validating them for all the various competition requirements, and ultimately producing a timetable for the preliminary round – negotiating along the way with problem times that might arise from the applicants. Finalists from the previous year have always been excused from the preliminary round as this seemed to be something of a formality. The competition administrator would update the committee about progress at its various meetings during the year, and also ask for any help which might be required. Other than that, the administrator has always had a degree of autonomy with the organisation of the competition, which otherwise would become cumbersome to run. On the competition days, a support team is organised to cover the duties of stewarding the competitors, ticket and programme sales, introducing the candidates, page-turning and looking after the adjudicators.

Ongar Music Club and the Essex Young Musician of the Year competition has always been exceedingly proud of its patron and close friend, John Lill, who has been unstinting in his support of the event and who has frequently joined the adjudication panel for the competition final – giving a great lift to the occasion. Many of the finalists have gone on to enjoy distinguished careers in the music profession. The very first winner was Anthony Marwood, a founder member of the Floristan Trio and a highly respected violinist.

In 2003, a young pianist of ten came before the panel who was still at primary school. His mother had rung the then administrator, Jean Hall, to say that he hadn't taken any graded exams, but he really wanted to enter. It had always been a recommendation that applicants would be of around Grade 8 standard, so Jean had some reservations. However, something told her that she should agree to the request, which she did, and he went on to win the competition – this was Benjamin Grosvenor, and he has developed a glittering international career. Many finalists have become members of major orchestras or ensembles. Others have excelled as solo singers or become members of international vocal ensembles such as The Kings Singers. A complete list of past finalists can be found in Appendix B.

Benjamin Grosvenor • Essex Young Musician of the Year 2003

One special feature of the main competition day has always been the tea between the semifinal and final rounds, which has been provided for the adjudicators along with the committee and their partners. For many years this was hosted by Anne Harries together with long term committee member Nicola Harries at her home in the High Street. This was quite a lavish affair which, for most years, was held outside on the lawn with a wonderful buffet. This was always the non-musical highlight of the day and greatly anticipated.

Although we were unable to run the competition in 2020 due to the COVID-19 pandemic, we did launch the event in 2021. There was a single preliminary round on 6th June followed by a final round on 4th July. By early July, many similar small-scale events were running live again with audiences, albeit in a controlled manner, and there were great hopes that the final would similarly be held live in Ongar. However, the trustees deemed it safest to run it online lest there be any concerns about safety. A big part of the ethos of the competition has always been to provide an opportunity for young musicians to have the experience of giving a performance in a concert hall to a live audience, and we trust that this will again be possible in 2022.

The club is hugely proud of the Essex Young Musician of the Year competition. Early in its history, the competition was attended by a representative of the Arts Council of Great Britain and ever since then, it has been included in their annual list of National Awards and Prizes. We hope that it will thrive for many years to come – supporting young Essex musicians with their hopes and musical aspirations.

Sarah-Jane Lewis, Essex Young Musician of the Year 2010, being award with her prize by chairman of the adjudicators, Neil Black • 4th July 2010

9. Young Music Makers

From very early days, Ongar Music Club was committed to providing special concerts specifically for young people. As with so many club ideas, this one came from founder-member Geoffrey Timms. Geoffrey's professional life had been spent in music education, and he was passionate about awakening young people to the power and delights of music. The first such concert was planned for 19th September 1976 and would involve Jean Hall *soprano* and Barrie Hall *piano & narrator* with Geoffrey Timms and myself playing the piano, and Colin Handley playing various brass instruments. There was also to be the showing of a filmstrip accompanying a recorded performance of one of the great children's stories, such as Peter and the Wolf. Ultimately, the performance took place on Sunday 28th November in the Arts Centre, with an audience of around 140, many asking for details of future concerts. This was to be the beginning of a tradition that would last for forty years and would

The first Children's Concert • 28th November 1976 • Arts Centre, Ongar • Performers: (c-r) Jean Hall, Colin Handley, Geoffrey Timms, Barrie Hall, Roderick Elms

indirectly be responsible for the launch of the Essex Young Musician of the Year competition. With such a clear marker of interest, it was decided to plan another such event for early 1977.

In fact, these concerts became an annual event, with many of them incorporating an art competition – the children bringing pieces of their artwork which would be judged by a local artist and prizes awarded. This pattern continued until 1985 when there came a low point, with a very small audience. These things can happen in the arts, as has been noted elsewhere, and for no obvious reason – circumstances simply conspire on a particular date. It had been decided to stop presenting these concerts, but something told Geoffrey to try again, with perhaps something of a twist. After all, the previous concerts had been remarkably successful and well attended. This new idea he tried in March 1986, but this time, not so much a performance for children but a performance *by* children – it was a great success and very well supported by parents and teachers alike.

In 1987 it was decided that due to the great success of this occasion, there would be additional concerts arranged for young people from the area. As well as the March concert, others would be held in late May/ June and November – the plan being that each of the concerts would have a different theme or instrumental bias, and there would also be extra encouragement to young performers with higher grades of ability who might be less confident in coming forward. Following a further concert in May, a children's concert was planned for 8th November, which would be the first of three planned for the 1987–1988 season. From this moment, these children's concerts were rebranded as Young Music Makers (YMM).

These concerts usually generated very large audiences, but the preparation required was significant. Not just in organising the performers but also liaising with teachers and planning the event. For many years, this was undertaken almost single-handedly by Geoffrey Timms, with a team helping with the all-important refreshments. These concerts were also quite a predictable source of income for the club, and at that time, the proceeds of the first YMM concert of the year were donated to a local charity. It was agreed that any surplus from the two subsequent concerts

The Butler family appearing at a Young Music Makers concert in 1997 • Amanda, Daniel, Stephen, Julia, Nigel, Jonathan & Katherine

in the year would be used to support the funding of the Essex Young Musician of the Year competition.

It was in June 1993 that Catherine Jennings first appeared on the committee as a guest, with a view to taking over the running of the Young Music Makers concerts. This was a result of Geoffrey Timms' announcement that he was moving to North Wales. Catherine has kindly provided some reminiscences:

> I first joined the committee in 1993 when I took over YMM from Geoffrey Timms. We were still at the Ongar Comprehensive School with the big hall and stage. We used to have children of all ages playing, though the older ones got progressively more nervous and sometimes dropped out. We had all different instruments, including piano duets. Many children played exam pieces as a practice run – I thought it was good for them to play in a concert without the exam pressure. I never thought I'd get enough to play, but at the very last minute I usually ended up with about twenty. I would contact their teachers well beforehand – some dropped out, and others dropped in, so I used to make up the program at the very last minute. They were each given a coloured badge with YMM. They used to collect different colours and pin them on their music bags! They had biscuits and orange in the interval. We later moved to the Budworth Hall where we were upstairs in the Concert Room. The children loved climbing up the surrounding balcony to watch, until health and safety arrived, and it was deemed too dangerous. My biggest group was Dr Butler and family – five kids and parents on various instruments (mum on the triangle). We did three concerts a year, and I worked out that I did around seventy over the years! We did have a few talented players. One singer went on to join Matthew Bourne's dance company!

In late 1998 the then chairman, Jean Hall, had lunch with representatives of the local Rotary Club at which they suggested a possible Rotary Club prize for under-19s be incorporated into the Essex Young Musician of the Year competition. They also made a proposal that their own Rotary young musician competition catchment area be extended to include Epping, as support had been poor from the local Ongar area. However, the committee foresaw numerous difficulties with this suggestion. It was therefore suggested to the Rotary Club that potential candidates could be asked to participate in the final Young Music Makers concert, which is only week before the main competition. It was thought that this could attract performers who might possibly find the major competition daunting. In addition, they would not have to pay the £25 entrance fee.

In early 1999 the Rotary had agreed to the club's proposal that their competition candidates be included in the final YMM concert, which, that season, was held on 20th June at 3:00pm. The judges were to be decided but would certainly include Catherine Jennings and John Harrop. The Rotary Club would send representatives, and it was agreed that it was up to the Rotary Club to get local teachers and schools to nominate entrants. This competition ran in this way, once a year for several years.

There was a disappointing entry for the Rotary Club competition held as part of the YMM event in May 2003. It was pointed out to the Rotary representative that Ongar no longer had a secondary school, and most

Catherine Jennings

young musicians from the Ongar area were going to school in Brentwood. They could therefore enter the Rotary competition elsewhere. However, it was decided to continue for now.

A little club history was made in December of that year when the YMM concert had to be cancelled due to many of the young competitors succumbing to the 'flu epidemic at the time. To go ahead was thought to be a 'step too far'. Fortunately the situation didn't repeat itself the following year, and there was a good entry in March 2004, although it was noted that many of the entrants had travelled quite a long distance.

The YMM concert in March 2005 recorded one of the highest audience levels in its history and an exceptionally high standard – this in stark contrast to the December occasion which had many problems of people arriving late or not turning up. The club had bought two new wooden music stands, which were inaugurated on this occasion and are still in regular use.

In December 2007, uncertainty arose concerning the Rotary Club competition in March. The Rotarians had previously expressed a desire that in 2008, entrants would only be accepted from Ongar and Epping. However, based on recent experience, the Music Club thought there would likely be none. It was subsequently agreed not to hold the Rotary competition in 2008, and the March performance was, in fact, very short – those performers present were very young, and almost all of them played the piano.

From around June 2010, it was becoming increasingly difficult to get a range of young performers, and it was agreed to hold just two concerts a year from then on. In 2013, for personal reasons, Catherine Jennings felt that she needed to step down, and another committee member, Carole Brown, took over the organisation with help from other committee members. Unfortunately, she too had to step down a year later for health reasons, and the organisation fell to another committee stalwart, Barbara Szymanek. By then, the concerts were becoming increasingly difficult to run, with a lack of young people able to take part. In the 2015–2016 season, there was just one performance, and for purely practical reasons, it was decided to discontinue the YMM events from the end of that season.

It was fairly clear that the steady decline in children coming forward to play was a direct result of fewer children being able to learn musical instruments at school. Local authority financial policies had resulted in savage cuts to the musical and instrumental provisions in schools. The direct result of those cuts being that so many young people lost the opportunity to discover the wonders of playing a musical instrument with its life-changing personal and social benefits. Who knows just how much talent was never discovered or allowed to grow to fruition. So frequently, the arts seem to be the first to lose support when challenges arise – this has been apparent in the current pandemic situation, with self-employed performers receiving very little acknowledgement. If only those in power had the perception and courage to realise the power of the arts, particularly music, on the human soul, and by extension, our everyday lives.

A number of the young people appearing in these children's and Young Music Makers concerts were destined to be very successful in their musical endeavours. Not least the viola player Helen Knief, who went on to become Essex Young Musician of the Year in 1988, and later, a member of the BBC Concert Orchestra.

A Young Music Makers concert from June 1999 • Concert Room, Budworth Hall, Ongar

10. Ongar Jazz Club

Jazz, and light-music in general, had featured occasionally in Music Club concerts since its early days when there had been a number of evenings which were not strictly classical in nature. These had included a Victorian evening and Old Time Music Hall events. With his own interest and performing experience in the field of light music, John Harrop had been keen on the idea of introducing some jazz events to the club's schedule (see chapter 5 for more detail regarding John Harrop's background). In early 1982, John brought this up for discussion. Although the membership of the club was very healthy, the committee agreed that some diversity of genre could only help to generate further interest and support in the club's activities. Also, any additional income would clearly be appreciated to support its activities.

John had mentioned the names of a few possible performers, including Dave Shepherd, one of the world's great jazz clarinettists who lived in Theydon Bois, relatively close to Ongar. It was discovered that his wife Mary worked at the Ongar Health Centre, so it was decided to make an informal approach to her with a view to her husband appearing for the club. The response was positive, and in April 1982, it was agreed that Geoffrey Timms would make formal contact with Dave Shepherd to arrange for him to play for the club. This he did in May of 1983, returning in many subsequent years – making a total of seven visits, the last being in 1989. This landmark concert by Dave Shepherd paved the way for appearances by other artistes in the years that followed. Eminent names from the world of jazz were frequently engaged for the Music Club's regular cabaret evenings, and the event on 2nd May 1986 was no exception, featuring the legendary Ronnie Scott and the Rainbow Dance Orchestra.

By April 1986, the committee had become aware of suggestions about the possible creation of a more formal jazz club in Ongar. This caused a degree of concern for the Music Club in respect of the impact on its own regular jazz evenings. There was also concern that there might be consequential effects on the Music Club's income, as the club's jazz evenings had been highly productive in supporting its more classical activities. Peter Lewis undertook to find out the intentions of the organisers and report back. Writing in the late nineties, Barrie Hall summarised the situation as follows:

> Peter [Lewis] reported [meeting, June 1986] regarding the proposed jazz club at the Budworth Hall. It would appear the be advantageous for the Music Club [and jazz group] to run parallel, having the same system for membership to the Music Club and Budworth Hall. A jazz date had been arranged for the 25th July 1986 [The Eastern All Stars]. The committee was all in agreement and wished the new venture every success. At a suggestion from Kenneth Bird, it was agreed that the Music Club should make a loan of £25 to cover expenses for the starting costs, advertising, etc. Also, if the jazz group should find themselves in difficulty regarding finances, they are to come to the Music Club who may be able to help. It was also agreed if money is held by the Music Club, a separate jazz club bank account should be opened.

Therefore discussions took place, and it was agreed that the new jazz club would be part of the Music Club. It would be known as the 'Jazz Section' and run as a non-profit-making organisation. The first formal concert was held on 25th July 1986 and featured an 'all star' lineup. This included such luminaries of the jazz world as Digby Fairweather *trumpet*, Dave Shepherd *saxophone* and Alistair Allan *trombone*. Alistair had been a pupil at Ongar Comprehensive School during the time that John Harrop was teaching science. He was to be involved in many subsequent

performances for Ongar Jazz Club. These visits frequently included the organisation of bands for many leading artistes, including the jazz club's president, Humphrey Lyttleton. Alistair was also involved in several evenings with bands organised by the great

Alistair Allan *trombone* (centre) with Humphrey Lyttleton *trumpet* and Martin Litton piano
June 1999 • Ballroom, Budworth Hall, Ongar

```
                        ONGAR  MUSIC  CLUB
                   President: Yehudi Menuhin K.B.E.
                          1982-83 SEASON
                       Friday 20th May 1983

                    THE DAVE SHEPHERD QUINTET

                   Dave Shepherd  (clarinet)
                   Roger Nobes    (vibes)
                   Brian Lemon    (piano)
                   Eddie Taylor   (drums)
                   Len Skeat      (bass)
```

DAVE SHEPHERD is, without doubt, the top jazz-influenced clarinettist in this country. Starting as he did at the age of 16 he found himself a broadcasting figure some two years later when, on joining the army, he quickly became part of a quartet formed by the British Forces Network. He spent two years with the quartet which broadcast programmes regularly from the B.F.N. station in Hamburg.

On leaving the services he played with many of the top professional bands in this country and continued his broadcasting career. He was also commissioned to make two LP records for the American market entitled "Tribute to Benny Goodman". As a result of these Dave Shepherd went to live in the States for a while working with many of the well-known musicians on the American Jazz scene.

Even after returning to England he continued to appear with American musicians and singers, notably Ella Fitzgerald. He led his own groups at home and abroad up to the present day. In the late 60's he toured in this country and abroad in company with Teddy Wilson, the original piano-playing member of the Benny Goodman Quartet. Dave represented Great Britain at the Montreux Jazz Festival in 1973.

He has made several other LP records including "Mr. Shepherd plays Mr. Goodman", "More Goodman Favourites", "Benny Goodman Classics", and there are also three albums with Teddy Wilson recorded at Montreux.

Renowned as a highly skilled musician who always gives an impeccable performance, Dave Shepherd collects around him musicians of similar outlook and ability, all of whom can boast of being 'professional' in every sense of the word.

jazz pianist Keith Nichols – Keith was from Ilford and local to where I lived for much of my life. They gave tribute concerts to both Bix Beiderbecke and Louis Armstrong, as well as presenting their special show, Jazz Classics Revisited. Also living in Ilford, and known to me, was the great jazz bass player, Len Skeat.

For many years the Jazz Club ran in this way as a partially separate entity, under the umbrella of Ongar Music Club. This new section had its own committee which reported to the Music Club committee, notably via Peter Lewis, who was involved in the Jazz Club from the very start and who served on both committees. Jean Hall served on the jazz section committee for a while as secretary and John Harrop as treasurer. This arrangement worked well for many years, with jazz evenings being presented every month over the six months from September – this later being increased to a nine-month period. In September 1986, Peter Lewis further reported:

```
                        JAZZ SECTION

Membership of Ongar Music Club now includes membership
of the newly-formed Jazz Section. As a result all
Music Club members are entitled to a 50p reduction on
the price of Jazz Section function tickets.

NEXT JAZZ SECTION FUNCTION


Friday, 2nd January 1987  (Budworth Hall  8.00 pm)

                  THE ALISTAIR ALLAN SEXTET
                     with guest soloist

            HUMPHREY LITTLETON

This should be a popular event.  Get your
tickets early.
```

... that the Jazz Club committee might contribute in some way to the organisation of the Music Club, perhaps by arranging the cabaret or our established jazz evening, or by introducing Jazz Club members to the Century Club.

From here on, the Music Club's finances increased steadily. At the 1987 AGM, John Harrop (treasurer) said that the last season's profits "have been considerably increased by Jazz Club and Century Club income". Peter Lewis reported on the Jazz Club at every committee meeting.

In April 1988, Peter reported that the March jazz concert had raised in excess of £1,000 for the Music Club's piano fund. He also reported that the Community Association was considering establishing a jazz section, looking into the possibility of holding regular Sunday afternoon jazz concerts. Peter Lewis stressed the undesirability of establishing a second source of regular jazz entertainment and suggested holding a "fair proportion of Music Club jazz events at the Budworth Hall to avoid any possible charge of ignoring the Community Association facilities".

In February 1989, Kenneth Bird wondered if the jazz committee was content with their current standing as part of the Music Club or whether they may wish to become independent. Peter reported that the current situation "is quite acceptable to the jazz committee and no splintering action is foreseen". Later that year, at the AGM, John Harrop explained that the Music Club would have ended the season on a shaky financial footing if the Jazz Club and Century Club had not produced such impressive takings. Barrie Hall continues:

> During 1990 we had a lot of problems with the bar. By now, the (comprehensive) school had closed, so both clubs met at the school for the 1990/91 and 1991/92 seasons. Due to the pressure of work, Peter Lewis left both committees in July 1991. For those two seasons, Ongar Jazz made big profits, lately because they got a licence and ran their own bar at the school. However, in 1992, they decided to return to the Budworth [Hall], preferring the atmosphere and being able to drown out the bar noise. We stayed at the school.

For many years the group operated under the name of the Jazz Section but, possibly aligned with the development of a new logo in 1995, it subsequently referred to itself as the Jazz Club. During the course of 1997, there had been ongoing meetings and discussions about aspects of the relationship between the Music Club and the Jazz Club. It had seemed to the Music Club that the Jazz Club wished to be autonomous yet remain part of Ongar Music Club. In many respects, that seemed to be a totally understandable position, as any such organisation is going to want to have control over its own activities, presentations and organisation. They had their own

Jazz Club president, Humphrey Lyttleton 'Humph' at the Lyric Theatre.

independent committee chaired by Howard Nicholson, and John Root had taken over as treasurer.

At the time, the Music Club had reserves of nearly £20,000. However, those reserves had been built up as a result of an enormous amount of hard work by both committees. As was noted at the time by the Music Club treasurer, John Harrop:

> It is quite possible that the present Jazz Club committee feels that they are subsidising us to quite a large extent. Barrie twice asked for television sets from members of his other club, the 'Television and Radio Industries'. Music Club members had been out selling tickets for the Grand Draw in the High Street. The Century Club and sponsorship have both taken a great deal of effort. OJC has benefitted from all these moneymaking activities organised by the Music Club. They charge more for their concerts, after costing them carefully, and usually are able to fill the hall, only rarely making a loss. I cannot see any reason why the funds shouldn't increase handsomely each year – to our mutual benefit.

Members of the Jazz Club were invited to join a special Music Club committee meeting at the Budworth Hall on 3rd February 1998 to discuss a request from 'Ongar Jazz' for day-to-day control of their finances. At the meeting, it was resolved that:

> ... Ongar Jazz Club should have day-to-day control over its financial affairs, including control over the Jazz Club Bank account, subject to the following conditions:
>
> 1. That regular statements are submitted to the Ongar Music Club treasurer.
>
> 2. An annual financial report is submitted to the Ongar Music Club treasurer for incorporation in Ongar Music Club's main accounts, which are audited and may be inspected by the Charity Commissioners.
>
> 3. Ongar Jazz Club's accounts are made available for inspection on request.
>
> These arrangements will come into effect for the financial year starting August 1998.

It was also agreed that a one-off capital sum of £5,000 would be transferred to the Ongar Jazz Club account, reflecting profits made since 1991. These arrangements were due to come into effect for the financial year starting August 1998. However, by June 1998, the Jazz Club was operating seemingly quite independently of the Music Club – planning its own events, social occasions and funding.

The Jazz Club was always a greatly valued and hugely successful part of the Music Club, and none of this history is in any way meant to suggest otherwise. I think this is just a natural result of two somewhat complementary organisations working independently, yet in some respects, together. From very early on, Ongar Music Club had always presented a number of evenings of a lighter nature. These were always very popular and generated a substantial income from ticket sales – supporting the more financially challenging classical concerts. It is a reality that the world of classical concert promotion is rarely self-supporting and relies on income from grants, sponsorship, advertising and other such sources. Ongar Music Club had always had a policy of trying to stand on its own two feet in so far as was possible, but clearly, certain aspects of its activities needed extra assistance.

For many years, the Jazz Club's president was the great jazz trumpeter Humphrey Lyttleton. Following his passing in 2008, the role was adopted by the legendary Digby Fairweather. Since 1986, Ongar Jazz Club has gained a formidable reputation and is one of the most respected jazz clubs in the country. Its list of star artistes reads like a 'Who's Who' of

The Frogg Island Jazz Band • 25th September 2020 • Budworth Hall, Ongar

the jazz world. It includes Kenny Ball, Acker Bilk, Maxine Daniels, Digby Fairweather, Cy Laurie, Humphrey Lyttleton, Keith Nichols, Ronnie Scott, Dave Shepherd, Monty Sunshine, Alex Walsh and Tommy Whittle.

Howard Nicholson has mentioned a memorable evening by Acker Bilk in January 1992 for which the great man had requested that a case of white wine be provided for the interval. This request was accommodated by the then chairman, Dr Geoffrey Tompkins, who had his own small vineyard. Apparently, Acker Bilk enjoyed the wine so much that he ordered and paid for a second case!

Since its inception, Ongar Jazz has made donations to various local and national organisations. A raffle has been held at their concerts that has provided the main revenue for these donations, which, between the years of 1998 and 2009, amounted to £19,845. Those supported include the National Jazz Archive, St Clare Hospice, St Francis Hospice, Budworth Hall, Comic Relief, Children in Need and Marie Curie.

Ongar Jazz Club is a story of great success and endeavour, in no short measure due to its hardworking committee and dedicated long-term chairman, Howard Nicholson. As with the Music club, the Jazz Club has been challenged by the events of 2020, although it did manage to start its new Budworth Hall season in September under strict domestic conditions. These included temperature checks, hand sanitising and distanced seating, either by the couple or singly. The guests on that occasion were The Frog Island Jazz Band which has an international reputation for its performances, reviving the spirit of 1920s and 1930s jazz. The band first visited Ongar Jazz Club in 1991, and three of the original 1962 members are still playing today.

I am indebted to Howard and Patti Nicholson, John Root and Alistair Allan for providing much valuable background information about the history and traditions of Ongar Jazz.

11. Committee Meetings

From the very start, committee meetings were held in the homes of committee members, on rotation – most usually on a Wednesday evening. Only 'extraordinary' or 'general' meetings would be held in a hall. Apart from being a rather more comfortable situation to conduct the club's business, this also eliminated the cost of hiring premises. Details of the venues were agreed upon at the start of the season and published to all members of the committee, together with (when Barrie Hall was secretary) very firm instructions to enter the dates into our diaries.

Until relatively recently, meetings were held monthly, with the exception of August, and the committee membership was very stable. Occasionally, during particularly busy periods, there would be two meetings in a month. Other meetings would be held by special sub-committees, such as for programme planning and those for the planning of special events. In writing this history, I have relied extensively on the minutes of committee meetings held between 1975 and 2015, which I inspected in the Essex Record Office, having been deposited there by the club for safe-keeping and without viewing restrictions. I have been struck by the great care taken by past secretaries, both in the content and in the presentation of the committee's decisions and actions, all clearly delineated and making it relatively straightforward to search for the required information. Had the minutes not been so painstakingly recorded and presented, my job would likely have been impossible.

Committee meetings during that period took on a consistent and traditional form which included the minutes of the previous meeting, and any matters and actions arising therefrom. The meeting would receive a treasurer's report and updates from other committee members about the progress or otherwise of their specific roles and duties. There would also be an assessment of the last recital and any conclusions drawn, not only about its musical success (or otherwise) but whether the artiste(s) might be invited back at a later date. The discussion would also consider any domestic aspects which might need addressing or improving for the future.

The meeting's agenda would include items detailing the progress of any special events such as the Essex Young Musician of the Year competition or social occasions – these might involve such crucial details as to who was to purchase the drinks and mince pies! The requirements for the next recital or event would be discussed, and these would include details of any particular layout necessary in the hall as well as any special lighting requirements. Piano tuning would also be arranged if required. Arrangements would be made as to who was organising the floral display at the front of the hall, as well as for the making of tea and coffee for the interval. Someone would be deputed to be on duty for ticket and programme sales, and occasionally, transport would be arranged when artistes needed collecting from the closest tube station (Epping). Many of the earlier concerts, and some of the later celebrity occasions, would also involve a post-concert party that needed to be planned.

A welcome highlight of each meeting was the provision of refreshment at its conclusion by the meeting's host. These would invariably include cake or other desserts, together with drinks as required. However, although regular committee meetings were conducted in comfortable, domestic surroundings, the meetings always proceeded in a totally business-like manner and occupied whatever time was required to deal with the agenda. Barrie Hall was remarkably effective (direct) when he felt a meeting might be heading off-course, and we would be dragged unceremoniously back to the matter in hand. Occasionally, when important issues needed to be discussed in depth, such as the concert venue situation of 1997, meetings could finish close to 11:00 pm – or even later.

Club Outings

Outings had been a regular aspect of the committee's agenda since the very first meeting – on that occasion to plan a visit to the Royal Festival Hall for a performance of Mozart piano concerti on 21st February 1975. The English Chamber Orchestra having been directed from the piano by Daniel Barenboim. This outing came before the club formally launched its own live concert performances later that year. Following that occasion, visits were regularly planned to a wide variety of productions. Many of these were in London and included recitals, orchestral concerts and operas. In the late 70s, there was something of a lull in concert outings, likely due to the degree of new concert activity in Ongar, much of which required a good deal of preparation, such as the recitals by Lord Menuhin and other large-scale events. Also, there needed to be someone on the committee with specific responsibility for organising the outings, and this was taken on by the irrepressible Arthur Pittock, who launched himself into the role with great gusto following his co-option onto the committee in October 1983.

Opera was to become a big feature of these club outings, and the first such occasion arose in January 1988 when a visit was planned to the London Coliseum to see a performance of Strauss' Der Rosenkavalier. Jean Hall made the excellent suggestion of an introductory evening ahead of the visit, in order to introduce the opera to those attending. Later that year, Arthur Pittock stood down from his role of organising outings, in which he had been quite remarkable. There is a considerable amount of work in planning such occasions, especially when you consider that in 1986 there were five outings, and four in 1987.

Jean Hall took over this task from the 1988–1989 season, and in October 1988, she made the suggestion of a trip to Glyndebourne. Set in wonderfully landscaped grounds near Lewes in East Sussex, this opera

Glyndebourne Opera House, East Sussex

house was once a country house. Since 1934, it has been home to this world-famous company which has a performance season during the early summer. Glyndebourne has been in the Christie family since its inception, and it was George Christie who, in 1966, decided to make their performances available to wider audiences by forming Glyndebourne Touring Opera – this started two years later. This company took performances around the country to local theatres, as well as giving performances in the opera house itself during the autumn – it was these latter performances that the club attended.

In 1989, the club made an outing to the annual Glyndebourne Prom at the Royal Albert Hall, in which one of the season's operas would be presented in a concert situation as part of the famous Henry Wood Promenade Concert seasons. Thereafter, there was an annual trip to East Sussex as well as a few other select concerts such as the Young Musician of the Year winner's recital in London. These outings invariably involved a coach leaving from Ongar, and there was a memorable occasion in 1996 when the coach didn't arrive in time, resulting in many people deciding to attempt the journey by car, becoming entwined in horrendous traffic and arriving very late – others simply gave up. Fortunately, due to great persistence and diplomacy on Nicola Harries' part, agreement and recompense were eventually agreed with the coach company.

There was a very special outing in 2011 when members travelled to the Royal Albert Hall to hear Benjamin Grosvenor play Liszt's second piano concerto with the BBC Symphony Orchestra at the 'First Night of the Proms'.

Nicola had taken over the organisation of the annual Glyndebourne trip in 2008 when it became difficult for Jean Hall to continue. Unfortunately, as the years went by, the age of those attending increased, and returning to Ongar in the early hours of the morning became less attractive. The outings had started with a full-size coach, but in later years, the coach size gradually reduced as interest waned. Nicola continued to organise these visits until the 2013 outing to a performance of Donizetti's *L'Elisir d'Amour*, which was the last visit to be made – at least for the time being.

Epilogue

There have been many changes in the Ongar area since 1975, but sadly, these didn't include the club's core audience. As people grew older, they were more reluctant to venture out at night. It was clear that a new approach and new management was needed if the club was to survive. Since 2019, the club has seen a number of significant changes in leadership and committee structure and its style of operation and concert presentation. For example, the 'Soundbites!' afternoon tea concerts proved to be very successful with the existing demographic until the arrival of the pandemic, which naturally provided further challenges to the organisation.

With these challenges came new opportunities to broaden the club's support by way of online-based musical events, giving the club another approach to its activities and widening its audience, though maybe slightly diluting the direct Ongar connection. These events have been greatly appreciated by the members and others, having music brought into their homes in difficult times, raising spirits and keeping them in touch with Ongar Music Club.

I'm sure that the club will focus on ways to develop opportunities for concert-giving with a return to live performance, post-covid – maybe alongside the existing online events. Possibly some live concerts could be streamed on the internet, offering a provision for those unable to attend concerts in person.

As shown by the club's founding fathers in 1975, music-making can hold a very special place in the heart of a community. However, it's crucial to find new avenues to explore and new ways to entice people into sharing the live concert experience with a changing demographic.

Appendix – A

ONGAR MUSIC CLUB CONCERTS

1975-76 SEASON

15th October • GSS
David Jewel *flute*, Hilary Jones *cello* and
Geoffrey Timms *piano*

19th November • AC
Quiz: Ladies vs Gentlemen followed by a Wine and
Cheese Party

17th December • GSS
Roderick Elms *piano*

14th January • GSS
Music Boxes: Bruce Moss

18th February • GSS
Keith Gurry *violin* and Margaret Kirby *piano*

14th April • AC
Barrie Hall: BBC Speaker (talk about Proms)

19th May • SMC
Choral Concert: Edna Graham *soprano*,
Frances Robinson *mezzo-soprano*
John Manuel *tenor*, Ivor Chapman *bass*,
The Aurelian Ensemble
Roderick Elms *organ continuo*,The Beal School Choir,
Geoffrey Timms *conductor*

18th June
South Bank Opera: Maureen Lake *piano*,
Tony Edwards *presenter*

9th July
Wine and Cheese Evening

1976-77 SEASON

22nd October • OCS
Antony Hopkins: Music in Question (BBC broadcast)

17th November • AC
Frances Robinson *mezzo soprano*, Charles Church *piano*

28th November • AC
Children's Concert: Jean Hall *soprano*, Barrie Hall *piano*
& *narrator*, Roderick Elms *piano*, Geoffrey Timms *piano*,
Colin Handley *brass*

17th December
Richard Deering*: Liszt – The Composer for Today lecture
recital*

21st January
Old Time Music Hall

18th February • BH
The Quintus Wind Ensemble: Penelope Feather *piano*
and flute, Jennifer Hall *oboe*, Jonathan Tribe *clarinet*,
Hilary Bailey *bassoon*, Uwe Radok *horn*

18th March
Keith Gurry *violin*, David Silkoff *piano*

3rd April • GSS
Rhondda Gillespie *piano* (Inauguration of the
Weber concert grand piano)

22nd April
Music Boxes: Bruce Moss

14th May • OCS
Orchestral Concert: 'Jubilee Concert'

24th June • BH
The Capella Group with Ann McLoughlin and
Olga Bennett

8th July • BH
Quiz

1977-78 SEASON

9th September • BH
David Silkoff *piano* (AGM)

7th October • OCS
Richard Baker

23th October • BH
Katharina Wolpa *piano* (for the club's piano fund)

11th November • BH
Gerald Tolan *guitar*

16th December • BH
Victorian Evening

13th January • BH
Allan Schiller *piano*

10th February • BH
Olde Thyme Music Hall

5th March • FBS
Children's Concert: George Lawrence *percussion*,
Helen Knief *viola and piano*, Ruth Turner *flute*

10th March
Charles Fox: jazz broadcaster/critic

18th March
Keith Gurry *violin*, David Silkoff *piano*

14th April • SMC
The Bochmann String Quartet: Michael Bochmann *violin*,
David Angel *violin*, Gustav Clarkson *viola*,
Sebastian Comberti *cello*

22nd April
Music Boxes

12th May • BH
Felix Aprahamian: talk on Beecham

8th June • OCS
Yehudi Menuhin and Pupils from the Menuhin School

1978-79 SEASON

15th September
David Silkoff *piano* (AGM)

27th October • OCS
Stephen Bishop-Kovacevich *piano*

17th November • BH
Cambiano Trio: Lucy Cartilage *flute*, Sophie Cartilage
harp, Nicholas Hooper *guitar*.
These artistes also gave a children's concert in the
afternoon at Ongar Primary School.

8th December
Fritz Spiegl, talk

14th January
Jean Woolhead *piano*

26th January • BH
Jane Manning *soprano*, Richard Rodney Bennett *piano*

16th March • BH
Melissa Phelps *cello*, John York *piano*

14th March
Old Time Music Hall

27th April • BH
The Quintus Wind Ensemble: Penelope Feather *piano and flute*, Jennifer Hall *oboe*, Jonathan Tribe *clarinet*, Hilary Bailey *bassoon*, Uwe Radok *horn*

11th May
Denis Matthews *piano*

15th June
Eric Fenby

30th June • SMC
The Aurelian Ensemble, leader Gerry Bates, conducted by Geoffrey Timms with Jonathan Small *oboe*

6th July
Musical Quiz and End-of-Season Social Evening

1979-80 SEASON

14th September • BH
Roderick Elms *piano* (AGM)

12th October • BH
Allan Schiller *piano* – Chopin

16th November • BH
James Blades *percussion*, Geoffrey Timms *piano*

20th January • BH
Children's Concert with Colin Handley *brass instruments*

1st February • BH
Steven Isserlis, *cello* Peter Evans *piano*

22nd February
College Opera Society: Olde Tyme Music Hall

21st March
Jack Brymer *clarinet* and John Harrop *piano*

18th April
Cormac Rigby: 'Ballet for Me'

9th May • SMC
Handel's Messiah: Beal School Choir and Orchestra conductor Geoffrey Timms
Ruth Saye *soprano*, Jean Hall *contralto*, Robert Muskett *tenor*, John Manuel *bass*

20th June
David Silkoff *piano*

4th July
Music Quiz with Cheese & Wine

1980-81 SEASON

19th September
Roderick Elms *piano* (AGM)

3rd October
Denis Matthews *piano*

31st October • OCS
An evening with Peter Pears – in association with Midland Bank celebrating ten years of service to Ongar

21st November
Avril Wood: talk by the daughter of Sir Henry Wood

12th December
Ongar Singers Christmas Concert with Jean Hall *mezzo-soprano* and Geoffrey Timms *piano*

18th January
Children's Concert with Music Wind Quintet

23rd January • BH
Keith Gurry *violin* Harold Lester *piano*

13th February • BH
Harlow Opera Company: An evening with Gilbert and Sullivan

20th March • BH
Roland Gallery *guitar*

10th April
Eric Shilling *baritone*, John Harrop *piano*, lecture recital

22nd May
Hanson String Quartet (Martin Loveday - cello)

12th June • BH
Katharine Wolpe *piano*

3rd July
Music Quiz with cheese & Wine

1981-82 SEASON

18th September
Eileen Broster *piano* (AGM)

23rd October
Anthony Hopkins: 'Music I Like'

20th November • BH
Graham Trew *baritone*, John Harrop *piano*

18th December
The Spirit of Christmas: Ongar Singers, Castle Players

29th January
David Ward: 'My Dearest Friend' Haydn and Mozart

7th February • BH
Children's Concert with 'The Gnaff Ensemble'

26th February • BH
Harry Mortimer OBE 'Man of Brass'

4th April • OCS
Harlow Symphony Orchestra, John Harrop *piano*

7th May • BH
Richard Kirkland *violin*, Geoffrey Timms *piano*

4th June • BH
Valerie Tryon *piano*

2nd July
Chairman's Quiz and Club Party with Cheese & Wine

1982-83 SEASON

17th September • BH
The Blue Birds: Jean Woolhead and her quartet of singers (AGM)

29th October
Graham Whettam: 'The Composer Speaks' Geraldine Allen *clarinet*, Andrew Whettam *percussion*

26th November
Eileen Broster *piano*

17th December • BH
Twelve Days: Music and Readings for Christmas,
The Ongar Singers, The Castle Players

28th January • BH
Barrie Hall: The Proms and the Man who Wrote it

29th January • BH
David Ward

6th February
Children's Concert with George Lawrence *percussion*

18th February • BH
Christopher Ackland *guitar*

18th March • BH
Meet the Marwoods: The Marwood Ensemble

22nd April • BH
An evening with Dame Eva Turner

20th May • BH
The Dave Shepherd Quintet

17th June • BH
Four Hands: Denis Matthews and Brenda McDermott
piano duet

8th July • BH
Chairman's Quiz with 'The Gnaff Ensemble'

1983-84 SEASON

30th September
Roderick Elms *piano* (AGM)

28th October
Eileen Broster *piano*

25th November • BH
Susan Baker: 'Violins, fiddles and follies',
Anthony Saunders *keyboards*

16th December
Christmas Cheer: The Castle Players and The Ongar
Singers, David Clegg (Chorister of the Year)

27th January • OCS
RAM Sinfonia with Nigel Hill *piano*, Lawrence Leonard
conductor – Mozart anniversary concert

12th February
Children's Concert: 'The Gnaff Ensemble'

24th February
Geoffrey Pogson *tenor*, Helen Robertson-Barker *piano*

23rd March • BH
Rainbow Dance Orchestra, Cabaret and Supper

27th April
William Grandison *guitar*

12th May • OCS
John Lill *piano*: Mozart, Beethoven, Chopin, Liszt

1st June • BH
The Jack Freestone Event: 'The Great Artists of
Post War Years'

22nd June • BH
Peter Wallfisch *piano*

20th July • BH
Essex Young Musician of the Year 1984

1984-85 SEASON

28th September
Three Competition prizewinners (AGM)

26th October
Allan Schiller *piano*

23rd November
Virginia Black *harpsichord*

21st December • BH
Carol Concert: Choir and Orchestra of Beal High School

25th January • OCS
David Abbott *flute*, Alvin Moisey *piano*

22nd February • BH
The Marwood Ensemble

1st March • BH
Anthony Marwood *violin*, Timothy Carey *piano*

10th March • BH
Children's Concert

19th April • BH
Dave Shepherd: Jazz Evening

3rd May • BH
Cabaret Evening with Tommy Whittle with fish and chip
supper

17th May • BH
Keith Gurry *violin*, David Silkoff *piano*

7th June • BH
Valerie Tryon *piano*

6th July • BH
Essex Young Musician of the Year Competition 1985

1985-86 SEASON

27th September • BH
Jane Webster *soprano*, Paul Turner *piano* (AGM)

25th October • BH
The Fairer Sax, Saxophone Quartet

22nd November • BH
Eileen Broster *piano*

29th November • BH
Dave Shepherd, Jazz Evening

13th December • BH
Christmas Concert, Chorister of the Year,
Stondon Singers

24th January • BH
Alison Baker *piano* • Essex Young Musician of the Year
1985

21st February • BH
The Troubadours

7th March • BH
How to Make a Violin: Edwin Dodd *violin* Demonstration
and Recital

16th March • BH
The Young Musicians of Ongar

11th April • BH
Alan Brown *piano*

2nd May • BH
Cabaret Evening with Ronnie Scott and Rainbow
Ballroom Orchestra

23rd May
Parnassus Ensemble

20th June
Alan Brind *violin* BBC Young Musician,
Elizabeth Burley *piano*

13th July
Essex Young Musician of the Year Competition 1986

25th July
The Eastern All Stars, Jazz Evening. First Concert of the newly formed Jazz Club #

1986-87 SEASON

26th September
Alvin Moisey *piano* (AGM)

17th October • BH
The Dussek Ensemble, led by Keith Gurry

21st November • BH
An evening with John Amis

5th December • BH
The Dave Shepherd Quintet #

19th December • BH
Stondon Singers Christmas Concert with Daniel Ludford-Thomas, Chorister of the Year

2nd January • BH
Jazz Concert #

23rd January • BH
Timothy Carey *piano*

13th February • BH
Jane Pembleton *flute*, and Fenella Haworth *piano*, Helen Knief *viola* and Daniel Schrôyens *piano*

13th March • BH
John Walsh Ensemble: members of the BBC Symphony Orchestra

22nd March • BH
The Young Musicians of Ongar

27th March • BH
Blue Magnolia, Jazz Evening #

10th April • BH
Denis Matthews: Mozart's Piano Concertos

8th May • BH
Cabaret, Rainbow Dance Orchestra Cabaret, Keith Nicholls *piano*

22nd May • BH
Jane Webster *soprano*, Nicholas Bosworth *piano*

31st May • BH
Children's Concert

19th June • BH
Peter Wallfisch *piano*

5th July • BH
Essex Young Musician of the Year Competition 1987

1987-88 SEASON

25th September • BH
Peter Sheppard *violin*, Rupert Burleigh *piano* (AGM)

23rd October • BH
Richard Baker: 'Music in my Life'

8th November • BH
The Young Musicians of Ongar

20th November • BH
Alison Baker *piano*

4th December • BH
Dave Shepherd Quintet: Jazz Evening

18th December • BH
Stondon Singers Christmas Concert with Adrian Philips - BET Choirboy of the Year

2nd January • BH
The Alistair Allan Sextet with Humphrey Littleton #

29th January • BH
The Quentin Poole Oboe Quartet with Miranda Fulleylove *violin*

19th February • BH
Pauline Dowse *cello* • Essex Young Musician of the Year 1987 with Simon Smith *piano*

18th March • BH
Humphrey Burton: 'Looking Back in Harmony'

20th March • BH
Young Music Makers (previously 'Children's Concert')

25th March • BH
Jazz Concert #

15th April
Colin Bradbury *clarinet*, Oliver Davies *piano* 'The Edwardian Clarinetist'

6th May
Cabaret with the Rainbow Dance Orchestra

20th May • BH
Parnassus String Ensemble

17th June
Alvin Moisey *piano*

10th July
Essex Young Musician of the Year Competition 1988

1988-89 SEASON

30th September • BH
Larissa Joy *clarinet*, James Vickers *piano* (AGM)

7th October • BH
Digby Fairweather, Jazz Concert #

21st October • BH
Anthony Hopkins: 'Beethoven – A Personal View'

30th October • BH
Young Music Makers 1

18th November • BH
David Silkoff *piano*

2nd December • BH
Dave Shepherd: Jazz Evening

16th December • BH
Christmas Concert: Allegro Singers with Sarah Ryan - BBC Choirgirl 1988

20th January • BH
Keith Nichols and Alan Elsdon, Jazz Evening #

27th January
The Troubadours: 'Music for Feasting and Brawling'

17th February • BH
Helen Knief *viola* • Essex Young Musician of the Year 1988, William Hancox *piano*

24th February • BH
College Operatic Society: Music Hall

5th March • BH
Young Music Makers 2

17th March • BH
Virginia Black *harpsichord*, Howard Davies *violin*

3rd March
Cy Laurie. Jazz Evening #

31st March • GSS
John Lill *piano:* Beethoven, Prokofiev, Chopin .

7th April • BH
Jane Webster *soprano*, Nicholas Bosworth *piano*

5th May • BH
Cabaret: Rainbow Dance Orchestra

19th May • BH
Alan Brown *piano*

4th June • BH
Young Music Makers 3

16th June • BH
Arthur Jacobs: 'Forty Years an Opera Critic'

7th July • BH
Kenny Ball: Jazz Evening #

9th July • BH
Essex Young Musician of the Year Competition 1989

1989-90 SEASON

22nd September • BH
Lucy Parham *piano* (AGM)

29th September • BH
Many Sunshine: Jazz Evening #

15th October • BH
Young Musician Makers 1

3rd November • BH
The Marwood Ensemble

17th November • BH
An evening with Dame Janet Baker

1st December • BH
Dave Shepherd, Jazz Evening

22nd December • BH
Allegro Singers' Christmas Concert

5th January • BH
Humphrey Lyttleton Jazz Evening #

8th January • Wigmore Hall
Alison Baker *piano* • Essex Young Musician of the Year 1985
Helen Knief *viola* • Essex Young Musician of the Year 1988 with William Hancox *piano*
Jane webster *soprano* • Essex Young Musician of the Year 1986 with Nicholas Bosworth *piano*

26th January
An Evening with Annetta Hoffnung

16th February
Allan Schiller *piano*

2nd March • BH
Terry Lightfoot: Jazz Evening #

4th March • BH
Young Music Makers 2

16th March • BH
Michael Berkeley: 'Mainly for Pleasure'

6th April • BH
An Evening with Brian Priestman

4th May • BH
Cabaret, Jane Webster *soprano*, Nicholas Bosworth *piano*

18th May • BH
Gregory Walmsley *cello* • Essex Young Musician of the Year 1989 with Jessica Butters *piano*

3rd June • BH
Young Music Makers 3

22nd June • BH
Alison Baker *piano*

8th July • BH
Essex Young Musician of the Year Competition 1990

1990-91 SEASON

28th September • OCS
Graham Trew *baritone*, John Harrop *piano* (AGM)

6th October
Blue Magnolia, Jazz Evening #

21st October
Young Music Makers 1

26th October
Fritz Spiegl: 'Mainly for Pleasure'

16th November • OCS
Trevor Wye *flute*, Robert Scott *piano*

30th November •OCS
Dave Shepherd Quintet: Jazz Evening #

21st December • OCS
Helios Singers and Brass Ensemble: Christmas Concert with Duncan Watts - BEF Choirboy of the Year

25th January • OCS
Nikos Zarb *viola* • Essex Young Musician of the Year 1990 with Andrew Rapp *piano*

22nd February • OCS
Andrew Marwood *violin*, William Howard *piano*

3rd March
Young Music Makers 2

15th March • OCS
John Lill *piano:* Mozart, Beethoven, Chopin, Prokofiev

25th March • Wigmore Hall
Anthony Marwood violin • Essex Young Musician of the Year 1984 with William Howard *piano*

16th April • OCS
Miami String Quartet: 4th prizewinners in the London International String Quartet Competition

10th May
Steve Lane's Famous Red Hot Peppers #

2nd June
Young Music Makers 3

21st June
Lucy Parham *piano*

28th June
Digby Fairweather: Jazz Evening #

13th July • SHC
Essex Young Musician of the Year Competition 1991

1991-92 SEASON

27th September
Daisy Jopling *violin*, Charles Mutter *piano* (AGM)

13th October
Young Music Makers 1

18th October • OCS
Alvin Moisey *piano*

22nd November • OCS
Sherherazade: Denise Dance *flute*, Veronica Chard
soprano, Fiona Clifton-Walker *harp*

20th December • OCS
Helios Singers and Brass Ensemble Christmas Concert
with James Elliott - BEF Choirboy of the Year
and Fyfield Handbell Ringers

10th January • OCS
Acker Bilk, Jazz Evening #

31st January • OCS
Claire and Antoinette Cann *piano duet*

14th February • OCS
Duncan Prescott *clarinet*, Scott Mitchell *piano*

22nd February
Essex Schools Musician of the Year

1st March
Young Music Makers 2

13th March • OCS
Alberni String Quartet

3rd April • OCS
Zoë Mather *piano* Essex • Young Musician of the Year 1991

15th May • OCS
Alison Buchanan *soprano* Maggie Teyte Prizewinner,
Eugene Asti *piano*

17th May
Young Music Makers 3

12th June • OCS
Jessica Butters *piano*

11th July • SHC
Essex Young Musician of the Year Competition 1992

1992-93 SEASON

2nd October • AEC
Emily Sheldrake *violin*, Geoffrey Timms *piano* (AGM)

11th October
Young Music Makers 1

16th October • BH
Tom Collins Jazz Band #

23rd October • AEC
Angela Lear *piano*

20th November
Dr. Mary Remnant: Medieval Minstrels and Instruments

27th November • BH
Monty Sunshine's Jazz Band #

18th December • OCS
Stondon Singers Christmas Concert with
Stephen Kay *piano*, Gavin Moralee - RCM Choirboy of
the Year and Fyfield Handbell Ringers

15th January
Alistair Allan and The Cotton Club Band #

29th January • OCS
Michael Broadway *pianola*

12th February • AEC
Sarah Barnes *cello* • Essex Young Musician of the Year
1992, Russell Lomas *piano*

20th February
Essex Schools Musician of the Year 1993

26th February • BH
Dave Shepherd and his Sextet #

5th March • Wigmore Hall
Gregory Bennett Walmsley *cello* • Essex Young Musician
of the Year 1989 with Anna Guijarro *piano*
Alison Baker *piano* Essex Young Musician of the Year 1985

7th March
Young Music Makers 2

26th March • OCS
Kerrie Alison *piano*

16th April • BH
Mike Daniels Delta Jazzmen #

30th April
Jane Webster *soprano*, Steven Naylor *piano* • OCS

16th May
Young Music Makers 3

28th May • OCS
Saxology: Saxophone quartet with Jeffery Wilson

18th June • OCS
The George Thorby Orchestra #

27th June •SHC
Essex Young Musician of the Year Competition 1993

1993-94 SEASON

1st October • OCS
Fiona Russell *recorders*, John Harrop *piano* (AGM)

10th October
Young Music Makers 1

22nd October
Antony Hopkins: 'Mozart, a Personal View'

29th October • BH
The Frog Island Jazz Band #

19th November
The Nadin Trio Comp *piano, cello, clarinet*

3rd December • BH
The Cotton Club Orchestra #

17th December
Stondon Singers Christmas Concert with
Stephen King *piano*, Gavin Moralee *treble*

7th January • BH
Terry Lightfoot and his Band, with Maxine Daniels #

28th January • AEC
William Hancox: Lecture/Recital on Mussorgsky's
'Pictures at an Exhibition'

18th February • OCS
Daniella Ganeva *marimba*, Graham Instrall *percussion*

6th March
Young Music Makers 2

18th March • BH
Digby Fairweather and the Superkings #

19th March
Essex Schools Musician of the Year 1994

25th March • OCS
Ian Watson *button accordion*

12th April • OCS
'Danel String Quartet' • 3rd prizewinners in the London
International String Quartet Competition

15th April
Hot Stuff #

13th May • OCS
New Edition: 'Harlow Opera Resurrected'
Gilbert & Sullivan

15th May
Young Music Makers 3

20th May
Cambridge City Jazz Band #

26th June • SHC
Essex Young Musician of the Year Competition 1994

1994-95 SEASON

23rd September • OCS
Kerry Sugden *piano*, Twig Hall *soprano*,
William Hancox *piano* (AGM)

21st October • OCS
Alison Baker *piano*

28th October • BH
Ken Collyer Trust Band #

20th November
Young Music Makers 1

25th November • OCS
Susan Blair *harp*

2nd December • BH
Maxine Daniels with the Ted Beamish Trio #

16th December • OCS
Stondon Singers Christmas Concert with Stephen King
piano, Michael Stokes *treble*

6th January • BH
Dave Shepherd Quintet #

14th January • OCS
Essex Chamber Orchestra, Simon Thompson *conductor*,
Siân Phillips *violin*

17th February • BH
Martin Litton's Red Hot Peppers#

24th February • OCS
Rachel Barnes *Bassoon* • Essex Young Musician of the
Year *1994*, Costas Fotopoulos *piano*

5th March
Young Music Makers 2

24th March • BH
Sonny See All-Stars #

31st March • OCS
Hugh Bean *violin*, Shelagh Sutherland *piano*

10th April 1995 • Wigmore Hall
Zoë Mather *piano* • Essex Young Musician of the Year 1991
Sarah Barnes *cello* • Essex Young Musician of the Year
1992 with Vanessa Perez *piano*

21st April • OCS
Pennyroyal: 'The Castle Walls'

12th May • BH
John Petters 'Boogie Woogie and All That Jazz' #

14th May
Young Music Makers 3

19th May • OCS
Alvin Moisey and Andrew Zolinsky *pianos:* Four Hands -
One Orchestra

25th June • AEC
Essex Young Musician of the Year Competition 1995

1995-96 SEASON

29th September • AEC
Edward Bale *violin*, Philippa Bale *piano* (AGM)

20th October • OCS
Duo Sevillanas – Hilary Palmer *oboe*,
Andrew Marlow *guitar*

22nd October
Young Music Makers 1 (opening event of the Ongar
Festival)

27th October • BH
The Original East Side Stompers #

17th November
The City Waites (presented as part of the Ongar Festival)

24th November • BH
Cotton Club Band #

15th December • OCS
Christmas Concert with the Salvation Army Romford
Citadel Band, Decorum, Edward Barrett *treble*

5th January • BH
The Monty Sunshine Band #

26th January • OCS
Paperhaus Duo: Barnaby Robson *clarinet*,
David Wickham *piano*

9th February • BH
Merseysippi Jazz Band #

23rd February • OCS
Robin Colvill *piano*, Kim Colvill *narrator:*
'Chopin's Last Tour'

15th March • BH
Riverside Jazz Band with Pam Coster #

3rd March
Young Music Makers 2

22nd March • OCS
James Scannell *saxophone* and *clarinet*, Ian Lake *piano*

19th April • OCS
Polished Brass

10th May • OCS
Tenth Season Celebration Evening #

12th May
Young Music Makers 3

31st May • OCS
Grange Piano Trio

30th June
Essex Young Musician of the Year Competition 1996

1996-97 SEASON

20th September • OCS
Alisdair Hogarth *piano* (AGM)

4th October • OCS
Barrie Hall, talking about the Proms

18th October • BH
Monty Sunshine and his Band #

25th October • OCS
The Eight Voices of Decorum: vocal octet

1st November • BH
Louis Lince's New Orleans Band #

16th November
Young Music Makers 1

22nd November • OCS
Felicity Vincent *cello*, Anthony Saunders *piano*

6th December • BH
Marilyn Middleton-Pollock with
Steve Mellor's Chicago Hoods #

20th December • OCS
Christmas Concert with the Salvation Army Romford
Citadel Band, Times and Seasons, Edward Barrett *treble*

18th January • OCS
Essex Chamber Orchestra: Simon Thompson *conductor*,
Sue Eversden *bassoon*

7th February • BH
Papa Joe's All Stars #

28th February • OCS
Patrizia Meier *harp*

3rd March
Young Music Makers 2

7th March • BH
Dave Shepherd Quintet #

21st March • OCS
Shelagh Sutherland *piano*

15th April • OCS
Belcea String Quartet, 3rd prizewiners in the London
International String Quartet Competition

18th April • BH
The President's Evening with Digby Fairweather #

2nd May • Purcell Room
Rachel Barnes *bassoon* • Essex Young Musician of the
Year 1994 with Steve Corley *piano*
Siân Philipps *violin* • Essex Young Musician of the Year
1993 with Lora Dimitrova *piano*

12th May
Young Music Makers 3

30th May • OCS
Margaret Archibold *clarinets* Illustrated talk

29th June
Essex Young Musician of the Year Competition 1997

1997-98 SEASON

15th September • BH
Clare Welfare *oboe*, Marcus Andrews *piano* (AGM)

19th September • BH
Terry Lightfoot and his Band

17th October • BH
'Hot Stuff'

24th October • BH
Joseph Tong *piano*

9th November • BH
Young Music Makers 1

21st November • BH
Bob Dwyer's 'Hot Six'

28th November • BH
Jupiter Ensemble *clarinet, viola, piano*

19th December • SMC
Salvation Army Romford Citadel Band Christmas
Concert with the Stondon Singers,
Rachel Barrett *soprano*

16th January • BH
Merseysippi Jazz Band

23rd January • BH
Courtlye Musick

20th February • BH
Siobhan Grealy *flute*, Karen Suter *piano*

27th February • BH
Bridget Metcalfe and the Mark Allaway Quartet

15th March
Young Music Makers 2

20th March • BH
Ian Lake *piano*

27th March • BH
Solebay Jazz Band

17th April • BH
Jane Webster *soprano*, Nicholas Bosworth *piano*

24th April • BH
The President's Evening with Digby Fairweather

15th May • BH
Fiona Harrison *guitar*

15th May • BH
Dinner Dance

21st June
Young Music Makers 3

28th June
Essex Young Musician of the Year Competition 1998

1998-99 SEASON

25th September • BH
Rebecca Thorn *clarinet*, Janet Walker *piano* (AGM)

23rd October • BH
Country House Opera

22nd November
Young Music Makers 1

27th November • BH
Anthony Woollard *cello*, Sarah Nicholls *piano*

18th December • SMC
Salvation Army Romford Citadel Band Christmas
Concert with the Cranbrook Singers, Rachel Barrett
soprano

22nd January • BH
Roderick Chadwick *piano*

26th February • BH
Marianne Olyver *violin*, Helen Ridout *piano*

12th March 1999 • St James' Church, Piccadilly
James Scannell *clarinet/alto saxophone* • Essex Young
Musician of the Year 1995
with Rika Smith *piano*,
Joseph Tong *piano* • Essex Young Musician of the Year
1996

14th March
Young Music Makers 2

26th March • BH
Helicon String Trio

16th April • BH
Quintessence: Wind and Brass Ensemble

28th May • BH
Tintagel: 'Notes on the Old Cross'

20th June
Young Music Makers 3, including Rotary Young Musician

27th June
Essex Young Musician of the Year Competition 1999

1999-2000 • 25th Anniversary Season

24th September
Magwitch Trio: two clarinets and bassoon (including past Chairmen playing Haydn's 'Toy Symphony' (AGM)

22nd October
Tammy Se *violin* • Essex Young Musician of the Year 1998, Kanako Shoda *piano*

26th November
Anthony Hopkins: 'How to be a successful failure'

28th November
Young Music Makers 1

17th December • SMC
Salvation Army Romford Citadel Band Christmas Concert, Times and Seasons,
David Wigram BBC 2 choirboy of the Year

28th January • BH
Anna Noakes *flute*, Gillian Tingay *harp*

25th February
Hatstand Opera: 'The Best of Gilbert and Sullivan'

22nd March • Brentwood Cathedral
John Lill *piano*: Ongar Music Club 25th Anniversary Recital

31st March • BH
Two-Piano Marathon • Concert Room, Budworth Hall
– Geoffrey Timms & Roderick Elms, Sarah Manning & Matthew Pengilly, Catherine Jennings & Geoffrey Tompkins, Valerie Manning & Catherine Jennings, Jean & Barrie Hall, John Harrop & Barrie Hall

9th April
Young Music Makers 2, including Rotary Young Musician

17th April
Con Tempo Quartet: 3rd Prizewinners in the International String Quartet Competition

19th May
Enterprise Brass

25th June
Young Music Makers 3

2nd July
Essex Young Musician of the Year 2000

2000-01 SEASON

22nd September
Vicki Tofts *flute*, You-Chiung Lin *piano* (AGM)

27th October
Clive Caroll *guitar*

19th November
Young Music Makers 1, including Rotary Young Musician

24th November
Sarah Beth Briggs *piano*

15th December • SMC
Christmas Concert: Cranbrook Singers with Harlow Brass and Oliver Lincoln *treble*

26th January
Enoch Arden: poem by Tennyson, music by Richard Strauss

23rd February
Rachel Brown *cornet, natural and modern trumpets*, Anne Smillie *piano and keyboard*

17th March 2001 • St Giles' Church, Cripplegate
Anthony Woollard *cello* • Essex Young Musician of the Year 1997 with Sarah Nicolls *piano*
Tammy Se *violin* • Essex Young Musician of the Year 1998 with Tom Blach *piano*

23rd March
Opera Exclusive!: 'The Lass with the Delicate Hair'

1st April
Young Music Makers 2, including Rotary Young Musician

6th April
The Brook Ensemble

18th May
Marianne Olyver *violin* Geoffrey Pratley *piano*

18th June
Young Music Makers 3, including Rotary Young Musician

1st July
Essex Young Musician of the Year 2001

2001-02 SEASON

28th September
Elspeth Taylor *horn*, Catherine Milledge *piano* (AGM)

26th October
Janey Miller *oboe* • Essex Young Musician of the Year 2000 with Sarah Nicholls *piano*

23rd November
Martyn Harrison – 'Overture and Beginners: The Everyday Life of an Opera Singer'

25th November
Young Music Makers 1

21st December
Christmas Concert with choir, Chelmsford Salvation Army Band and Oliver Lincoln *treble*

18th January
Ian Fountain *piano*

15th February
Hilsa Flute & Harp Duo
Rachel Hilsa Smith *flute*, Emma Ramsdale *harp*

15th March
Felicity Vincent *cello*, Geoffrey Pratley *piano*

14th April
Young Music Makers 2, including Rotary Young Musician

26th April
Eden Stell *guitar duo*

17th May
Southend Girls' Choir

16th June
Young Music Makers 3

30th June
Essex Young Musician of the Year 2002

2002-03 SEASON

27th September
Patrick McCarthy *tenor*, Alison Baker *piano* (AGM)

25th October
Tubalaté *brass quartet*

22nd November
Jane Stoneham *percussion* • Essex Young Musician of the Year 2001, and friends

1st December
Young Music Makers 1

20th December • SMC
Christmas Concert with Brentwood School Choir and Chelmsford Citadel Salvation Army Band

24th January
Piano4Hands: Joseph Tong and Wake Hasegawa *piano duet*

14th February
The Romantic Viola: Stephen Tees *viola*, Ian Gammie *guitar*

14th March
Kim and Robin Colvill: 'Romantic Piano Classics'

11th April
The Karillon Trio

13th April
Young Music Makers 2, including Rotary Young Musician

14th May 2003 • St Giles' Church, Cripplegate
Janey Miller *oboe* • Essex Young Musician of the Year 2000 with Sarah Nicholls *piano*
Clive Carroll *guitar* • Essex Young Musician of the Year 1999

23rd May
Tim Hurst-Brown and Peter Hewitt: 'Here's a How-de-do'

22nd June
Young Music Makers 3

29th June
Essex Young Musician of the Year 2003 (twentieth competition)

2003-04 SEASON

19th September
Leanne Dobinson *soprano*, John Harrop *piano* (AGM)

24th October
Zephyr Ensemble

28th November
Raymond Banning *piano*

7th December
Young Music Makers 1 - cancelled due to a 'flu epidemic

19th December
Christmas Concert with the Ursuline School Choir and the Salvation Army Band

30th January
Anne Allen *flute*, Yeu-Meng Chan *piano*

27th February
Victoria Goldsmith *violin*, Inga Goldsmith *piano*

26th March
Woollard Trio: Tony Woollard *cello* with flute and piano

28th March
Young Music Makers 2, including Rotary Young Musician

30th April
Mary Remnant – lecture recital

28th May
Patrick McCarthy *tenor*, Alison Baker *piano*

20th June
Young Music Makers 3

27th June
Essex Young Musician of the Year 2004

2004-05 SEASON

24th September • BH
Suzanne Thorn *oboe*, Janet Walker *piano* (AGM)

22nd October • BH
Carlos Bonell *guitar*

19th November • BH
Benjamin Grosvenor *piano* • Essex Young Musician of the Year 2003

5th November • BH
Young Music Makers 1

17th December • URC
Carol Concert with the Salvation Army Band

28th January • BH
Lucy Wakeford *harp*, Susan Thomas *flute*

25th February • GS
John Lill *piano* 60th Birthday Recital

18th March • BH
The Crayford Duo: Marcia Crayford *violin*, Helen Crayford *piano*

20th March
Young Music Makers 2, including Rotary Young Musician

29th April • BH
The Artaria Piano Trio: Farran Scott *violin*, Nicholas Stringfellow *cello*, Eleanor Hodgkinson *piano*

20th May • BH
The Aurora Ensemble: Andrew Mason *clarinet*, Gwenllian Davies *oboe*, Connie Tanner *bassoon*, Joanna Smith *piano*

12th June • BH
Young Music Makers 3

3rd July • BH
Essex Young Musician the Year Competition 2005

2005-06 SEASON

23rd September • BH
Sophie Biebuyck *soprano*, Joanna Smith *piano* (AGM)

28th October • BH
Patricia Spero *harp* and Kate Cuzner *flute*

25th November • BH
Victoria Goldsmith *violin*, Inga Goldsmith *piano*

4th December
Young Music Makers 1

16th December • BH
Hatstand Opera: 'Love, Lust and a Damn Good Chardonnay'

27th January • BH
Keyboard Konnections I: Joanna Smith and
Roderick Elms *piano duo*

17th February • BH
Robert Bourton: 'Meet the Bassoon'
with John Alley *piano*

17th March' • BH
Michael Round: 'Villa-Lobos and his World

26th March • BH
Young Music Makers 2, including Rotary Young Musician

28th April • BH
Gregory Bennett Walmsley *cello* & Andrew West *piano*

19th May • BH
Mixed Doubles: Stephen Bell and Charlotte Lines *horn*,
Joanna Smith and Roderick Elms *piano*

18th June • BH
Young Music Makers 3

2nd July • BH
Essex Young Musician the Year Competition 2006

2006-07 SEASON

29th September • BH
Anthony Sabberton *violin*, Julie Coucheron *piano* (AGM)

27th October
Suzanne Thorn *oboe*, Daniel Smith *piano*

17th November • BH
Piano4hands: Joseph Tong and
Waka Hasegawa *piano duo*

3rd December
Young Music Makers 1

15th December
Clive Carol *guitar*

19th January
'Rags to Riches': Helen Crayford, *piano and trumpet*

23rd February
Sarah Williamson *clarinet* and Richard Evans *piano*

16th March
Mark Wilde, *tenor* and Helen Sanderson, *piano*

25th March
Young Music Makers 2

20th April
'Travelling by Tuba' I – Chris Cranham and Stewart Death

18th May
Amici Piano Trio

10th June
Young Music Makers 3, including Rotary Young Musician
(last competition in Ongar)

1st July • BH
Essex Young Musician the Year Competition 2007

2007-08 SEASON

21st September
Fergal O'Mahony *piano* (AGM)

26th October
Sophie Biebuyck *soprano* & Amit Yahav *piano*

30th November
Saxology: Saxophone quartet with Jeffery Wilson

2nd December
Young Music Makers 1

21st December
Gabriella dall'Olio *harp* and Maya Sapone *soprano*

18th January
Keyboard Konnections II – Joanna Smith and
Roderick Elms *piano duo*

22nd February
Duo Rosa

9th March
Young Music Makers 2, including Rotary Young Musician
(last competition in Ongar)

14th March
The Manovitz Duo

25th April • BH
The Aurora Ensemble

16th May • BH
Marianne Olyver Piano Trio

15th June • BH
Young Music Makers 3

29th June • BH
Essex Young Musician of the Year 2008

2008-09 SEASON

19th September • BH
Lindsey Isles *clarinet* and Joanna Smith *piano* (AGM)

31st October • BH
Bizet to Bernstein: Jane Webster *soprano* and
Nicholas Bosworth *piano*

21st November • BH
Carlos Bonell, guitar

7th December • BH
Young Music Makers 1

19th December • BH
'Travelling by Tuba' II – The Sequel

20th February • BH
Andrew Mason *clarinet* and Joanna smith *piano*

20th March • BH
The Harpham String Quartet

29th March • BH
Young Music Makers 2

17th April • BH
Tamsin Thorne *bassoon* • Essex Young Musician of the
Year 2008 and Daniel Smith *piano*

15th May • GS
John Lill *piano*

14th June • BH
Young Music Makers 3

5th July • BH
Essex Young Musician of the Year 2008

2009-10 SEASON

25th September • BH
Christopher Bearman *tuba* and Joanna Smith *piano*
(AGM)

23rd October • BH
The Conservatoire Series: Students from the
Trinity College of Music – Katharine Carter *flute*,
Ian Richardson *piano*

27th November • BH
TenStringFever: Jane Miller *violin* and
Terry Spooner *guitar*

6th December • BH
Young Music Makers 1

18th December • BH
Christmas Concert with The Stondon Singers and
Brentwood Brass

26th February • BH
Blowing His Own Trumpets – Martin Hurrell *trumpet* and
Elizabeth Burley *piano*

19th March • BH
Michael Round: An Evening with Percy Grainger and
friends

28th March • BH
Young Music Makers 2

23rd April • BH
Joanna Marie Skillett *soprano* • Essex Young Musician of
the Year 2009 with Melanie Jones *piano*

21st May
Keyboard Konnections III: Joanna Smith and
Roderick Elms *piano duo*

20th June • BH
Young Music Makers 3

4th July • BH
Essex Young Musician of the Year 2010

2010-11 SEASON

17th September • BH
Matthew Lewis *trombone* and Jennifer Hughes *piano*
(AGM)

15th October • BH
Siân Philipps *violin* and Sophia Rahman *piano*

12th November • BH
Sarah-Jane Lewis *mezzo-soprano* • Essex Young
Musician of the Year 2010 with Kentaro Nagai *piano*

5th December • BH
Young Music Makers 1

17th December • BH
The Foxtons' Ensemble

18th February • BH
David Campbell *clarinet*, David McArthur *piano*

18th March • BH
The Conservatoire Series: Students from the Royal
Academy of Music – Lauren Steel *cello*,
Carson Becke *piano*

15th April • BH
Roger Montgomery *guitar*

13th May • BH
Trillogy

22nd May • BH
Young Music Makers 2

3rd July • BH
Essex Young Musician of the Year 2011

2011-12 SEASON

23rd September • BH
Joanna Smith and Roderick Elms *piano duo*
Inauguration of the club's newly refurbished Bechstein
grand (AGM)

28th October • BH
Carlos Bonell *guitar*

18th November • BH
Madeleine Mitchell *violin* and Andrew Ball *piano*

27th November • BH
Young Music Makers 1

18th December • BH
The Spirit of Christmas: Cantate Alumni Choir with
Michael Kibblewhite *music director*

17th February • BH
Matthew Lewis *trombone* • Essex Young Musician of the
Year 2011 with Jennifer Hughes *piano*

23rd March • BH
The Aurora Ensemble with Joanna Smith *piano*

20th April • BH
The Conservatoire Series: Students from the Royal
College of Music – Anna Anandaraja *soprano* and
Yunhee Choi *piano*

18th May • BH
Alisdair Hogarth *piano* Runner-up in the 1996 Essex
Young Musician of the Year competition

20th May • BH
Young Music Makers 2

1st July • BH
Essex Young Musician of the Year 2012

2012-13 SEASON

21st September • BH
Helen McKeon *clarinet* and Joanna Smith *piano* (AGM)

26th October • BH
Susanna Hurrell *soprano* and Sebastian Wybrew *piano*

16th November • BH
Adam Brown *guitar*

2nd December • BH
Young Music Makers 1

23rd December • BH
More Christmas Spirit: Cantate Alumni Choir with
Michael Kibblewhite *music director*

1st February • BH
Celebrity Recital: Benjamin Grosvenor *piano* •
Essex Young Musician of the Year 2003

15th March • BH
The Conservatoire Series: Students from the Guildhall
School of Music and Drama –
Lauren Reeve-Rawlings *french horn*, Seb Grand *piano*

26th April • BH
Matthew Paris *double-bass* • Essex Young Musician of the
Year 2012 with Robert Hunter *piano*

19th May • BH
Young Music Makers 2

24th May • BH
The Rose Trio: Suzanne Thorn *Oboe*, Rebecca Thorn
clarinet, Tamsin Thorn *bassoon*

7th July • BH
Essex Young Musician of the Year 2013

2013-14 SEASON

27th September • BH
William Knight *clarinet* and Joanna Smith *piano* (AGM)

25th October • BH
Joseph Tong *piano*

15th November • BH
Hanna Hipp *mezzo-soprano* and Emma Abbate *piano*

1st December • BH
Young Music Makers 1

22nd December • BH
By Popular Demand: Cantate Alumni Choir with
Michael Kibblewhite *music director*

21st February • BH
The Goldman Ensemble

14th March • BH
The Damask Ensemble

4th April • BH
The Williams/Kelleher Duo

9th May • BH
Charlotte Ashton *flute* and Chad Vindin *piano*

18th May • BH
Young Music Makers 2

6th July
Essex Young Musician of the Year 2014

2014-15 SEASON

19th September • BH
Elodie Chousmer-Howelles *violin* and Tim Carey *piano*
(AGM)

17th October • BH
Celebrity Recital: The Endellion String Quartet

5th December • BH
Barrie Hall Memorial Concert: A Musical Celebration

21st December • BH
By Even More Popular Demand – Cantate Alumni Choir,
Michael Kibblewhite *music director*

8th February • BH
Young Music Makers

13th March • BH
Rebecca Leung *piano* • Essex Young Musician of the
Year 2013

24th April • BH
Shakespeare in Song

5th July • BH
Essex Young Musician of the Year 2015

2015-16 SEASON

25th September • BH
Cameron Davies *baritone* and Catherine Davies *piano*
(AGM)

13th November • BH
William Knight *clarinet* • Essex Young Musician of the
Year 2014 with Joanna Smith *piano*

20th December • BH
By Even More Popular Demand – Cantate Alumni Choir
Michael Kibblewhite *music director*

26th February • BH
Espérance

13th March • BH
Young Music Makers

29th April • BH
Marianne Olyver and her Orchestra

3rd July • BH
Essex Young Musician of the Year 2016

2016-17 SEASON

7th October
Joanna Smith and Roderick Elms *piano duo* (AGM)

2nd December
Joseph Tong *piano*

2017-18 SEASON

15th September
Felicity Latham *flute*, Joanna Smith *piano* (AGM)

4th May • St John's Arts and Recreation Centre, Harlow
(ARC)
Kayleigh McEvoy *soprano* • Essex Young Musician of the
Year 2017 with Mikey Panda *piano*

2018-19 SEASON

26th April
Jessica Hope *soprano,* Alisdair Hogarth *piano* (AGM)

5th July • ARC, Harlow
Jamie Cochrane *piano* Essex Young Musician of the
Year 2018

Events presented by Ongar Jazz Club are indicated # in green. These are included for the period during which the Jazz Club's events were promoted within the Ongar Music Club brochure.

Soundbites!

2019-20 SEASON

26th June • BH
Gregory Walmsley *cello*

10th September • BH
Jessica Edom *soprano*, Jamie Cochrane *piano*

24th September • BH
Alisdair Hogarth *piano*

29th October • BH
The Countess of Wessex's String Orchestra (quartet)

26th November • BH
Janet Fairlie *soprano*, Christopher Duckett *piano*

17th December • BH
Simeon Wood *flautist and entertainer*

28th January • BH
Xander Benham *piano*

18th February • BH
Dominic Natoli *tenor*, Nicholas Reading *piano*

Unfortunately, the *Soundbites!* events scheduled from March 2020 had to be postponed due to the COVID-19 situation

Venues

AC – Arts Centre	FBS – Fyfield Boarding School	OCS – Ongar Comprehensive School
AEC – Adult Education Campus	GS – Great Stony	SHC – Spire Hall, Chelmsford
ARC St John's – Harlow	GSS – Great Stony School	Jazz Club events are shown in green

Appendix – B

Essex Young Musician of the Year
Finalists: 1984 – 2019

1984
Anthony Marwood *violin*
Peter Sheppard *violin* (joint second)
Gregory Walmsley *cello* (joint second)

1985
Alison Baker *piano*
Pauline Dowse *cello*
Jane Webster *soprano*

1986
Jane Webster *soprano*
Catherine Bell *flute*
Hannah Bell *soprano*

1987
Pauline Dowse *cello*
Larissa Joy *clarinet*
Helen Knief *viola*

1988
Helen Knief *viola*
Carole Court *soprano*
Larissa Joy *clarinet*

1989
Gregory Walmsley *cello*
Philip Sheppard *cello*
Richard Ashton *horn in F*

1990
Nikos Zarb *viola*
Daisy Jopling *violin*
Deborah Fink *soprano*
Rosemary Lindsell *bassoon*
Philip Harper *E flat tenor horn* (Hugh Terry)

1991
Zoe Mather *piano*
Andrew Webster *clarinet*
Vanessa Cozens *mezzo soprano*
Sarah Barnes *cello*
Gurminder Kaur Bhogal *piano* (Hugh Terry)

1992
Sarah Barnes *cello*
Philippa Bale *piano*
Emily Sheldrake *violin*
Anthony Woollard *cello*
Joanna Smith *piano* (Hugh Terry)

1993
Siân Philipps *violin*
Rachel Barnes *bassoon*
Daisy Jopling *violin*
Louisa Oakley *piano*
Fiona Russell *recorders* (Hugh Terry)

1994
Rachel Barnes *bassoon*
Daisy Jopling *violin*
Louisa Oakley *piano* (joint third)
Warwick Potter *bassoon* (joint third)
Ian Watson *free base accordion* (Hugh Terry)

1995
James Scannell *saxophone*
Ian Watson *free base accordion*
Kerry Sugden *piano*
Edward Bale *violin*
Kelly-Ann Harrison *E flat tenor horn* (Hugh Terry)
Timothy Birchall *violin* (James Dace)

1996
Joseph Tong *piano*
Alisdair Hogarth *piano*
Anthony Woollard *cello*
Kerry Sugden *piano*
Elizabeth Allen *flute* (Hugh Terry
Dominique Pecheur *cello* (James Dace)

1997
Anthony Woollard *cello*
Joanna Smith *piano*
Jacqueline Roach *violin*
Anita D'Attellis *piano*
Emily Sutcliffe *clarinet* (Hugh Terry)
Colin Davis *piano* (James Dace)

1998
Tammy Se *violin*
Ian Watson *free base accordion*
Clare Welfare *oboe*
Alisdair Hogarth *piano*
Alexandra Oyston *violin* (Hugh Terry)
Rebecca Thorn *clarinet* (James Dace)

1999
Clive Carroll *guitar*
Jane Stoneham *marimba*
Sarnia Scott *oboe*
Emily Sutcliffe *clarinet*
Heidi Sutcliffe *trumpet* (Hugh Terry)
Poppy Walshaw *cello* (James Dace)

2000
Janey Miller *oboe*
Vicki Tofts *flute*
Kaspars Vilnitis *viola*
Helen Randall *soprano*
Suzanne Thorn *oboe* (Hugh Terry)
Carrie Fisher *flute/piccolo* (James Dace)

2001
Jane Stoneham *marimba*
Rebecca Walker *cello*
Dominique Pecheur *cello*
Elspeth Taylor *French horn*
Paul Vowles *clarinet* (Hugh Terry)
James Dace prize not awarded

2002
Thomas Oxley *bassoon*
Clare Welfare *oboe*
Benjamin Hulett *tenor*
Emily Sutcliffe *clarinet*
Christopher Stokes *piano* (Hugh Terry)
Sarah Whitbread *violin* (James Dace)

2003
Benjamin Grosvenor *piano*
Suzanne Thorn *oboe*
Victoria Goldsmith *violin*
Leanne Dobinson *soprano*
Sophie Biebuyck *soprano* (Hugh Terry)
Madeleine Ridd *cello* (James Dace)

2004
Victoria Goldsmith *violin*
Suzanne Thorn *oboe*
Katy Elman *marimba/xylophone*
Christopher Stokes *piano*
Christina Shand – soprano (Hugh Terry)
James Dace prize not awarded

2005
Suzanne Thorn *oboe*
Anthony Sabberton *violin*
Sophie Biebuyck *soprano*
James Hughes *percussion*
Alexander Baker (not traced) (Hugh Terry)
Matthew Lewis *trombone* (James Dace)

2006
Sophie Biebuyck *soprano*
Anthony Sabberton *violin*
Christopher Bearman *tuba*
James Hughes *percussion*
Tamsin Thorn *bassoon* (Hugh Terry)
William Church *piano* (James Dace)

2007
Timothy Wayne-Wright *counter tenor*
Fergal O'Mahony *piano*
Tristan Stocks *baritone*
Lindsey Iles *clarinet*
Nathan Steele *piano* (Hugh Terry)
Antony Camillo *piano* (James Dace)

2008
Tamsin Thorn *bassoon*
Christopher Bearman *tuba*
Lindsey Iles *clarinet* (joint third)
Tristan Stocks *baritone* (joint third)
William Newell *violin* (Hugh Terry)
Matthew Strover *cello* (James Dace)

2009
Joanna Skillett *soprano*
Christopher Bearman *tuba*
Lindsey Iles *clarinet*
Matthew Lewis *trombone*
William Knight *clarinet* (Hugh Terry)
David Albon *flute* (James Dace)

2010
Sarah-Jane Lewis *mezzo-soprano*
Matthew Lewis *trombone*
Christopher Bearman *tuba*
Ross Ramgobin *baritone*
Ben Gershinson *oboe* (Hugh Terry)
James Dace prize not awarded

2011
Matthew Lewis *trombone*
Ben Gershinson *oboe*
Emily Onsloe *soprano*
James Priest *baritone*
Harry O'keefe *violin* (Hugh Terry)
James Dace prize not awarded

2012
Matthew Paris *double bass*
Helen McKeown *clarinet*
Carina Gascoine *flute*
Emily Onsloe *soprano*
Christopher Burt *oboe* (Hugh Terry)
William Knight *clarinet* (James Dace)

2013
Rebecca Leung *piano*
William Knight *clarinet*
Elitsa Bogdanova *viola*
Elodie Chousmer-Howelles *violin*
Hannah McNaboe *soprano* (Hugh Terry)
Lydia Dunn *flute* (James Dace)

2014

William Knight *clarinet*
Elodie Chousmer-Howelles *violin*
Corinna Wilson *soprano*
Irena Klimach *oboe*
David Cox *trombone* (Hugh Terry)
Keenan Ngo *piano* (James Dace)

2015

Elodie Chousmer-Howelles *violin*
Cameron Davies *baritone*
Ashley Blasse *guitar*
No fourth prize
David Cox *trombone* (Geoffrey Timms)
Rebecca Rimmington *flute* (Hugh Terry)

2016

Rebecca Silverman *soprano*
Harry O'Keefe *violin*
Eleanor Austin *soprano*
Michael Hollette *bassoon*
Jamie Cochrane *piano* (Geoffrey Timms)
Francesca Slater *flute* (Hugh Terry)

2017

Kayleigh McEvoy *soprano*
Jessica Hope *soprano*
Felicity Latham *flute*
Michael Hollette *bassoon*
Alex Usher *clarinet* (Geoffrey Timms)
Abbie Ward *soprano* (OMC)

2018

Jamie Cochrane *piano*
Esme Smith *soprano*
Ralph Thomas Williams *counter tenor*
Rachael Bull *cello*
Alex Usher *clarinet* (Hall Memorial)
Vivien Wong *clarinet* (Geoffrey Timms)

2019

Michael Lafferty *baritone*
Alexander Benham *piano*
Jessica Edom *soprano*
Joanna Lam *piano*
Callum Sherriff *violin*
Vivien Wong *clarinet* (Hall Memorial)
Alanna Crouch *piano* (Geoffrey Timms)

2020

Cancelled due to the pandemic

2021

Madeline Robinson *soprano*
Holly Putt *mezzo-soprano*
Melinda Blackman *violin*
Justin Man *piano*
Isabella Pincombe *oboe*
Amy Wood *flute*
Elizabeth Loboda *oboe* (Geoffrey Timms Memorial Prize)
Nell Ramdenee *oboe* (Bert Webster Memorial Prize)

A name in brackets signifies the name of the prize awarded.
These are the junior prizes are awarded to performers under the age of nineteen.
In 2019 there were five prizes plus two junior prizes awarded.
In 2021 there were six prizes plus two junior prizes awarded.

Essex Schools' Musician – Finalists

1992	1993	1994
Anthony Woollard – cello	Fiona Russell – recorders	Ian Watson – freebase accordion
Pippa Stewart – flute	Joanna Smith – piano	Susan Fitzgerald – flute

Essex Young Musicians of the Year – London Recitals

8th January 1990 • Wigmore Hall
Alison Baker *piano* • Essex Young Musician of the Year 1985
Helen Knief *viola* • Essex Young Musician of the Year 1988 with William Hancox *piano*
Jane Webster *soprano* • Essex Young Musician of the Year 1986
with Nicholas Bosworth *piano*

25th March 1991 • Wigmore Hall (sponsored by the Essex Chronicle Group)
Anthony Marwood *violin* • Essex Young Musician of the Year 1984
with William Howard *piano*

5th March 1993 • Wigmore Hall
Gregory Walmsley *cello* • Essex Young Musician of the Year 1989
with Ana Guijarro *piano*
Alison Baker *piano* (1985 EYMY and a last minute replacement for Zoë Mather
who was forced to withdraw due to personal circumstances)

10th April 1995 • Wigmore Hall
Zoë Mather *piano* • Essex Young Musician of the Year 1991
Sarah Barnes *cello* • Essex Young Musician of the Year 1992 with Vanessa Perez *piano*

2nd May 1997 • Purcell Room
Rachel Barnes *bassoon* • Essex Young Musician of the Year 1994
with Steve Corley *piano*
Siân Philipps *violin* • Essex Young Musician of the Year 1993 with Lora Dimitrova *piano*

12th March 1999 • St James' Church, Piccadilly (the last London concert)
James Scannell *clarinet/alto saxophone* • Essex Young Musician of the Year 1995
with Rika Smith *piano*
Joseph Tong *piano* • Essex Young Musician of the Year 1996

17th March 2001 • St Giles' Church, Cripplegate
Anthony Woollard *cello* • Essex Young Musician of the Year 1997
with Sarah Nicolls *piano*
Tammy Se *violin* • Essex Young Musician of the Year 1998 with Tom Blach *piano*

14th May 2003 • St Giles' Church, Cripplegate
Janey Miller *oboe* • Essex Young Musician of the Year 2000 with Sarah Nicholls *piano*
Clive Carroll *guitar* • Essex Young Musician of the Year 1999

Essex Young Musician of the Year – Number of Entrants

1984	1985	1986	1987	1988	1989	1990	1991
–	18	14	20 (-3)	17	20	15	–

1992	1993	1994	1995	1996	1997	1998	1999
13	17 (-1)	16 (-1)	17 (-2)	25	21	21	22

2000	2001	2002	2003	2004	2005	2006	2007
20	20	18	23	13	17 (-1)	16 -1)	17 (-2)

2008	2009	2010	2011	2012	2013	2014	2015
17	12	13 (-1)	15	14	9	13 (-20)	5 (-2)

2016	2017	2018	2019	–	2021		
13 (-1)	14	13 (-1)	15 (-1)		21		

Essex Young Musician of the Year – Judges

1984
Eileen Broster, Chris Green, Bramwell Tovey, John White,
Geoffrey Timms

1985
Roderick Elms, Peter Pople, Geoffrey Timms,
Graham Trew

1986
Roderick Elms, Keith Gurry, Barrie Hall, Geoffrey Timms,
Graham Trew

1987
Harry Blech, Roderick Elms, Barrie Hall, Linden Harris,
Russell Jordan, Geoffrey Timms, Graham Trew

1988
Harry Blech, Roderick Elms, Barrie Hall, David Thomas,
Geoffrey Timms, Graham Trew

1989
John Lill, Roderick Elms, Barrie Hall, Robert Hill,
David Strange, Geoffrey Timms, Graham Trew

1990
John Lill, Roderick Elms, Barrie Hall, David Strange,
Geoffrey Timms, Bramwell Tovey, Graham Trew,
Margaret Watson

1991
Roderick Elms, Barrie Hall, Simon Joly, Kieron Moore,
David Strange, Geoffrey Timms, Graham Trew

1992
Roderick Elms, Barrie Hall, John Harrop, Simon Joly,
David Strange, Geoffrey Timms, Graham Trew

1993
Michael Boyle, Douglas Cummings, Roderick Elms,
Barrie Hall, John Harrop, Simon Joly, Geoffrey Timms,
Graham Trew

1994
Michael Boyle, Roderick Elms, Barrie Hall, John Harrop,
Simon Joly, Nona Liddell, Geoffrey Timms, Graham Trew

1995
John Lill, Alison Baker, Michael Boyle, Roderick Elms,
Barrie Hall, John Harrop, Simon Joly, Nona Liddell,
Geoffrey Timms,

1996
Virginia Black, Barrie Hall, John Harrop, Simon Joly,
David Strange, Geoffrey Timms, Graham Trew

1997
Michael Boyle, Roderick Elms, Barrie Hall, John Harrop,
Simon Joly, Alison Kelly, Geoffrey Timms, Graham Trew

1998
Michael Boyle, Roderick Elms, Barrie Hall, John Harrop,
Simon Joly, Nona Liddell, Geoffrey Timms, Graham Trew

1999
John Lill, Michael Boyle, Roderick Elms, Barrie Hall,
John Harrop, Simon Joly, Nona Liddell, Geoffrey Timms,
Graham Trew

2000
Michael Boyle, Roderick Elms, Barrie Hall, John Harrop,
Simon Joly, Alison Kelly, Geoffrey Timms, Graham Trew

2001
Michael Boyle, Barrie Hall, John Harrop, Simon Joly,
Alison Kelly, Geoffrey Timms, Graham Trew

2002
Michael Boyle, Roderick Elms, Barrie Hall, John Harrop,
Simon Joly, Nona Liddell, Geoffrey Timms, Graham Trew

2003
Roderick Elms, Barrie Hall, John Harrop,
Catherine Jennings, Thea King, Brian Priestman,
Marianne Olyver, Jane Webster

2004
Barrie Hall, John Harrop, Catherine Jennings, Thea King,
Peter Pople, Jane Webster

2005
Colin Bradbury, Roderick Elms, Barrie Hall, John Harrop,
Catherine Jennings, Marianne Olyver, Jane Webster

2006
Roderick Elms, Barrie Hall, John Harrop,
Catherine Jennings, Thea King, Marianne Olyver

2007
Colin Bradbury, Stephen Bell, Roderick Elms,
Marianne Olyver, Jane Webster

2008
Neil Black, Simon Channing, Roderick Elms, Keith Gurry,
Marianne Olyver, Jane Webster

2009
Neil Black, Elizabeth Burley, Roderick Elms,
Martin Hurrell, Marianne Olyver, Jane Webster

2010
Neil Black, Roderick Elms, Marianne Olyver, John Sibley,
Jane Webster

2011
Neil Black, Elizabeth Burley, Roderick Elms,
Martin Hurrell, Marianne Olyver, Jane Webster

2012
John Lill, Neil Black, Roderick Elms, Alasdair Hogarth,
Marianne Olyver, John Sibley, Jane Webster

2013
Neil Black, Alasdair Hogarth, Marianne Olyver,
John Sibley, Jane Webster

2014
Lindsay Benson, Karen Jones, Marianne Olyver, John Sibley

2015
John Anderson, Rebecca Bottone, Roderick Elms, Marianne Olyver, John Sibley, Geoffrey Timms

2016
John Anderson, Roderick Elms, Marianne Olyver, John Sibley, Jane Webster

2017
John Anderson, Roderick Elms, Alasdair Hogarth, Marianne Olyver, John Sibley, Jane Webster

2018
Janet Hilton, Roderick Elms, Marianne Olyver, John Sibley, Jane Webster

2019
John Anderson, Roderick Elms, Marianne Olyver, John Sibley, Jane Webster

2020
Cancelled

2021
John Anderson, Roderick Elms, Marianne Olyver, John Sibley, Jane Webster

---

ONGAR MUSIC CLUB

Programme 1994-1995

All concerts take place in the main hall of the Ongar Adult Education Campus, except 10 April

Friday 23 September at 8.0
Kerry Sugden (piano) Twig Hall (soprano) with Michael Hall (piano)

A short AGM followed by a recital. Kerry Sugden was a semifinalist in this year's Essex Young Musician; she plays a Beethoven sonata, Chopin Nocturne and Fantaisie-Impromptu. Twig and Michael Hall perform Mozart's Exsultate, Jubilate (Alleluia) and Schubert Songs. Twig sings with early music groups including the Taverner Singers and Monteverdi Choir; in opera and concerts and radio and TV here and abroad, and on several CDs. £3

Friday 21 October at 8.0
Alison Baker (piano)

A staunch supporter of the Club since becoming the 1885 Essex Young Musician, and now soloist, accompanist, teacher, adjudicator and composer. Alison returns with sonatas by Schubert and Beethoven, and works by Liszt, Brahms and Bartók, on the 16th anniversary of her first London concert. £6

Sunday 20 November at 3.0
Young Music Makers 1

We have had piano, violin and orchestras. If you know players, a choir, and an orchestra, if you wish, contact Catherine Jennings (see back page) preferably at least a month in advance.
(See also 5 March, 14 May.) Adults £1.50 Children 90p

Friday 25 November at 8.0
Susan Blair (harp)
(NPWINNER55O YOUNG ARTIST)

Susan Blair adds the National Federation of Music Societies' Award to her already impressive list of prizes. Starting at 12, she has studied with Marisa Robles and Nicanor Zabaleta, played on TV and before H.M. The Queen, and in December gives a Purcell Room recital. Tonight's delightful varied programme includes Bach, Fauré and Glinka; and she will also talk about her instrument. £6

Friday 16 December at 8.0
Christmas Carol Concert

This ever-popular event is again given by the Stondon Singers, conductor Simon Berridge, and our Chairman. The audience will be invited to join in singing well-loved carols; and interval punch and mincepies are included. In our usual Rattle precede to British Society for Music Therapy, which helps children and adults suffering from many kinds of handicap. £8

Saturday 14 January at 8.0
Essex Chamber Orchestra
Simon Thompson (conductor)
Siân Philipps (harp)

It is many years since our last orchestral concert. The Essex Chamber Orchestra assembles three times a year for intensive rehearsal followed by two concerts. They play Weber's Der Freischütz overture, Brahms's third symphony, and Mendelssohn's violin concerto with 1993 Essex Young Musician of the Year, Siân Philipps. Best booking advised. £6

Friday 24 February at 8.0
Rachel Barnes (bassoon) Essex Young Musician of 1994
Costas Solopoulos (piano)

Don't be content – Rachel Barnes won this year, her sister Sarah won in 1992 and plays at the Wigmore Concert on 10 April. There is another sister, Maryse, who plays clarinet. Rachel's achievement is impressive: scholarship winner 1992 BBC Young Musician; last year's English Speaking Union scholarship winner, which took her to Canada, broadcasts on Radio 3, Classic fM and TV.
Programme includes works by Pierné Tansman, Berwald, and piano solos. £6

Sunday 5 March at 3.0
Young Music Makers 2
(See 20 November)

Friday 31 March at 8.0
Hugh Bean (violin)

Hugh Bean has led the Philharmonia, BBC Symphony, and London Symphony Orchestras, as well as playing chamber music and giving solo recitals. He was a founder member of the Music Group of London and professor for many years at the RCM. Tonight he plays and introduces sonatas by Beethoven (7 in C minor) Fauré (No. 1) and the ever-popular César Franck. £6

Monday 10 April at The Wigmore Hall, London, 7.30
Zoë Mather (piano)
Sarah Barnes (cello) and Vanessa Perez (piano)

Two of our Essex Young Musician winners, 1991 & 1992, Zoë, whose final Guildhall School recital gained her a First, has a Radio 3 Young Concert Artists Forum scheduled for October '94, and a Countess of Munster Trust Award for postgraduate study. She plays Beethoven, Liszt and Ravel, and three Cole Porter arrangements made for Joanna MacGregor – Zoë calls them 'beautiful and hilariously difficult' Sarah will play the Chopin and Prokofiev sonatas.

Coaches will be organised – contact Chairman Jean Hall (0277 899337) £4.50, £6, £7.50 and £9. Also coaches from the Wigmore Hall (071-935 2141) or at the door on the night.

Friday 21 April at 8.0
'The Castle Walls' with Pennyroyal

The Castle Walls presents renaissance masterpieces with simple folk melodies, linked by a fascinating story-line, guaranteed to soothe and stimulate the senses. By Pennyroyal, four players who include flute, guitar and a singer, and music by Byrd, Dowland, Gibbons among others. £6

Sunday 14 May at 3.0
Young Music Makers 3
(See 20 November)

Friday 19 May at 8.0
Alvin Moisey & Andrew Zolinsky
Four Hands — One Orchestra

Alvin Moisey, old friend of the Club, with his partner Andrew Zolinsky, in the second 'orchestral' concert this season – arrangements, as far as possible by the composers themselves, of works better known in orchestral form, including Ravel's Mother Goose Suite and Stravinsky's The Rite of Spring. All for four hands at one piano. £6

Essex Young Musician of the Year 1995 (Twelfth Competition)

Saturday 24 June
Preliminaries at 2.0   Admission free

Sunday 25 June
Semi-finals at 2.0   All-day ticket £5, with concessions
Finals at 7.50

(All at the Adult Education Campus, Ongar)
This prestige event returns to Ongar for the greater convenience of Club members. Five previous winners in this season – Music Makers nights. Rachel and Sarah Barnes, Zoë Mather – provide sufficient evidence of the high standards achieved. Professional adjudicators choose the John Lill winner. This year's winner takes part immediately after an always exciting finale. Can you pick here?

(Entry forms for competitors from Geoffrey Timms, Ty Camp, Clocaenog, nr. Ruthin, Clwyd LL15 2AT (Tel and Fax 0824 750 503).

ONGAR JAZZ

A Section of Ongar Music Club

President: Humphrey Lyttelton

Secretary: Mrs. Jean Ball, 4 Bowes Drive, Ongar, Essex CM5 9AU (0277 362309)

Treasurer: John Harrop (0277 364255)
Committee: Fred Eastland (0277 362453)
John Sibson (0277 362173)
Howard Nicholson (0277 899504)
Steve Welch (0277 363282)

All concerts take place in the Budworth Hall

Friday 28 October at 8.0
Ken Colyer Trust Band
Authentic New Orleans Style at its best
members £6   non-members £7

Friday 2 December at 8.0
Maxine Daniels with the Ted Beamish Trio
One of Britain's finest Jazz singers making her first appearance at this Club
members £6   non-members £7

Friday 6 January at 8.0
Dave Shepherd Quintet
Always welcome at Ongar, this award-winning clarinettist with his excellent Quintet play 'Benny Goodman Style' Jazz.
members £8   non-members £9

Friday 17 February at 8.0
Martin Litton's Red Hot Peppers
Remember the visit by The Superkings ? We now have the opportunity to hear this young pianist virtuoso with his own band. Not to be missed!
members £8   non-members £9

Friday 24 March at 8.0
Sonny Dee All-Stars
A first visit to Ongar for this very popular traditional Jazz Band.
members £8   non-members £9

Friday 12 May at 8.0
John Petters 'Boogie Woogie and All That Jazz'
We close the season with something different but special, another piano wizard, Duncan Swift, with John Petters.
members £8   non-members £9

Tickets for Ongar Jazz events can be obtained from Jean Ball (0277 362309) and Highway Travel, High Street, Ongar (0277 363665) – s.a.e. please if you want your tickets posted to you.

(Please note that once purchased, tickets may not be returned except in the case of a cancelled concert.)

Appendix – C

COMMITTEES

1975 - Initial Meeting
David Kirkwood (Chairman/Secretary), Betty Greatrex (Treasurer), Arthur Bennett (Press Secretary)

AGM 17th September 1975 - Formal Committee Elected
David Kirkwood (Chairman–Secretary), Betty Greatrex (Treasurer), Arthur Bennett Press (Secretary) Sylvia Terry (Membership Secretary), Phoebe Musgrave, Geoffrey Timms

1976-77
Executive Committee
David Kirkwood (Chairman), Mrs J Wilson (Secretary), Betty Greatrex (Treasurer), Sylvia Terry (Membership Secretary), Barrie Hall (Publicity Secretary), Geoffrey Timms (Artistic Adviser)

Concerts Committee
Phoebe Musgrave, Mrs Fox, Miss Skrimshire, Mr Roberts, Diedre Ratcliffe

1977-78
David Kirkwood (Chairman), Mrs J Wilson (Secretary), Betty Greatrex (Treasurer), Sylvia Terry (Membership Secretary), Barrie Hall (Publicity Secretary), Geoffrey Timms (Artistic Adviser), John Harrop, Joyce Perry

1978-79
John Harrop (Chairman), Joyce Perry (Secretary), David Kirkwood (Treasurer), Sylvia Terry (Membership Secretary), Barrie Hall (Publicity Secretary), Geoffrey Timms (Artistic Adviser), Betty Greatrex, Phoebe Musgrave (Concert Hostesses), Kenneth Bird, Peter Lewis

1979-80
John Harrop (Chairman), Joyce Perry (Secretary), Peter Lewis (Treasurer), Sylvia Terry (Membership Secretary), Barrie Hall (Publicity Secretary), Geoffrey Timms (Artistic Adviser), Betty Greatrex, Phoebe Musgrave (Social Secretaries), Kenneth Bird, Frank Spinks

1980-81
John Harrop (Chairman), Joyce Perry (Secretary), Peter Lewis (Treasurer), Sylvia Terry (Membership Secretary), Barrie Hall (Publicity Secretary), Geoffrey Timms (Artistic Adviser), Betty Greatrex, Phoebe Musgrave (Social Secretaries), Kenneth Bird, Frank Spinks

1981-82
Barrie Hall (Chairman/Publicity Secretary), Geoffrey Timms (Vice-Chairman/Artistic Adviser), Daphne Tinsey (Secretary), Archie Norrie (Treasurer), Sylvia Terry (Membership Secretary), Betty Greatrex, Phoebe Musgrave (Social Secretaries), Kenneth Bird, John Harrop, Peter Lewis

1982-83
Barrie Hall (Chairman/Publicity Secretary), Geoffrey Timms (Vice-Chairman/Artistic Adviser), Daphne Tinsey (Secretary), Janice Tompkins (Treasurer), Sylvia Terry (Membership Secretary), Betty Greatrex, Margareta Walker-Arnott (Social Secretaries), Kenneth Bird, John Harrop, Peter Lewis

1983-84
Barrie Hall (Chairman/Publicity Secretary), Geoffrey Timms (Vice-Chairman/Artistic Adviser), Daphne Tinsey (Secretary), Janice Tompkins (Treasurer), Sylvia Terry (Membership Secretary), Betty Greatrex, Margareta Walker-Arnott (Social Secretaries), Kenneth Bird, John Harrop, Peter Lewis

1984-85
Geoffrey Timms (Chairman/Artistic Adviser), Peter Lewis (Vice-Chairman), Daphne Tinsey (Secretary), Janice Tompkins (Treasurer), Sylvia Terry (Membership Secretary), Barrie Hall (Publicity Secretary), Betty Greatrex (Social Secretary), Kenneth Bird, John Harrop, Arthur Pittock, Grace Darnley

1985-86
Geoffrey Timms (Chairman/Artistic Adviser), Daphne Tinsey (Secretary), John Harrop (Treasurer), Sylvia Terry (Membership Secretary), Barrie Hall (Publicity Secretary), Betty Greatrex (Social Secretary), Kenneth Bird, Roderick Elms, Peter Lewis, Arthur Pittock, Janice Tompkins

1986-87
Geoffrey Timms (Chairman/Artistic Adviser), Daphne Tinsey (Secretary), John Harrop (Treasurer), Sylvia Terry (Membership Secretary), Barrie Hall (Publicity Secretary), Betty Greatrex (Social Secretary), Kenneth Bird, Roderick Elms, Peter Lewis, Arthur Pittock (Outside Activities), Ian Allen

1987-88
Geoffrey Timms (Chairman/Artistic Adviser), Daphne Tinsey (Librarian), John Harrop (Treasurer), Sylvia Terry (Membership Secretary) , Barrie Hall (Publicity Secretary), Kenneth Bird (CA Liaison), Peter Lewis (Jazz Club), Arthur Pittock (Outside Activities), Roderick Elms, Ian Allen, Valerie Chetham, Geoffrey Tompkins (from 2.1.87)

1988-89
Barrie Hall (Chairman/Publicity), Geoffrey Timms (Vice-Chairman/Artistic Adviser/Century Club/YMM), Ian Allen (Secretary), John Harrop (Treasurer), Daphne Tinsey (Librarian), Valerie Chetham (Social Secretary), Sylvia Terry (Membership Secretary), Kenneth Bird (CA Liaison), Roderick Elms (Musical Adviser), Peter Lewis (Jazz Club), Geoffrey Tompkins, Patti Nicholson, Jean Hall Outings (from 12.10.88)

1989-90

Dr Geoffrey Tompkins (Chairman), Barrie Hall (Vice-Chairman/Publicity), Geoffrey Timms (Century Club/YMM), Ian Allen (Secretary), John Harrop (Treasurer), Patti Nicholson (Librarian), Valerie Chetham (Social Secretary), Sylvia Terry (Membership Secretary), Roderick Elms (Musical Adviser), Peter Lewis (Jazz Club), Jean Hall (Outings)

1990-91

Dr Geoffrey Tompkins (Chairman), Barrie Hall (Vice-Chairman/Publicity), Geoffrey Timms (Century Club/YMM), Ian Allen (Secretary), John Harrop (Treasurer), Patti Nicholson (Librarian), Valerie Chetham (Social Secretary), Sylvia Terry (Membership Secretary), Roderick Elms (Musical Adviser), Jean Hall (Outings)

1991-92

Dr Geoffrey Tompkins (Chairman), Barrie Hall (Vice-Chairman/Publicity), Geoffrey Timms (Century Club/YMM), Ian Allen (Secretary), John Harrop (Treasurer), Patti Nicholson (Librarian), Adèle Dimmock (Social Secretary), Sylvia Terry (Membership Secretary) Roderick Elms (Musical Adviser), Jean Hall (Outings), Valerie Chetham, Mauro Sheehan

1992-93

Jean Hall (Chairman/Outings), Barrie Hall (Secretary/Publicity), Geoffrey Timms (Century Club/YMM), John Harrop (Treasurer), Patti Nicholson (Librarian), Adèle Birch Social (Secretary), Sylvia Terry (Membership Secretary), Roderick Elms (Musical Adviser), Valerie Chetham, Colin Bailey, Geoffrey Tompkins

1993-94

Jean Hall (Chairman/Outings), John Harrop (Vice-Chairman/Treasurer), Barrie Hall (Secretary/Publicity), Patti Nicholson (Librarian), Adèle Birch (Social Secretary), Roderick Elms (Musical Adviser), Valerie Chetham, Nicola Harries, Geoffrey Tompkins, Catherine Jennings, Janet Pope (from 23.9.94), Peter Jackson (from 23.9.94)

1994-95

Jean Hall (Chairman/Outings), John Harrop (Vice-Chairman/Treasurer), Barrie Hall (Secretary/Publicity), Adèle Birch (Social Secretary), Roderick Elms (Musical Adviser), Patti Nicholson (Librarian), Valerie Chetham, Nicola Harries, Peter Strickland, Geoffrey Tompkins, Catherine Jennings, Janet Pope, Peter Jackson

1995-96

Janet Pope (Chairman), Jean Hall (Vice-Chairman/Outings), Peter Jackson (Secretary), John Harrop (Treasurer), Barrie Hall (Secretary/Publicity), Adèle Birch (Social Secretary), Roderick Elms (Musical Adviser), Valerie Chetham, Nicola Harries, Peter Strickland, Catherine Jennings

1996-97

Janet Pope (Chairman), Jean Hall (Vice-Chairman/Outings), Peter Jackson (Secretary), John Harrop (Treasurer), Barrie Hall (Secretary/Publicity), Adèle Birch (Social Secretary), Roderick Elms (Musical Adviser), Valerie Chetham, Nicola Harries, Catherine Jennings

1997-98

Janet Pope (Chairman), Jean Hall (Vice-Chairman), Adèle Birch, Valerie Chetham, Barrie Hall, Nicola Harries, John Harrop (Treasurer), Catherine Jennings, Peter Jackson (Secretary)

1998-99

Jean Hall (Chairman), Janet Pope (Vice-Chairman), Barrie Hall (Secretary), Peter Jackson (Secretary), John Harrop (Treasurer), Roderick Elms (Music Adviser), Adèle Birch, Valerie Chetham, Stan Cornhill, Nicola Harries, Catherine Jennings, Brian Lawrence

1999-2000

Jean Hall (Chairman), Janet Pope (Vice-Chairman), Barrie Hall (Secretary), Peter Jackson (Secretary), John Harrop (Treasurer), Roderick Elms (Music Adviser), Adèle Birch, Valerie Chetham, Stan Cornhill, Nicola Harries, Catherine Jennings, Brian Lawrence

2000-2001

Jean Hall (Chairman), Janet Pope (Vice-Chairman), Barrie Hall (Secretary), Peter Jackson, John Harrop (Treasurer), Roderick Elms (Music Adviser), Adèle Birch, Stan Cornhill, Nicola Harries, Catherine Jennings, Brian Lawrence

2001-2002

Catherine Jennings (Chairman), Nicola Harries (Vice-Chairman), Barrie Hall (Secretary), John Harrop (Treasurer), Peter Jackson, Roderick Elms (Music Adviser), Adèle Birch, Jean Hall, Rosalie Ritson, Brian Lawrence

2002-2003

Catherine Jennings (Chairman), Nicola Harries (Vice-Chairman), Barrie Hall (Secretary), John Harrop (Treasurer), Peter Jackson, Roderick Elms (Music Adviser), Adèle Birch, Jean Hall, Rosalie Ritson, Brian Lawrence

2003-2004

Catherine Jennings (Chairman), Nicola Harries (Vice-Chairman), Barrie Hall (Secretary), John Harrop (Treasurer), Peter Jackson (Century Club – Raffle), Roderick Elms (Music Adviser), Adèle Birch, Jean Hall (Sponsorship – Outings), Rosalie Ritson, Brian Lawrence

2004-2005

John Harrop (Chairman & Treasurer), Nicola Harries (Vice-Chairman), Adèle birch, Jean Hall, Catherine Jennings, Janet Pope, Roderick Elms, Rosalie Ritson, Joanna Smith, Peter Jackson, Brian Lawrence and Barrie Hall (Secretary)

2005-2006

John Harrop (Chairman), Nicola Harries (Vice-Chairman & Hon. Treasurer), Adèle birch, Jean Hall, Catherine Jennings, Janet Pope, Roderick Elms, Rosalie Ritson, Joanna Smith, Peter Jackson, Brian Lawrence and Barrie Hall (Secretary)

2006-2007

John Harrop (Chairman), Nicola Harries (Vice-Chairman & Hon. Treasurer), Roderick Elms, Joanna Smith, Jean Hall, Barrie Hall, Peter Jackson, Catherine Jennings, Brian Lawrence, Janet Pope (Secretary), Rosalie Ritson and Barbara Szymanek and Adèle Birch

2007-2008

John Harrop (Chairman), Nicola Harries (Vice-Chairman & Hon. Treasurer), Roderick Elms, Joanna Smith, Jean Hall, Barrie Hall, Peter Jackson, Catherine Jennings, Brian Lawrence, Janet Pope (Secretary), Rosalie Ritson, Barbara Szymanek and Adèle Birch

2008-2009

Nicola Harries (Chairman), Janet Pope (Vice-Chairman & Secretary), Peter Jackson, (Hon. Treasurer), John Harrop, Brian Lawrence, Rosalie Ritson, Barrie Hall, Jean Hall, Roderick Elms, Catherine Jennings, Joanna Smith, Adèle Birch and Barbara Szymanek

2009-2010

Nicola Harries (Chairman), Peter Jackson (Vice-Chairman & Treasurer), Janet Pope (Secretary), John Harrop, Roderick Elms, Catherine Jennings, Brian Lawrence, Joanna Smith, Barrie Hall, Jean Hall, Rosalie Ritson and Barbara Szymanek.

2010-2011

Nicola Harries (Chairman), Peter Jackson (Treasurer), Janet Pope (Secretary), John Harrop, Catherine Jennings, Barbara Szymanek, Rosalie Ritson, Roderick Elms, Joanna Smith, Eric Crook, Jean Crook

2011-2012

Nicola Harries (Chairman), Peter Jackson (Treasurer), Janet Pope (Secretary), Catherine Jennings, Barbara Szymanek, Rosalie Ritson, Roderick Elms, Joanna Smith, Eric Crook, Jean Crook

2012-2013

Peter Jackson (Chairman), Eric Crook (Treasurer), Janet Pope (Secretary), Nicola Harries, Catherine Jennings, Barbara Szymanek, Rosalie Ritson, Roderick Elms, Joanna Smith, Jean Crook

2013-2014

Peter Jackson (Chairman), Eric Crook (Treasurer), Janet Pope (Secretary), Nicola Harries, Catherine Jennings, Barbara Szymanek, Rosalie Ritson, Roderick Elms, Joanna Smith, Jean Crook

2014-2015

Peter Jackson (Chairman), Eric Crook (Treasurer), Janet Pope (Secretary), Nicola Harries, Catherine Jennings, Barbara Szymanek, Roderick Elms, Joanna Smith, Jean Crook

2015-2016

Peter Jackson (Chairman), Eric Crook (Treasurer), Janet Pope (Secretary), Nicola Harries, Catherine Jennings, Barbara Szymanek, Roderick Elms, Joanna Smith, Jean Crook

2016-2017

Janet Pope (Chairman), Peter Jackson (Treasurer), Nicola Harries (Secretary), Barbara Szymanek, Roderick Elms, Joanna Smith

2017-2018

Janet Pope (Chairman), Peter Jackson (Treasurer), Nicola Harries (Secretary), Barbara Szymanek, Roderick Elms, Joanna Smith

2018-2019 (November)

Janet Pope (Chairman), Peter Jackson (Treasurer), Nicola Harries (Secretary), Barbara Szymanek, Roderick Elms, Joanna Smith

2019 (March)-2020 (October)

Jane Webster (Chairman), David Haniball (Treasurer), Nicola Harries (Secretary), Roderick Elms, Joanna Smith

2020 (January)-2020 (October)

Jane Webster (Chairman), David Haniball (Treasurer), Carol Pummell (Secretary), Roderick Elms, Joanna Smith

2020 (January)-2020 (October)

Jane Webster (Chairman), David Haniball (Treasurer), Carol Pummell (Secretary), Alisdair Hogarth, Andy King

Appendix – D

CLUB OUTINGS

1975 21st February RFH Mozart Piano Concerti

8th May Visit to Brentwood School Music Society Concert

1976 15th December, South Bank Opera Company

1983 10th July Thaxted Church

23rd October Snape Maltings

1984 15th July Thaxted Church Arthur Pittock

1985 14th July Thaxted Church Arthur Pittock

1986 22nd April Yehudi Menuin Birthday Festival Concert

1st July Thaxted Church, John Lill

13th September Chelmsford Cathedral, Essex Youth Orchestra

19th November RFH

1987 16th May Chelmsford Cathedral

14th June Jazz Meadway cruiser

11th July Thaxted Church, John Lill

16th September Chelmsford

1988 20th January Coliseum *Der Rosenkavelier*

29th April Colliseum *Cosi Fan Tutti*

2nd July Thaxted Festival Nigel Kennedy

1989 9th January Wigmore Hal, EYMY Concert

9th March Royal Naval College, Greenwich

11th June Barbican, Leningrad Philharmonic Orchestra

1989 31st August RAH, Glyndebourne Prom

22nd November RFH, St Ceclia's Day Concert

1990 8th January Wigmore Hall EYMY Winners

12th October, Glyndebourne Fidelio

1991 12th June Kings College Cambridge CUMS

25th March Wigmore Hall, EYMY Winner

12th October Glyndebourne *La Boheme*

1992 10th March RFH ,John Lill Brahms 2

21st November Barbican

11th December Blackheath ASMF

1993 5th March Wigmore Hall EYMY Winners

1994 26th October Glyndebourne *The Barber of Seville*

1995 10th April Wigmore Hall EYMY Concert

14 October Glyndebourne *La Bohème*

1996 18 October Glyndebourne *The Marriage of Figaro*

1997 2nd May Purcell Room EYMY Winners

20th October Glyndebourne *Il Seraglio*

1998 12th October Glyndebourne *Cosi fan Tutte*

1999 12th March St James', Piccadilly EYMY Winners

September Finchcocks Museum

26th October Glyndebourne Pelléas et Mélisande

2000 22nd March Brentwood Cathedral John Lill

21st May Cliffs Pavillion, Southend

20th October Glyndebourne *Don Giovani*

2001 17th March St Giles, Cripplegate EYMY Winners

16th October Glyndebourne Fidelio

2002 27th July Barbican, Academy of St Martin

23rd October Glyndebourne *Albert Herring*

2003 14th May St Giles, Cripplegate EYMY Winners

14th October La Traviata

2004 8th October Glyndebourne *Magic Flute*

2005 24th April Cliffs Pavillion, Southend, Benjamin Grosvenor

25th October Glyndebourne *La Ceneretola*

2006 19th March Cliffs Pavilion, John Lill Mozart

22nd October Glyndebourne *Die Fledermaus*

2007 22nd October Glyndebourne *L'Elisir d'Amour*

2008 21st October Glyndebourne *Carmen*

2009 31st October Glyndebourne *Falstaff*

2010 28th January Philharmonia concert

10th October Glyndebourne *La Cenerentola*

16th January RFH Budapest Festival Orchestra

2011 30th April Chatham, RPO

15th July Benjamin Grosvenor, Royal Albert Hall First Night of the Proms

8th October Glyndebourne *La Bohème*

2012 20th October Glyndebourne *The Marriage of Figaro*

2013 13th October Glyndebourne *L'Elisir d'Amore*

Photographs

Abbreviations

AGM — Annual General Meeting
ARC — Arts & Recreation Centre (Harlow)
CA — Community Association (Ongar)
ECG — Essex Chronicle Group
ECC — Essex County Council
EFDC — Epping Forest District Council
EYMY — Essex Young Musician of the Year

NFMS — National Federation of Music Societies
OJC — Ongar Jazz Club
OCA — Ongar Community Association
OMC — Ongar Music Club
PRS — Performing Rights Societ
YMM — Young Music Makers

Index

SPONSORS

The organisation of a competition like that for The Essex Young Musician of the Year would not be possible without financial help from outside. ONGAR MUSIC CLUB is most grateful to the businesses and individuals who have contributed funds, and appreciates their generosity. For this year's competition, all prizes have been sponsored as follows:

1st Prize   £500   **M and G Group, plc.** (Chelmsford)

2nd Prize   £300   **Nortel Technology** (Harlow)

3rd Prize   £200   **Raggett, Tiffen & Harries** (Ongar)

4th Prize   £125   **Mr & Mrs G. Chetham** (Ongar)

The Hugh Terry Prize £100 **Rhône-Poulenc Agriculture Ltd.**
(Ongar)

The James Dace Prize £100 **James Dace & Son** (Chelmsford)

Just a Little From the Top is the title of Roderick Elms' memoirs, chronicling his love of music from childhood, through school and college, ultimately leading to a career spanning more than forty years, in which he has worked at the highest levels of music-making in London.

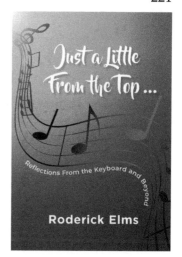

It gives a unique insight into many aspects of the workings of the profession and contains a multitude of anecdotes, many humorous, about his fascinating life journey. These include occasions when things have gone wrong, sometimes as a result of practical or mechanical failures, others due to poor leadership.

What people say

A truly enjoyable account of Roderick Elms' life in music, peppered with stories, from the hilarious to the educational! This lively account of the life and times of a valued friend includes plenty of entertaining anecdotes, plus details of musical mishaps and triumphs along the way. A great read for anyone interested in the workings of today's classical music world.

Aled Jones

If you want an intimate glimpse behind the scenes of the fascinating world of orchestral musicians then look no further than Roderick Elms' hugely entertaining book. Even if you've never met him, you'll get to know him very well and if you have (and worked with him, as I've been lucky enough to do on many occasions) then it will remind you – with enormous pleasure – of good times past.

Brian Kay

Roderick Elms' book is a real delight for musicians and non-musicians alike – packed full of wonderful memories and anecdotes from a much-admired musician and composer.

Debbie Wiseman OBE

'Just a Little From the Top' can be bought discounted, from www.masterkeyboards.co.uk or from usual outlets.